Child Health Policy In An Age of Fiscal Austerity:

CRITIQUES OF THE
SELECT PANEL REPORT

CHILD AND FAMILY POLICY

SERIES EDITORS
JAMES J. GALLAGHER AND RON HASKINS

VOLUME I

MODELS FOR ANALYSIS OF SOCIAL POLICY:
AN INTRODUCTION

Ron Haskins and James J. Gallagher

VOLUME II

CHILD HEALTH POLICY
IN AN AGE OF FISCAL AUSTERITY:
CRITIQUES OF THE
SELECT PANEL REPORT

Ron Haskins

VOLUME III

PARENT EDUCATION
AND PUBLIC POLICY

Ron Haskins

CHILD HEALTH POLICY IN AN AGE OF FISCAL AUSTERITY:

CRITIQUES OF THE SELECT PANEL REPORT

RON HASKINS
EDITOR

ABLEX Publishing Corporation
Norwood, New Jersey 07648

Copyright © 1983 by Ablex Publishing Corporation

Printed in the United States of America.

Library of Congress Cataloging in Publication Data
Main entry under title:

Child health policy in an age of fiscal austerity.

(Advances in child and family policy; v. 2)
Papers from a colloquium series held during the spring of 1982 in Chapel Hill.
Includes indexes.
1. Child health services—Government policy—United States—Congresses. I. Haskins, Ron. II. United States. Select Panel for the Promotion of Child Health. III. Series.
RJ102.C48   1981   362.1'9892'000973   82-22820
ISBN 0-89391-118-6

ABLEX Publishing Corporation
355 Chestnut Street
Norwood, New Jersey 07648

Contents

ELEVEN

PRESIDENTIAL AND CONGRESSIONAL COMMISSIONS:
THE SELECT PANEL IN CONTEXT   **162**
Ron Haskins

APPENDIX A

SUMMARY AND CRITIQUE OF THE
SELECT PANEL'S RECOMMENDATIONS   **198**
Charles K. Burnett

PREFACE TO THE SERIES

JAMES J. GALLAGHER

Emergence of the new field of social policy analysis, starting in the 1960s, but accelerating in the 1970s, is an intriguing phenomenon in the academic world that is worthy of study in its own right. This evolving discipline is clearly multidisciplinary in nature, drawing interest and contributions from such diverse bedfellows as the health sciences, economics, sociology, psychology, and education, among others.

Even more interesting than this multidisciplinary thrust from the academic community is that those in positions of power seem to be aware of this new movement and are generally attentive. The relationship between the keepers of knowledge and holders of power has always been a strained one. Truth, particularly when unpleasant, has rarely been welcomed by those at the seat of power. Those messengers who deliver such unpleasant truths run some very real risks, more psychological than physical these days. On the other hand, the academician rarely has a sense of the multitude of conflicting pressures and compromises that are the daily menu of the practicing politician, and often doesn't appreciate the many changes in directions that often must be taken to reach a political (policy) goal.

To appreciate this continued strain between knowledge and power, one need not invoke the memories of Galileo or Sir Thomas More. The current difficulties are well expressed in the agonies of the atomic scientists, aptly delineated in an extraordinary series of novels by C. P. Snow. Given this obvious and continued strain, why is there a current interest in pursuing what academia can bring to social policy formulation and implementation?

My own view is that the public policies of the 1960s are the stimuli for this review of relationships. Those policies were, by and large, designed to lead to a better life for all our citizens through improving the delivery of health, social, and educational services. The consensus held by both the political community and the lay public appears to be that after 15 years, the programs have largely come to grief, or have attained much less than was originally intended. Whether this outcome is the result of unrealistic expectations, poor policy formulation, or inadequate policy implementation is still a matter of personal interpretation.

Currently, there is a growing realization that attempts to improve American society can no longer be based on a "seat-of-the-pants," largely uncorrelated, and uncontrolled set of innovations. Such a strategy yields uncontrolled budgets and a corrosive cycle of over-expectation, disappointment, and despair. There appears to be a new willingness, tinged with some skepticism, to pursue what academia has to offer in improving policy design and implementation. What does academia have to offer? What it always has—the ability to organize systems of ideas into a pattern that allows us to bring order and new insights to the phenomenon under study.

This series on social policy analysis summarizes some of the latest ideas and methods that are being utilized by those social and health scientists most directly concerned with policy relating to children and families. Each volume in the series will be built around a particular theme so that contributors to a given volume will be focusing on a common topic. In this first volume, the theme is the development of models for analyzing social policy. Such model development is presented from a multidisciplinary perspective as we seek some usable procedures to bring clarity and comprehension to complex policy topics. In subsequent volumes, we will focus upon policy issues such as parent education, the needs of handicapped children and their families, maternal and child health, and children and families in poverty. In each of these volumes, there will be a mixture of general descriptions on the topic area plus the inclusion of specific policy analyses that attempt to bring insight into particular topics within the theme.

It would be inappropriate to conclude these introductory remarks without giving credit to the Bush Foundation of St. Paul, Minnesota, whose forward thinking has provided financial support for much of the analytic work that will be included in these volumes. The Bush Foundation has established training programs at four major universities—Michigan, Yale, UCLA, and North Carolina—and while the papers in this series will be based, to a large degree, on the work at North Carolina, the ideas and concepts in this series will undoubtedly reflect the interests of all four Bush centers.

PREFACE TO VOLUME II

Ron Haskins

This volume of papers critically analyzing the Report of the Select Panel for the Promotion of Child Health is an ideal choice for the second volume in this series on analysis of social policy. In the first volume, we provided an overview of the emerging field of social policy analysis, and outlined a number of policy analysis models. Although none of the chapters in this volume uses a formal analysis model to examine Select Panel recommendations, there is much discussion of the elements of typical analysis models—especially values, criteria, and alternative policies. This second volume, then, is a series of papers that critically assess the policy recommendations of a major document on child health policy.

Appointed by Secretary of Health, Education, and Welfare Joseph Califano at the direction of the Congress in 1978, the Select Panel for the Promotion of Child Health was charged with developing "a comprehensive plan to promote the health of children and pregnant women in the United States." Nineteen months later, the Panel published its elaborate four-volume study which carefully analyzes the status of maternal and child health, examines programs bearing on the health of mothers and children (especially Title V of the Social Security Act; Early and Periodic Screening, Diagnosis, and Treatment; the Special Supplemental Food Program for Women, Infants, and Children; P.L. 94-142; and Community Mental Health Centers), and brings together a thorough and comprehensive set of data on the status of American mothers and children. In addition, the final volume of the Select Panel Report contains 22 background papers commissioned by the Panel that deal with a broad array of maternal and child health issues.

Given the tendency of government reports to reside unobtrusively on library shelves, Dr. Arden Miller and others on the Bush faculty at the University of North Carolina determined that the Select Panel Report deserved a better fate. The Select Panel was, after all, the first major federal commission directed specifically at a policy issue concerning children and families. Thus, we decided to invite a number of scholars and practitioners to critically examine particular aspects of the Select Panel Report, to present the results of their examination in a colloquium series held during the Spring of 1981 in Chapel Hill, and to publish the papers as part of our series on child and family policy. A brief overview of the resulting volume is now in order.

The first chapter provides background on the Select Panel and its Report. Ms. Lisbeth Schorr, chairperson of the Panel, outlines the composition of the Panel, traces its congressional origins during the Carter administration, specifies the nature of the Panel's congressional charge, and outlines the Panel's major conclusions. With regard to the latter point, Schorr identifies six major areas in which the Panel made recommendations: providing basic minimal services; promoting coherence and coordination among health programs; improving environment, nutrition, and health behavior; expanding the availability of psychosocial services; improving the organization of health services; and achieving a more equitable, reliable, and dependable means of financing health services.

The primary objective of the second chapter is to provide a framework within which the Panel's Report can be critically analyzed. More specifically, Arden Miller establishes the context for health policy in the 1980s by defining and exploring six major dilemmas of health policy: impingement of societal responsibility for child health on the freedoms and prerogatives of parents; the disjunction between factors that are known to be major deterrents of health (e.g., nutrition, sanitation, and reproductive behavior and fertility) and the types of health services that currently enjoy funding priority (e.g., high technology treatment of disease); the respective effects of comprehensive services on the one hand and categorical services on the other; methods by which people's behavior can be changed to improve their health; the perplexing mix of partnership and adversarial conflict between local, state, and federal governments; and the relative virtues and problems of selected and universal services.

The five chapters that follow Miller's present thoughtful—and in some cases, sharp—critiques of the Select Panel Report. Mrs. Beverlee Myers, director of health for the state of California, is the senior author of the first of these five chapters. Not surprisingly, the focus of Myers' criticism is the Panel's view of federal-state relations. In general, Myers and her colleague, David Hayes-Bautista, believe the Select Panel did not demonstrate adequate appreciation of the "economic and political situation" (p. 40) that must condition health policy in the 1980s. More specifically, they argue that Select Panel recommendations are a prescription for "more of the same" (p. 41)—more large-scale programs initiated at the federal level, and imposed on the states primarily through inflexible regulations. By contrast, Myers and Hayes-Bautista hold that a new logic should provide the basis for federal-state relations in an era of "Kemp-Roth, Proposition 13, and many other tax revolt measures" (p. 41). As a step toward defining this new logic, the authors propose that the federal government should be responsible for four primary functions, namely: planning, financing, establishing standards, and monitoring performance. The states, in turn, should be responsible for the actual design and implementation of health programs within their jurisdiction. This system of federal-state relations would be characterized by decentralized government; specific program details arrived at through a process of federal-state negotiation; and a wide latitude for states in selecting program goals, in designing health programs, and in using federal money. All in all, the federal-state relations envisioned by Myers and Hayes-Bautista amount to a very substantial change in the status quo.

By contrast, the Marmor and Greenberg chapter provides few specific suggestions for changes in current federal policy. Rather, these authors carefully scrutinize the Select Panel recommendations concerning regulation. Regulatory issues are at the heart of current battles concerning the new federalism, primarily because many social critics—especially those of the right and New Right—view federal regulation as both noxious and a fundamental cause of inefficiency. Regulations that bear directly or indirectly on health are held by these critics to be confusing, costly, contradictory, and short-sighted.

Marmor and Greenberg present a succinct and unbiased assessment of the Select Panel approach to regulation. After proposing that two general types of regulations must be addressed; namely, those pertaining specifically to health (and especially health financing) and those pertaining to more general issues that are not health per se but nonetheless have a major impact on health, Marmor and Greenberg present a very useful classification and summary of the specific recommendations for regulatory change set forth by the Select Panel.

First, they identify six Panel recommendations addressed specifically to safeguarding mothers and children (e.g., auto and home safety, day care centers, prescription drugs for pregnant women); second, they identify five recommended changes in regulation addressed to the entire population, mothers and children included (e.g., speed limits, fire hazards in the home, hand guns, lead levels in the air and water); third, they identify two Panel recommendations that, although addressed to mothers and children, would probably need to be formulated in such a way that all members of the population would be affected (e.g., x-rays, pesticide exposure, and food dyes).

The authors then proceed to the identification of several regulatory issues they feel were ignored by the Select Panel, including abortion, midwifery, smoking in public places, and flex time for mothers and pregnant women. One gathers, though Marmor and Greenberg do not say so explicitly, that they feel the Select Panel committed a serious oversight in not dealing with these regulatory issues.

Perhaps the most original and useful undertaking of this excellent chapter is the authors' identification of criteria by which analysts should assess the case for any of the regulatory changes suggested or ignored by the Panel. These include the potential health impact of a given regulatory change, the ease of implementation and enforcement of the regulation, the question of whether health is the pivotal concern of the regulation, and the possible secondary or unintended consequences of the regulation.

In turning to the chapter by Eli Newberger and his colleagues, we are faced with a complex approach to a complex problem. Roughly speaking, the problem is this: first, is each of us our brother's keeper; second, if so, how can we translate intention into action; third, are we even more our brother's keeper if he happens to be a child? This last issue is especially tricky since children, due to immaturity, are not capable of making informed choices. As applied to health behavior, this means that adults must assume responsibility for immunizations, good child care, use of seat belts or car seats, good nutrition, and so on.

But what if adults, and in particular, parents, do not fulfill these responsibilities? Take the case of seat belts. I doubt there will be a single parent who reads this book who has not, on at least a few occasions, allowed her child to ride in a car without wearing a seat belt. Yet as we all know full well, such a decision is extremely irresponsible. The data on seat belt use by children is incontrovertible. Thus, a child's chances of dying or sustaining serious injury in an auto crash are slashed at least

50% by seat belt use. Can there, then, be any excuse for a parent's failure to require seat belt use by his children? Less dramatically, we can apply the same line of reasoning to argue that parents must insure that children be immunized, fed properly, and taken for regular checkups. Parents may be the first line of attack, but what if they fail? Then who is responsible? And what if parents have their own problems that interfere in fulfilling their responsibilities toward their children? Or what if they cannot afford adequate care in our largely private, fee-for-service, medical care system?

Newberger and his colleagues examine the Select Panel's approach to these questions by presenting case studies of children and families. Each case study is selected to illustrate various facets of the "whose responsibility?" question. Further, the authors propose three levels of responsibility for each case, namely, responsibility at the social and environmental level, at the family level, and at the level of the individual child.

The case studies prove to be an excellent device for showing the complex interaction between federal and state laws, local institutions (such as hospitals), medical professionals, and parents in assuring the health of our nation's children. Newberger and his colleagues also use the case study technique to raise several questions about the Select Panel's approach to the issue of responsibility for child health.

Though Newberger and his colleagues find several points of disagreement with the Select Panel, perhaps the most fundamental of these is the issue of non-medical services. In particular, they feel the Panel did not sufficiently recognize the importance of non-medical services; moreover, the Report "degrades these vital supports for child health by referring to them as boundary services" (p. 79). The authors go on to argue that so far from being boundary services, social services are a critical part of preventive and therapeutic medical care without which most medical treatments are little more than stopgag measures.

Schorr counters this charge rather sharply in her summary chapter by arguing that the Panel makes frequent reference to the critical importance of non-medical services, and even suggested that such services should play a "more central role" in health care. She then proceeds to reference several places in the Report that spell out the specific types of non-medical services that the Panel believed most vital.

In a closely related criticism, Newberger and his colleagues also indicate dissatisfaction with the Panel's failure to strongly endorse large-scale attacks on poverty through some type of income maintenance program. In this case, Schorr counters that such a proposal would have taken the Select Panel beyond its congressional mandate.

The two chapters following Newberger's are addressed to the

health manpower recommendations of the Select Panel. Although Fernando Guerra indicates general satisfaction with the Panel's Report and policy recommendations, he does identify a number of problems concerning health manpower that, in his view, were inadequately covered in the Report. Guerra's major criticism is that he feels the Report insufficiently recognized and discussed manpower productivity problems. Because our current health care system is characterized by "waste, abuse, duplication, confusion, and inappropriate health care utilization" (p. 96), Guerra believes that attention to productivity is the first order of business for those concerned with health manpower. In a word, we should determine ways to get the most out of the health personnel already available before we plan for additional personnel.

Guerra is also concerned that the Panel failed to pay adequate attention to the issue of health personnel distribution. It is widely known that pediatricians and other health providers prefer urban and suburban settings to conduct their practice, thereby leaving large numbers of mothers and children in rural areas with inadequate service. In addition, Guerra claims that many doctors prefer not to serve the type of children and families eligible for Medicaid reimbursement. The point here is that aggregate data on health providers per person in the population are likely to provide a misleading basis for health manpower projections. Merely increasing the number of health personnel available to serve mothers and children will not insure adequate service for demographic groups such as the urban and rural poor.

Like most professionals concerned with child health, Guerra believes the Panel's emphasis on the "new morbidity" is well justified. Certainly, there is a need for more and better services to attack problems such as emotional disturbance, poor health behavior, and school learning and behavior deficits. Guerra's concern is that the Panel, in emphasizing the need for new health personnel to address these problems, was not specific in identifying the numbers and types of personnel needed, nor in providing analyses of the training needed by such personnel.

The chapter by Carolyn Williams is an extensive treatment of one aspect of the health manpower problem, namely, the nurse practitioner movement. Nurse practitioners—nurses who have received additional training that allows them to provide services and make "assessment and management decisions formerly reserved for physicians" (p. 104)—are a partial solution to one cause of inflated medical care costs. Not only do nurse practitioners provide many of the same services as medical doctors at reduced cost, they also apparently produce health outcomes at least as good as those produced by physicians. Indeed, studies reviewed by Williams demonstrate that some of their services are even more effective than those provided by physicians—particularly in the areas of health prevention, patient compliance, and behavioral outcomes for patients suffering from chronic diseases. There are at least some data which suggest that both patients and physicians accept and are satisifed with the expanded role of nurse practitioners.

It might be expected, then, that the nurse practitioner movement would be undergoing substantial expansion. Such, however, is not the case. Williams argues that there seems now to be significant "retrenchment" (p. 107) on the issue of an expanded role for nurse practitioners. Indeed, there is disturbing evidence that physicians and health administrators are returning to an earlier view that nurse practitioners were but a stopgag measure against a shortage of physicians. But as Williams shows, recent projections indicate that we will soon enter an era of physician surplus—one result of which is the building pressure to limit the expansion of nurse practitioners.

Thus, although generally impressed by the scope and insight of the Select Panel Report, Williams expresses disappointment in the Panel's rather tepid support of the nurse practitioner movement. Because the Panel's major recommendations concerned the universal availability of precisely those services in which nurse practitioners excel (e.g., prenatal and postnatal care, comprehensive health care for children, and family planning), and because of the historical and philosophical compatibility between the nurse practitioner movement and services for mothers and children, Williams believes the Select Panel to have been entirely too circumspect in its support of nurse practitioners. Schorr's half-hearted rebuttal of Williams's criticisms (pp. 153–154) leaves me with the impression that Schorr is sympathetic with Williams's argument, and perhaps even wishes the Panel had taken a stronger stand in support of the nurse practitioner movement.

Following these five chapters in which criticism of the Select Panel Report is the primary order of business, we have included two chapters that speak to broader issues that will condition reaction to the Select Panel Report. The first of these, by Lewis Margolis, provides an epidemiological assessment of the long-term consequences of failing to implement the major Select Panel recommendations. The second chapter, by Jonathan Kotch, examines a major element of the political context in which the Report was published, namely, the New Right.

Although the word "provocative" is much overused these days, I feel this term is precisely the one required to characterize the chapter by Margolis. Perhaps no economic aphorism is more celebrated by repetition and violated by practice than the dictum that policymakers should attempt to spend the last dollar of public money where it will do the most good. There may be few advantages in the kind of economic calamity that our nation is now experiencing, but such times at least have the salubrious effect of forcing us to set funding priorities. Further, such an atmosphere is conducive to careful analysis of the outcomes of social programs. When money is available, we want everything; when money is tight, we try to save only the best programs. The Margolis chapter is an excellent example of the thinking that should now pervade the field of policy analysis. Margolis raises the straightforward question: If we maintain the status quo in health programs, what will be the effect on subsequent mortality and morbidity among the nation's children?

Some might wish to quibble with Margolis's numbers, or with his methods of estimation and projection, or with the soundness of primary sources he uses to derive his estimates. But the basic message seems quite clear—in fact, all too clear. Using the device of taking the 1985 birth cohort, and, based on current knowledge of leading causes of childhood mortality and morbidity, projecting forward to kindergarten entry in 1990, Margolis determines that about 6,000 children will have died unnecessarily in birth-related casualties and childhood accidents; another 75,000 will suffer preventable handicaps because of birth trauma, accidents, and malnutrition.

We should not, of course, suffer under the impression that an academic analysis such as this will have a major influence on public policy—especially during a period of rather frenzied budget cutting. Nonetheless, it is difficult to resist the impression that the Margolis analysis is fundamentally sound. One is then likely to be afflicted by the realization that Margolis's projections are based on the situation in 1980—even before the first round of Reagan budget cuts in programs such as Title XX, school lunch, and food stamps. As the country now looks "forward" to further cuts over the next several years, one concludes that we are likely to have the opportunity to subject the Margolis analysis to an empirical test.

Not the least of the reasons for this likelihood is the existence of the New Right. The chapter by Jonathan Kotch provides an overview of the New Right, with special attention to the history of right-wing groups in American politics, to the political methods used by these groups, and to prominent individuals and organizations in the New Right.

A central point emphasized by Kotch, and one directly pertinent to future action on Select Panel policy recommendations, might be called the "psychology" of people who support or join radical right-wing groups such as the Moral Majority. These people, in the memorable phrase of Ben Wattenberg, are "unyoung, unpoor, and unblack." As Kotch points out, they are "recent migrants to the world of middle-class perquisities" (p. 137). As such, they are threatened by the upward striv-ings of minorities, by attacks on their recently achieved middle-class values, and by economic uncertainties.

These uncertainties provide the grist for what Kotch calls, quoting Alan Crawford, the "politics of grievance." Thus, New Right organi-zations do not stand for a particular political agenda as much as they stand against anything that threatens traditional values and their view of the American way of life. Underlying these grievances is the resent-ment of minorities and other unwashed groups who benefit from public programs.

The primary message Kotch draws from his analysis of the New Right is that supporters of Select Panel recommendations may be able to capitalize on the very fears which provide the underlying support for New Right organizations. The strength of the Report is its emphasis on "universal health services for all pregnant women and children" (p. 142). By emphasizing that the policy objective is to insure certain basic medical services for all families—and not just poor families—Kotch be-lieves that advocates could count on substantial support from people who are normally attracted to the New Right.

As might be expected, we asked Ms. Schorr to respond to the various criticisms and comments about the Select Panel Report outlined above. She gladly agreed; her Commentary and Afterword may be found in Chapter Ten. Having already referred to a number of Schorr's ar-guments and counterarguments, while discussing the individual chap-ters, I do not intend to recapitulate her various positions here. Suffice is to say that Schorr is as capable of defending the Select Panel Report against its critics as she was of leading a group of 18 disparate individuals to produce this remarkable document in the first place.

I would, however, call attention to the final point emphasized by Schorr. Despite the Select Panel's emphasis on universal services, she identifies equity as a central goal of American health policy. Her eloquent statement concerning our responsibilities toward the "most vulnerable" (p. 159) members of our society is particularly important in the current climate of tax breaks for corporations and the rich justified, not as conces-sions to avarice and greed, but as the true path to plenty for all. Un-fortunately, the early stages of implementing this policy seem notable for the sinking of many small boats. It seems increasingly unlikely that public policy can promote equity by helping the rich.

Two other features of this volume merit brief attention. In the final chapter, I analyze the value of presidential and congressional commis-sions as a tool in producing good public policy. My major purpose is to emphasize the fact that commissions such as the Select Panel are ultimately to be judged on the wisdom of their policy recommendations. Examining previous commissions, with special attention to their recommendations and to short- and long-term responses to their recommendations, enables us to evaluate the effectiveness of commissions as an approach to policy analysis, and to draw some speculative conclusions about the fate of Select Panel recommendations. All in all, I find it difficult to conclude that commissions are a very effective way to formulate or influence public policy.

The Appendix by Charles Burnett provides a topical classification of all Select Panel recommendations. As the reader will quickly understand, locating, organizing, and summarizing the Select Panel recommendations was a formidable undertaking. Burnett not only does it well, but also provides additional information concerning who is responsible for implementing each recommendation, and whether each recommendation would require a new policy or program, or modification of extant policies and programs.

Producing a volume such as this could easily be damaging to an editor's health. Surprisingly, however, this volume was produced without trauma—thanks largely to the timely and efficient efforts of many people. Of greatest importance, the authors were reasonable in their responses to editorial suggestions, and were extremely prompt in their writing and rewriting.

A major share of the credit for this volume should go to Arden Miller and Lisbeth Schorr. It was Dr. Miller's original idea to provide critiques of the Select Panel Report, and he played a leading role in selecting the authors of individual chapters. Lisbeth Schorr also helped select the critics, wrote two of the chapters, and was extremely gracious in responding to the various criticisms of the Select Panel's work.

As usual, our staff of secretaries did a marvelous job of typing and retyping the manuscripts. Flo Purdie, Sherree Payne, and Amy Glass were especially helpful. Nor can I fail to mention the extremely competent editorial help and proofreading given by Susann Hutaff.

Finally, we wish to acknowledge the financial assistance provided by the Bush Foundation of St. Paul, Minnesota.

Child Health Policy In An Age of Fiscal Austerity:

CRITIQUES OF THE
SELECT PANEL REPORT

One

Background and Highlights of the Report of the Select Panel

Lisbeth Bamberger Schorr

Introduction

In late 1978, Congress created a Select Panel of 12 private citizens and 5 public officials to develop "a comprehensive plan to promote the health of children and pregnant women in the United States." Members of the Panel were appointed in the spring of 1979 and worked diligently for 19 months. The completed report (Select Panel, 1981) was transmitted, in accordance with our congressional mandate, to the Congress and the Secretary of Health and Human Services on December 2, 1980.

Soon after commencing our work, we came to be concerned about what would ultimately become of our product. The heavy investment in this report included not only $800,000 of the taxpayers' money, but also the intense commitment of an unusually dedicated group of Panel members and staff. In addition, we discovered that the chance to participate in designing the foundations of a renewed national effort to improve the health of our nation's children permitted us to mobilize the contributions of hundreds of individuals and organizations throughout the country who are engaged in large and small ways in understanding and serving the health needs of the country's children and families.

We knew that despite all these efforts, it was possible that our finished report might sink without a trace. Very little is known about what makes the difference between a report that is acted on and one that fails to capture the attention of those who commissioned it, between a report whose ideas become part of the fabric of social discourse, and one which is ignored and left to gather dust on a shelf.

Concerns about the ultimate impact of our report grew as the political climate seemed to become increasingly inhospitable to some of the proposals emerging from our discussions and consultations. Panel members were concerned that the political climate was growing ever more skeptical about new or strengthened social programs and significant increases in public spending and federal authority. As a result of the election of November, 1980, many of those in both the legislative and executive branch of the federal government most receptive to our recommendations were no longer in positions to take effective action. Nevertheless, we believe that much of what we have found and what we recommend is highly relevant and timely.

It is true that many of the changes we recommend involve expansion of government authorities as well as increased spending, neither of which, it now seems clear, will be legislated by the federal government in the immediate future. However, the assessment of current services, programs, problems, and performance on which these recommendations for change are based can be used by advocates and policymakers in assessing proposals to cut back existing programs and in modifying existing authority over many of these programs. Thus, we expect our report will be of considerable immediate usefulness and there is evidence that it is, in fact, being widely utilized.

Nevertheless, we are doubly glad that we decided early in our deliberations to take both a short-run and a long-run perspective and put our highest priority on the formulation of sound long-term recommendations and directions for change, allowing for the possibility of fundamental changes over time in the way health policy issues are perceived, in how health services are utilized and paid for, and in the priority given to maternal and child health by citizens and policymakers.

We expect our report to help bring about some of the needed long-term changes. If it is to do so, of course, it must become part of the dialogue which engages both thinkers and doers in the health field. I can think of no more effective way of getting that process started than the dissemination and consideration of the papers assembled in this volume. I must convey not only my own gratitude for this effort, but that of my fellow Panelists and other colleagues who worked so hard on this report. This book will be a major contribution toward making certain that the proposals outlined in our report will get a fair hearing and thorough analysis, and that the most substantial of our proposals will be acted on in the next decade.

First, I will consider the background and scope of the report and then our findings and recommendations.

COMPOSITION OF THE SELECT PANEL

The congressional action establishing the Panel provided that the then Secretary of HEW, Joseph A. Califano, Jr., appoint the membership from categories which included "representatives from the scientific, medical, dental, allied health, mental health, preventive health, public health, and education professions," as well as "consumers and state and local health agency representatives." The mere selection of such a group is obviously a formidable undertaking, especially when one contemplates the complexities of filling these slots while simultaneously achieving geographic, ethnic, and gender representation.

We ended up with an interesting, broadly representative, and committed group of Panel members. The Panel's vice chairman was a past president of the American Academy of Pediatrics, and the Panel included five other pediatricians: JoAnne Brasel, past president of the Society for Pediatric Research, now at UCLA; Roger Herdman, Commissioner of Health of the State of New York when he was appointed, and now Vice President of Sloan-Kettering; Aaron Shirley, the director of a remarkable community health center in Jackson, Mississippi; George Lythcott, an administrator of the Health Services Administration of the Public Health Service; and Julius Richmond, Assistant Secretary for Health and Surgeon General of the United States.

The Panel also included a practicing obstetrician–gynecologist, Frank Hardart of New York; an eminent specialist in mental retardation from UCLA, George Tarjan; a distinguished developmental psychologist from Vanderbilt University, Nicholas Hobbs; the Dean of the School of Social Work at Columbia University, Mitchell Ginsberg; the distinguished nurse practitioner and Professor of Nursing at the University of North Carolina, Katherine Nuckolls; the Dean of the School of Dentistry at Howard University, Jeanne Skinford; the founding chairperson of the Council on Maternal and Infant Health of the State of Georgia, Charlotte Wilen; the Administrator of the Health Care Financing Administration, Howard Newman; and the Assistant Secretaries for Planning and for Human Development in the Department of Health and Human Services, John Palmer and Cesar Perales.

No one in this highly diverse group came out of our experience together unchanged. What we saw and heard, as well as our exchanges with one another, caused each of us to modify previously held convictions. One of the strengths of our report is the fact that it reflects a consensus fashioned by the interplay of a broad spectrum of interests, concerns, and ideologies.

CONGRESSIONAL ORIGINS

Many of us have speculated about why Congress decided to set in motion a comprehensive assessment of where the nation stands in maternal and child health and where we should be going. In retrospect, I think there are probably two primary concerns which underlay the congressional decision to set up the Select Panel.

The first is the recent enormous increase in awareness of the potential effectiveness of greatly enlarging national efforts at health promotion and disease prevention: if the many demonstrably effective forms of health promotion and disease prevention were more available (especially to children and pregnant women) and more widely utilized, health would be markedly improved. Many also believe that, over the long run, perhaps some money would even be saved. Second, acute concern has developed in Congress and elsewhere that increased investment in maternal and child health over the past two decades has been accompanied by growing duplication, fragmentation, and overlap in program governance and oversight. There is a pervasive sense that programs do not work in relation to one another in ways that assure the most effective expenditure of available funds.

Three additional concerns emerged quite clearly as our Panel conducted hearings and site visits around the country, reviewed an extensive body of research and policy analyses, and talked with a wide range of individuals engaged in efforts to improve the health of mothers and children.

First, though universal lip service is paid to the family as the primary source of health care for children, there is widespread failure to recognize this central role of the family in the provision of health services. Second, while the burden of childhood illness and disability has changed significantly since 1900, partly as a result of spectacular successes in combating infectious disease, the organization and financing of child health care have not been adapted to deal effectively with the complicated interplay of physiological, genetic, psychological, social, and environmental factors which are now major determinants of child health status. Third, not all groups have shared equally in the dramatic improvement which has occurred over the past two decades in the general health status of American children. Sharp disparities persist between the haves and the have-nots in this country—between rich and poor, white and nonwhite, inner-city dwellers and suburbanites.

Together, these five concerns became our central themes and underlie the findings and recommendations contained in the first volume of our report, which is intended primarily to present a coherent national strategy to improve child health.

The second volume contains proposals for specific improvements in five major existing federal programs: Medicaid, Title V of the Social Security Act, P.L. 94–142 (Education of all Handicapped Children Act), the Mental Health Systems Act, and the Special Supplemental Food Program for Women, Infants, and Children (WIC). A third volume, consisting primarily of statistical tables, is probably the most comprehensive single compilation of data on child health and related issues yet published. A fourth volume includes the many extraordinarily valuable background papers prepared for the Panel's use.

SCOPE OF THE SELECT PANEL REPORT

Our recommendations cover an extremely broad range of issues, including the physical environment, health behavior, nutrition, needed health services, organization and financing of services, structure of governmental arrangements, manpower considerations, and research. Addressing such a wide-ranging array of issues proved extremely difficult. Many times during the year and a half of our work we—together with members of our overburdened staff—wondered whether we had been too ambitious, but we kept returning to the conviction that comprehensiveness and specificity were both essential to fashioning an effective national strategy and to complying with our mandate.

Those who read our report carefully will discover our findings and recommendations not only are far-ranging, but also include many subtleties necessitated by the complexities we found. For example, while we make the case for comprehensive health care, we also recommend categorical support for a new preventive dental program for school-age children and urge continued support and expansion of categorical family planning programs. While we oppose the isolation of individual service components from what should be coordinated care, we focus on home visiting as an especially promising means of reaching pregnant women and infants with needed services. Similarly, while emphasizing the improvements needed in the primary care parts of our health system, we note the astonishing achievements in specialized medical care, recommend better links between primary and more complex care, advocate firm and continued support of secondary and tertiary care, and take up the issues raised by hospitalized infants and children and the need for regionalizing complex services. Although our recommendations are mainly in the realm of public policy, we also direct attention to issues which are most effectively dealt with in the family setting. Furthermore, whereas most of our proposals involve changes in the health system, many involve policy changes in agriculture, transportation, and environmental protection. And finally, though much of what we recommend is intended for implementation in the public sector, very little of importance will happen unless we are heard also by the private sector.

MAJOR CONCLUSIONS

Although a succinct summary of our work is difficult, in the following sections I will briefly describe a few of our major conclusions.

Basic Minimal Services

Three categories of health services are so demonstrably effective and so important that it is no longer acceptable for any individual to be denied them. These are: (1) prenatal care and delivery; (2) comprehensive health services for children through age 5; and (3) family planning services. Public policy until now has been limited to efforts aimed at expanding the availability of these services, and not always in a systematic fashion. Our Panel concluded that—at least with respect to these sets of minimal basic services—the current passive governmental posture is no longer tenable. Some of us pushed for a Panel recommendation that the federal government actually guarantee receipt of these services, but the fears of unacceptable invasions of privacy and confidentiality that such a policy might entail, coupled with the anticipated furor that the implication of a court-enforceable universal right to these services might call forth, culminated in a compromise position. We unanimously agreed to recommend that access to, as well as availability of, these basic essential services should henceforth be assured. This assurance would require a series of steps, including removal of financial barriers through improvements in Medicaid, private insurance and grants programs, expansion and strengthening of provider arrangements, and clear designation of the ultimate governmental responsibility for assuring that these services are actually available and accessible.

Coherence Among Programs

To simplify the work of state and local agencies while still maintaining accountability, we concluded that the federal government must establish concrete goals and develop accountability mechanisms which stress broad but measurable performance objectives and urged that states be given greater autonomy to determine how they go about attaining these goals. At each level of government, functions must be defined more clearly so that programs reinforce each other, rather than conflict in ways that frustrate users, providers, and program administrators. New pressures must be created to encourage the development of joint eligibility determinations, reporting requirements, and accountability procedures. We recommend new organizational and oversight mechanisms to bring these about, including a Maternal and Child Health Administration, a Maternal and Child Health Advisory Commission, and periodic congressional oversight hearings. But in doing so, we emphasize that the existing plethora of programs reflects neither past ignorance nor ineptitude, but a legitimate variety of policy objectives and differences in political priorities, as well as a traditional preference for incremental change.

Our Panel's call for a new national commitment to protect and promote maternal and child health is reflected in our recommendations for organizational changes to insure greater visibility and more coherence in the administration of maternal and child health programs. We concluded that such coherence and efficiency would require careful planning at all levels of government, rather than a weakening of the governmental role at the federal, state, or local level.

Environment, Nutrition, and Health Behavior

A third set of major recommendations revolves around the steps that social institutions—including schools, industry, the media, and voluntary associations, as well as individuals and the health system—must take to reduce accidents and risks in the physical environment, improve nutrition, and promote healthier ways of living. Our proposals in each of these areas emphasize the importance of social and structural changes. Often the most effective strategy involves environmental change. Better motor vehicle design, for example, may be the best way to reduce car injuries and deaths. Limiting the temperature on hot water heaters may be the most effective way of preventing burns, just as mandatory window guards in New York City seem to reduce deaths and injuries from falls.

The Panel also focused considerable attention on the crucial role of behavior in shaping health, especially during pregnancy, infancy, and adolescence. We found hopeful signs of effective interventions, especially in reducing teenage smoking, but there is still an urgent need for better understanding of the many complex determinants of health behavior.

   We concluded that to help famillies provide a nurturant, safe, and stimulating environment for their children at every stage of development, parents should have better access to programs of preparation for childbirth and parenting and to community support programs. We emphasize that the degree of personal control over health behavior is not evenly or randomly distributed throughout society, and that the health system, schools, the media, industry, and voluntary associations should all be part of efforts to help individuals live healthier lives.

   The Panel gives particular attention to nutrition because of its importance to growth and development, especially in pregnant women, infants, and children, and because of the mounting evidence associating various dietary patterns, often set in childhood, with the development of chronic degenerative diseases in later life. We concluded that existing governmental food programs have contributed much to improve child health and that such programs must be maintained and expanded. We also outlined a variety of strategies to make adequate nutrition a more central element in policies and programs to improve health.

Importance of Psychosocial Services

   The fourth set of major recommendations to be emphasized derives from our conclusion that a broader array of appropriate services addressed to health problems with significant psychosocial and behavioral components (e.g., child abuse, pregnancy among young teenagers, the management of chronic illness) must be made widely available. This requires changes in the organization and financing of health services, the training and utilization of health professionals, and the processes for defining such services and the circumstances in which they are best paid for by third-party payers.

   As Dr. Robert Haggerty wrote several years ago (and as was confirmed by our Panel wherever we turned), the current major health problems of children are those that would have been barely mentioned a generation ago:

- Up to a million children each year are the victims of child abuse;
- Each year some 11,000 children are born to girls under 15 years old;
- Sixty percent of seventh-grade boys and 75% of eighth-grade boys drink alcohol; and 5% of seventh-grade boys and 16% of eighth-grade boys were classified in a national survey as "problem drinkers."

It is possible to look at data like these, as well as data on disparities in infant mortality and incidence of low birth weight by race, and rising death rates from homicide, suicide, and accidents, and conclude, as many have done, that medicine has already made its full contribution to the improvement of child health, and that, at least in this country, further improvements await changes in social conditions we seem unwilling to make. It is true, of course, that if we could eliminate poverty and racism in our society, if teachers and schools were more effective, and if we had full employment and every young person could look forward to productive work, the current predominance of negative health statistics would change and the gaps between population groups would be reduced. But, our Panel asked, is this the only way for child health to improve?

We concluded that the answer to that question is a very clear "no," and we were determined to direct public attention to the extensive opportunities for improving child health by improving health policies and programs, so long as health services and policies are defined broadly.

An impressive array of data shows that health services can make a difference; we already know a great deal about how to modify the health system to reduce gaps among population groups, to prevent the preventable tragedies, diseases, and disabilities, and to provide services that respond to the changing needs of today's children and families.

Implications for Organizing and Financing Health Services

Our Panel concluded that much of what must be done to make a broader array of services available to all who need them is entirely consistent with what must be done to make minimum basic services universally available, as well as to assure access to groups traditionally considered "hard to reach." Let me review the implications for the organization of health services financing which flow from this conclusion.

It is quite clear that barriers to making needed health services more widely available and accessible can be overcome. These barriers have been overcome in community health centers, children and youth centers, maternal and infant care centers, Health Maintenance Organizations (HMO's), and other organized settings where physicians, nurse practitioners, and a wide variety of health professionals work collaboratively—and often with trained lay persons—to provide a broad range of services. These organizations have also demonstrated their capacity to reach out and establish working partnerships with neighborhood organizations, community mental health centers, school systems, correctional systems, and social service systems. Based on clear evidence of their success in conducting a wide range of programs, we recommended that these programs be strengthened and expanded.

Let me cite just a few examples of successful efforts conducted by these types of programs:

1. In Cleveland, those patients enrolled in a maternal and infant care

project receiving patient education, nutrition counseling, social services, appointment follow-up, and special services for adolescents
experienced 60% less perinatal mortality than a matched group of
patients being seen in the same hospital and not receiving these
additional services (Select Panel, 1981, Vol. I, p. 237);

2. In Alabama, under the leadership of a vigorous new director of
maternal and child health, the health department substantially extended and upgraded its services, establishing prenatal care clinics
in ten of the poorest counties where none had existed previously.
Within 4 years, infant mortality in Alabama has been reduced from
20 to 14.3 per 1,000—very close to the national average. This is, of
course, an extraordinary accomplishment, in view of the fact that
Alabama is 46th among the states in per capita income (Select Panel,
1981, Vol. I, p. 244);

3. In Denver and Cincinnati, integrated networks of neighborhood
health services have markedly lowered differentials in infant mortality between races and between low-income and more affluent
areas (Select Panel, 1981, Vol. I, p. 244);

4. Home visiting programs in Montreal, Denver, Rochester, and rural
Appalachia—which are among the few sites that have produced
evaluation data—have improved some significant aspects of health
outcomes for pregnant women and infants, children at risk of abuse,
or chonically ill children and their families (Select Panel, 1981, Vol.
I, p. 205, p. 259).

American communities vary so widely in their needs and resources
and prize so highly the diversity of their own ways of solving problems
that it seemed to us neither feasible nor wise to attempt to move the
nation toward one standard way of delivering health services to mothers
and children. However, we did identify specific organizational attributes
which we recommend for incorporation in all primary care units. These
organizational attributes include comprehensive services, accessibility,
capacity for outreach, coordination of services, continuity of care, appropriate personnel arrangements, accountability, consumer participation, and partnership with parents.

We also concluded that the effective organization and structuring
of services is especially important for families with handicapped, chronically ill, or severely ill children; for pregnant women who, for social or
medical reasons, are at high risk; and for low-income families, who have
greater needs for health and related services and fewer resources to
negotiate their way through a complicated maze of fragmented health
services. Since these categories of families include perhaps 20% of all
children and pregnant women at any one time, and 25–33% over a period

of years, it seemed to us that the need for more highly organized primary care is not circumscribed, but spread widely throughout the population.

We were aware, and took account of the fact, that most primary care is not provided in organized settings. But we believe that with a little ingenuity, it may be possible for providers in much smaller settings (e.g., solo or small group practice), to respond more effectively to patients' psychological and social needs. This could be achieved both directly and by creating a network that reaches beyond the walls of providers' offices, by mobilizing the services needed by a pregnant woman who wants to stop drinking or smoking, by the family of a malnourished and neglected infant, by a child with learning difficulties, or by a family in need of genetic counseling.

Current financing arrangements make all this very difficult, of course, even in settings supported by grant funds. The full array of health services needed by children and pregnant women will not be adequately available without broad changes in the policies and practices of third-party payers, including restructuring of fee schedules, wider use of lump-sum and capitation payments, and use of other techniques that make economic incentives more consistent with health objectives. Nor will such an array of services be available unless we can redress the balance between the rewards for performance of technical procedures and the more time-consuming interventions such as counseling and teaching.

Our financing recommendations reflect our judgment that the way health services are financed is the single most important determinant of how the health system operates, what services are available, which professionals provide those services, and who will receive them. Current public and private third-party payment plans and programs provide incentives that result in an allocation of physician time, a distribution of physicians by specialty and location, and a manner of providing health services that collectively is unresponsive to a significant part of patient needs—especially those of children and pregnant women—and that unnecessarily drives up health care costs. We recommend that (1) purchasers of health insurance, public and private third-party payers, and health care providers take steps to modify and create alternatives to prevailing methods of reimbursing health professionals and institutions; and (2) a mechanism be created to provide expert guidance concerning which services are, in fact, needed, who is qualified to provide them and under what circumstances, and the likely effects that various payment policies and practices will have on the availability of needed services, professional personnel, facilities, and other components of the health care system.

Because current financing arrangements leave millions of Americans without public or private health insurance (and many millions more with grossly inadequate coverage), we advocate immediate improvement in both private insurance and Medicaid. But even if these improvements are made, some people will remain uncovered by any form of health insurance and many families will still be barred from needed health services or forced to choose between health care for their children and the purchase of other necessities. The inefficiencies of multiple and conflicting eligibility determinations and fragmented sources of financing will continue.

It is the Panel's conviction that the health care needs of children and pregnant women will be best served over the long run by a national health financing program that ensures entitlement to needed health services for all Americans. If such a plan cannot be put in place relatively soon, the Panel urges enactment of national health insurance for pregnant women and children under age 18. If it proves necessary to phase in eligibility even for this population, the Panel recommends starting with a program covering all pregnant women and children through age 5.

Allocating Resources

In concluding this brief sketch of our findings and recommendations, I want to put our financing recommendations into the more general context of decision-making regarding resource allocations.

Targeting funds and services. We hear increasingly about the urgent need for better and more precise targeting of our resources. In my view, it is extremely important to distinguish clearly among various kinds of targeting. The implications of targeting resources on undeserved geographic areas or on all children and pregnant women are very different from targeting programs to serve only those individuals and families which meet narrow definitions of medical, social, or economic need. The pressures to allocate scarce resources are very real, but they must not be glibly translated into ever more restrictive eligibility requirements that will then become increasingly formidable barriers to the receipt of prompt and appropriate services.

The cost of certain forms of targeting must be considered along with the savings. Costs of targeting include the increased probability of a given individual falling through the cracks between programs and therefore not receiving needed services, the lack of public support for programs limited to the poor, and the expense of sorting and resorting large numbers of families that move in and out of poverty and risk status.

Thus, it is possible to advocate, as the Panel did, targeting resources to assure that a range of particularly effective services is available to all in need and to assure that resources are made available in underserved areas. We conclude, on the other hand, that with regard to long-term financing of personal health services, a program of universal entitlement is decisively preferable to one directed solely at the poor. When eligibility for a health financing program is tied to poverty status, the results are so detrimental to the quality, continuity, and appropriate use of care, to incentives for economic independence, to public support, and to administrative efficiency, that the price of targeting in this instance is too high.

More refined targeting has also been advocated for supplemental food programs of all kinds, including Food Stamps, WIC, and school lunch and breakfast programs. Before substantial changes are made in these programs, however, it is important to consider their accomplishments and how their proven effectiveness would be impaired by proposed changes. The accomplishments of food programs are well documented by two Field Foundation surveys of hunger in America, the first undertaken by a group of physicians in 1967, and the second repeated 10 years later, after the enactment of WIC and the major expansion of other federal food programs, including Food Stamps. In 1977, the Field Foundation medical team reported their "overwhelming impression" that there were:

> . . . far fewer grossly malnourished people in this country today than there were ten years ago . . . . In the Mississippi Delta, in the coal fields of Appalachia and in coastal South Carolina—where visitors ten years ago could quickly see large numbers of stunted, apathetic children with swollen stomachs and the dull eyes and poorly healing wounds characteristic of malnutrition—such children are not to be seen in such numbers. (Kotz, 1979, p. 9)

The Field observers concluded that "the facts of life for Americans living in poverty remain . . . But in the area of food there is a difference" (Kotz, 1979, p. 9).

One can only hope that the architects of new attempts to cut and target food programs take such findings into account.

Reliance on market mechanisms.   Market mechanisms have worked in our health system to produce excellent health services, although often limited in range, for many Americans. Families and individuals having the requisite money or insurance coverage and the necessary information to negotiate the system, and who live in places and circumstances that are attractive to physicians, can get excellent health care, especially for acute illness. It is tempting, therefore, to place an uncritical reliance on present or future market mechanisms to generate answers to heretofore unsolved problems. However, market forces are unlikely to distribute resources to geographic areas that need them most, or to make available an array of services which are well-matched to the array of needs in the population.

The assumption of those who look to the market as the mechanism for allocating health care resources is that there is a certain sanctity inherent in services purchased by people with their own money and through third-party reimbursement plans which they or their employers have purchased. This argument further assumes that these services are chosen by consumers in preference to other services.

The weakness of this reasoning lies in the fact that consumers of health services, individually or in groups, rarely possess the information they need to make reasonable and rational decisions in their own and their families' interest. In particular, most consumers lack the requisite expertise to evaluate medical information, and most consumers also have had only a narrow range of choices available to them. For example, parents of children with asthma, juvenile-onset diabetes, or other chronic conditions often assume, on the basis of their experiences with physicians who deal only with the narrow, medical aspects of these diseases, that they cannot expect their needs for counseling, advice, and support could be met through the health system.

The range of services currently available to most consumers may be only tangentially related to actual consumer preferences. They are more likely to be the products of such factors as:

- Whether they are the kind of services which providers have been traditionally trained to provide (resulting in an emphasis on high-technology, in-hospital, tertiary care services);
- Whether the services are expensive and unpredictable enough to conform to the principle of "the insurable risk," which third-party payers have traditionally underwritten in preference to coverage of more routine services, that are more likely to be under some control by the insured;
- Whether the services are relatively easy for third-party payers to define and establish uniform standards for.

Furthermore, much advertising and other media messages, many aspects of our culture, and some parts of the medical world have successfully conveyed to consumers a worship of medical technology, a hope for the "magic bullet" that will cure, and a general outlook on life that is not conducive to consumers' demanding—or sometimes even supporting—interventions aimed at anything short of rapid, miracle cures.

In fact, largely because of the pressure of market forces, our health system has been shaped in such a way that it works better for saving 1,000-gram infants than for reducing the incidence of births to young teenagers; it works better for the pregnant woman who needs a Caesarian section than for one who needs the help of a home visitor in preparing to nourish and nurture a new baby; and it works better for the child who needs a fiber-optic gastroscopy than for the one whose parents need help in coping with his chronic illness.

The mismatch between needed and available services is greater for children than for most other population groups, while a high proportion of children's health care is paid for out-of-pocket. This combination of circumstances provides additional evidence of the ineffectiveness of the marketplace in providing the appropriate array of needed services.

Current proposals to introduce more marketplace competition into the health system are unlikely to change these forces, including their impact on health services. Proposals for basing health financing programs on competition (or "consumer choice") rely heavily on the advantages of Health Maintenance Organizations (HMO's), which—together with other organized settings—the Panel has identified as an effective delivery mechanism. However, unrestrained provider competition entails clear dangers to the health of mothers and children. If new proposals based on provider competition were nevertheless adopted, community health centers, hospital outpatient departments, and health departments should be assured a chance to participate in the competition with HMO's. Even under those circumstances, however, it is unlikely that unregulated competition would involve much more than a contest among providers to see who can most sharply cut short-run costs for a narrowly defined, traditional set of medical services, without much reference to long-range effects on either costs or health.

PROSPECTS FOR THE FUTURE

As we contemplate the future from our vantage point in 1981, it seems a number of urgent and immediate tasks emerge from the Panel's conclusions. Foremost among these is that we must make certain that current attempts to streamline programs and make them more efficient are undertaken with full understanding of: (1) the accomplishments of existing programs; (2) the opportunities for better coordination through such mechanisms as joint reporting, joint eligibility determinations, and better definitions of roles among programs and among levels of government; (3) the illusoriness of savings that can be expected from cutbacks in essential services; (4) the clear need for certain minimum improvements in existing programs; and (5) the dangers of more and greater inequities resulting from the withdrawal of federal authority over

a number of specific functions, such as the setting of performance standards and health goals.

Among the longer-range tasks that emerge from our report, several
seem to me of particular importance. First, we must take steps to increase
the understanding by policymakers and the public that our nation can,
and must, create a less narrowly medical system of health services;
furthermore, pressures on third-party payers and on purchasers of
health insurance must go beyond cost containment and aim at harness-
ing the health financing system to health objectives. Second, we must,
with whatever local, state, federal, or private funds are available, encourage activities to document the effects of large-scale (state-wide or
region-wide) interventions aimed at such major problems as health behavior in pregnancy, child safety, assuring basic minimal services to
entire populations, home visiting to pregnant women and newborns,
and forging better linkages between private physicians on the one hand
and health departments, out patient departments, welfare agencies, and
similar community services on the other hand. Third, we must, again
with whatever funds are available, support the development of local
community efforts, ranging from making hospital policies more responsive to the needs of children and families to monitoring the health-related
arrangements for children who are being cared for through public institutions and agencies.

The times we live in are hardly optimal for those of us who believe
that our arrangements for shared responsibility for the young—under
both public and private auspices—are not only essential, but must be
extended. We hope that our Panel has contributed to illuminating the
specifics of what needs to be done to improve child health and has
provided some of the documentation to make it possible to continually
broaden the consensus needed for constructive action. Let us work together in the years ahead to make certain that the child health policies
and programs shaped in the 1980's respond adequately and wisely to
the needs of all our children.

REFERENCES

Kotz, N. *Hunger in America: The federal response.* New York: Field Foundation, 1979.
Select Panel for the Promotion of Child Health. *Better health for our children: A national strategy* (4 vols.). Washington, D.C.: U.S. Printing Office, 1981.

TWO

CONSCIENCE, CONTROVERSY, AND CHILDREN

C. ARDEN MILLER

INTRODUCTION

Formulations of public policy for the health of children address two separate records of relevance: what we do and what we say we do. Characterizations from these two domains can be termed "operational policy" and "nominal policy," respectively. Though they are not unrelated to each other, their linkages are inconstant. Disparity between word and deed in children's policy was not great in this country prior to a hundred years ago, because childhood as a social issue is barely that old (Takanishi, 1978). Before that time, the prevailing nominal policy regarding children accurately reflected the dominant practice: children were a responsibility, and sometimes a resource, for their parent's concern; societal attention to the young grew only as children survived to achieve social and economic independence from their parents.

Focus on children as a social concern brought a view of childhood as a critical period for the reform of society. Conditions surrounding children were a prime target for reform movements in early twentieth-century America (Takanishi, 1978). Tension developed between old and new conceptions of children:

> The old view argued that children were economic assets who had an obligation to compensate their parents for raising them . . . . central to child labor reform was the conceptualization of childhood as a formative period during which physical development was strengthened and orientation and skills for life work were established through educational programs. Children were not to be "wasted" during their early years since they were important as trained adults for the progress of the society. (Takanishi, 1978, p. 15)

Within recent decades, a perspective has developed that children have rights of their own, independent either of parental or societal interests (Feshbach & Feshbach, 1978; Caldwell, 1980). The case for such rights is argued on behalf of children as individuals, rather than for their potential to protect the security of aging parents or to improve the future for society at large. To whatever extent children are accorded such rights, there follows a societal responsibility to safeguard them.

The tensions surrounding opposing orientations on the status of children became manifest in diverse ways. These opposing views have come to represent a cluster of unresolved policy dilemmas regarding children's health. Any responsible effort to understand or cope with the health of children must deal with these dilemmas. Indeed, these dilemmas represent a thorny legacy of controversy for the work of the Select Panel for the Promotion of Child Health. In this paper, then, I will identify these dilemmas, characterize their many programmatic manifestations, and examine the prospects for their resolution as one way to measure the potential contribution of the Select Panel Report. The major assumption of this paper is that the Select Panel's Report, if it is to provide direction for child health policy in the decade ahead, must help us understand and resolve the persistent policy dilemmas which have caused child health programs to be reshaped from time to time by prevailing sociopolitical orientations and at other times to be immobilized by contradictory approaches and by political antagonisms.

The issues of interest are in substantial measure matters of conscience. Well-intentioned people examine the same circumstances and draw diametrically opposed conclusions. Arguments tend to invoke value judgments; new research data, important as it is to elevate the argumentation, seldom are so conclusive as to refute one set of values in favor of another.

Many of the issues are not unique to concerns about health or to programs for children. Health agencies nevertheless have become important arenas for debate and negotiation of these issues, and children are commonly the vulnerable victims of unresolved controversy. Even considering many important improvements in the status of children's health the record of progress is uneven and troubling, especially when comparing subgroups within our population. Some critics hold that large numbers of American children are the victims of a socially-sanctioned paralysis in health policy which perpetuates deficiencies in essential services and programs. But other critics hold that those very services and programs rob children and their families of freedom and self-reliance.

The Select Panel's Report sets forth the best available compilation on the status of children's health and the condition of programs which have been designed to improve it. A full recapitulation of that record is not necessary, but parts of it will be invoked as the dilemmas of health policy are identified and elaborated. These dilemmas include: impingement of societal responsibility on parental freedoms and prerogatives; disharmony between known determinants of health and program development; comprehensive and family-focused vs. categorical services; behavior and health—individual choice or imposed patterns; federal, state and local government—partners or adversaries; selected or universal services.

IMPINGEMENT OF SOCIETAL RESPONSIBILITY ON PARENTAL FREEDOMS AND PREROGATIVES

The first dilemma is basic and underlies the others to a significant degree. This issue weighs individual freedoms against the dependence that may result from protective and supportive services provided under governmental authority. One side of the issue was recently described with beautiful clarity in Ludington's (1980) biography of John Dos Passos, a chronicle which serves in significant respects as twentieth-century America's intellectual history. Dos Passos, always concerned about individual liberties, came to believe in a conspiracy of bureaucratic repression. As Ludington (1980) puts it, "utterly committed to individual freedoms, [Dos Passos] interpreted conspiracy when society infringed on the rights of the individual. He understood that an increasingly complex society was bound to put strains on libertarianism; yet he could only decry those pressures" (p. 430).

Others have seen that social justice and equity require a society dominated by entrepreneurial advantage and rugged individualism to take systematic steps to protect the well-being of the least rugged. In the competitive allocation of resources and services which so much characterizes operational health policies in this country, some population groups are persistently neglected. These include infants, children, poor people, minority groups, the elderly, and women, especially if they are young and poor. Do these groups require an organized effort to help assure that they receive basic services and benefits?

The tension between individual or parental freedoms and the exercise of some degree of collective responsibility is especially poignant in the history of public health; there is virtually no public health measure of consequence that does not in some measure, according to someone's view, limit individual freedoms. The history of public health can be written as a chronicle of tradeoffs between individual freedom and societal responsibility to protect health. A few examples will illustrate that point.

A hundred years ago, efforts to collect data on epidemic disease by requiring that physicians report cases of tuberculosis, plague, and cholera were bitterly fought as an invasion of privacy and a disruption of the doctor–patient relationship. Court rulings ultimately supported the right of public agencies to require the reporting of disease in order to help curb epidemics. Collective protection took precedence over individual freedoms. This conflict was rekindled recently in California when revisions of the birth certificate were considered by the state legislature. A politically potent group argued that any information beyond simple recording of a birth constituted invasion of privacy and enlarged the potential for bureaucratic interference and control, especially of nonconforming persons.

The most fundamental regulations on disposal of waste and use of water supplies also restrain personal action and individual freedoms. Although controversy over regulating household privies and community sewage now seems quaint, the controversy emerges with new relevance in efforts to curb pollution of air, water, and land by industrial toxins, either potential or real, which proliferate faster than understanding of their possible hazards. For example, what curbs will be imposed, whose land will be condemned, and whose health will be jeopardized by storage of poison from industrial waste?

Early efforts to regulate private property in order to protect the public's health were met with violent opposition. Requirements for safety doors on elevators were viewed as an unnecessary expense which impinged on the rights of property owners to spend their own money in their own ways. Courts upheld the government's stance in protecting public safety even at the expense of regulating private property. Similar controversy persists surrounding regulations which would compel construction of safer automobiles. Mandatory emission control standards, use of seat belts, and speed limits have all been resisted by the auto industry and often by portions of the public whose safety was presumably being protected.

Control of epidemic disease at times imposed control of personal behavior and even enforced treatment over objections from the client.

Arrests and fines for spitting on the sidewalk, for example, were a well-intentioned effort to curb the spread of tuberculosis. Such control of behavior was resisted by many people who cherished liberty even more than sanitation or aesthetics. Enforced hospitalization for active cases of tuberculosis was also deemed necessary in the public interest, in spite of resistance by many. In current times, laws requiring that children be immunized or be excluded from school represent a clear restraint on freedom. These and similar restraints can be circumvented only by strenuous objection. Fluoridation of water, well-defended for promoting dental health, is fought on grounds that it eliminates individual choice about medication.

Government action restraining child labor is a classic issue which pits the protective role of government against the rights of parents to decide the fate of their own children. Restrictive laws were passed by Congress and later declared unconstitutional, the classic test case originating from the textile mills of North Carolina (Bremner, 1971, pp. 710–717). Efforts in 1915 to amend the Constitution in order to establish the protective role of government were fought with an acrimony which exceeded by far the current intensity of debates on the Equal Rights Amendment. Once again, although the controversy over child labor now seems archaic, it continues in subtle forms. Every summer legislatures in states depending on migrant labor for their agricultural harvest debate resolutions setting aside child labor restraints. Arguments in favor of deregulation cite the character-building effects of hard work and the undesirable alternative of coping with shiftless children with too much time on their hands. Is the current proposal to set aside the minimum wage for children an example of this same conflict? Does such action represent expanded job opportunity for children or a resurgence of their economic exploitation?

Projections on premature deaths and disability from automobile accidents suggest that the compulsory use of seat belts for infants and children would have a dramatically beneficial effect. Several states have experimented with laws requiring that children be restrained in automobiles. Proposals for these laws are ordinarily bitterly contested not only because of difficulties with enforcement, but also because of the implications of bureaucratic control over individual behavior. Proposals for such a law in North Carolina, for example, have been consistently thwarted. A law was passed in Tennessee, but it was modified to allow an infant to be held in the mother's arms, although abundant evidence indicates that, on impact, the arms will not restrain the child from flying through the windshield.

The use of motorcycle helmets is another example of restrictions on personal behavior for a common good which is poorly understood and not always accepted. At one time all states but two had laws requiring motorcyclists to wear helmets. Such laws have been repealed in 18 states on the grounds that they unnecessarily restrict individual freedoms and that a motorcyclist should be allowed to place his own head at risk if he desires. The countervailing view argues that an injured motorcyclist will expect that community services (e.g., emergency medical care, intensive treatment units, and rehabilitative services) be available, when necessary. According to this view, costly services should not inflate the public tax burden unnecessarily. Furthermore, if the deceased motorcyclist has a family, an appropriate expectation holds that society will provide care and sustenance for surviving children. Thus, arguments can be marshalled to demonstrate that society has a stake in the degree of risk which a motorcyclist chooses for himself.

Community action to prevent child abuse is one of the most fascinating examples of societal interference with personal or parental rights. For many decades, physicians who saw large numbers of children were aware that many suffered "accidents" and injuries which strongly suggested abuse. Careful investigations were seldom made and certainly no community action was mounted to cope with the problem, because it was widely believed that parental control over children was absolute—even at the expense of occasionally absued children. The matter became a legitimate target for societal intervention only when Dr. Henry Kempe gave emphasis to child abuse as a problem requiring concern for parents (Helfer & Kempe, 1976, p. 183). He characterized child abuse as a plea by the parent for help. In a sense, when the victim was defined as the parent rather than the child, intervention became permissible without carrying the threat of interference with parental rights.

John Lennon's murder and, more recently, the attempted assassination of President Reagan have once again triggered concern about handguns. Data have been persuasive for many years that such guns are not effective protectors of private property or of personal safety, and the extent to which such guns are used in sport clubs appears to be quite small (Pasternack, 1973). Rather, handguns find distressing use as instruments of murder or accidental death, most often between close friends and family members. In spite of this knowledge, the view has prevailed that government must not interfere with an individual's right to bear arms, notwithstanding the fact that even tiny guns and tiny bullets represent substantial hazards to the freedom and life of others.

Two especially timely examples which pitted government-sponsored protective services against individual freedoms were exemplified by President Nixon's veto message of the 1971 Comprehensive Child Development Act. The message explained that providing group care for children of working mothers threatened to weaken the fiber of the

American family. The communal care of children was identified with communes, and communes, at least by inference, with communism. Senator Walter Mondale, who had sponsored the legislation, reported that nothing in his entire political career had brought down a more vigorous and vituperative campaign of abuse than his proposals for expanded funding of day care centers. The legislation had been carefully framed as an effort to strengthen and support families by providing them with essential services. Such an argument, however, was not politically persuasive.

One astonishing example of the controversy between personal freedoms and government intervention was prompted by the recent North Carolina Child Health Plan (Kotch & Johnson, 1981). The plan was a carefully worked out proposal which defined the substantial health problems and health needs of North Carolina's children. Among other proposals, the plan suggested that every child should have a "medical home" and that children who were not served by existing provider systems should enjoy the benefits of expanded, publicly-sponsored, medical service programs. The metaphor of a medical home was seized upon by conservative libertarians as an example of bureaucratic intrusion into the sanctity of the family and was linked with the threat of removing children from their own parental homes to something like a government-sponsored medical orphanage. The cause was promptly abandoned and a child health plan for North Carolina was demonstrated to be politically risky.

The particular way these examples are formulated may reflect a bias in favor of government action to protect and serve neglected people, while simultaneously minimizing the risks to important liberties that ensue from assuring that people receive demonstrably necessary care. Nevertheless, tradeoffs between individual freedom and public responsibility are involved in each example, and they indicate all too clearly that designing government programs for those in need can be tricky and surprising business. Reports recently circulated about a Texas town in which a newspaper advertisement invited inquiry about abortion. Women who responded to the advertisement were promptly visited by someone who was authorized by court order to serve as guardian for the continued health and safety of the unborn fetus. To most people, this sad event represents a corruption of the protective intent of government—at the expense of the pregnant women's liberties. But where is the dividing line between protection and persecution? It is not precise, and in a free society it must be established by political negotiation. Some tradeoffs are involved in protecting the public's health; it is important and fascinating work. Adherents to a wide range of political perspectives will agree that the best tradeoffs have not always been made; convincing examples can be cited in support of different kinds of conscience.

DISHARMONY BETWEEN KNOWN DETERMINANTS OF HEALTH AND PROGRAM DEVELOPMENT

The second major dilemma of health policy has to do with the disjunction between known determinants of health on the one hand and the resource allocation and program development proposed to promote health on the other. The initiatives most effective in improving children's health have to do with food and nutrition, reproductive behavior, and improved sanitation. Further efforts in these endeavors are well justified and almost certainly would be rewarded by further improvements in health. Even more dramatic improvements might come from injury prevention and improved safety in the home, at job sites, and on the highways. Most of these interventions require a publicly sponsored service or a degree of regulation which is strenuously resisted by some people.

Medical care on the other hand, important as it is for humanitarian reasons and for lifesaving and rehabilitation of selected individuals, is an expensive and not-too-promising approach to improving health for entire populations. There is room here for controversy. One of the dramatic achievements in recent years has been the improved survival rates of low birth weight infants in this country by means of expensive and elaborate medical interventions. This achievement highlights a related problem, namely, that an excessive proportion of American babies continue to be born at low birth weights. Efforts to treat the problem have gained support far in excess of efforts to prevent it. The nation seems to be involved in a medical arms race in which few, if any, restraints are placed on the development and application of costly technologies. Is there an implicit hope that good health can be achieved through medical care, even at great expense, thereby making it unnecessary to undertake difficult and painful social reforms that would be necessary to prevent the same problems? Prevention would involve assuring participation by all populations in essential services such as prenatal care, family planning, and well child supervision. Some special assurances on behalf of the poor and minority groups would be required. Income supplements might be necessary. These are the very interventions which some libertarians view as threatening—and dependency-producing—rather than protective.

The possibility that expanded medical care is being used as a surrogate for social reform focuses attention not only on a difficult role for professional providers but on the inconsistencies of a society which thrusts large responsibilities on the healing professions and then increasingly blames them for the frustrations and expense which result.

COMPREHENSIVE AND FAMILY-FOCUSED VS. CATEGORICAL SERVICES

A third dilemma splits the camp which holds that organized community supports and services are essential for children's health. Should those services be limited to certain populations or to certain problems which can be readily identified and addressed in piecemeal ways, or should the services be comprehensive, in the sense that all known health benefits are provided under one system of care and, when possible, under one roof? Supportive evidence is flawed for both the categorical and comprehensive approaches. A categorical label has come to characterize the public health approach, largely because money has been made available for specific services as new needs have been identified or supported. Family planning, venereal disease control, mental health, mental retardation, perinatal care, well child services: all these causes have been more often advanced separately than together and have usually been advocated by strong pressure groups working on behalf of some neglected sector of the population. Categorical services have come to be identified with fragmentation, discontinuity, gaps in service, unintended duplications, and sometimes with a demeaning, impersonalized approach.

The origins of comprehensive services can be traced back to the early days of public health, but they received their greatest impetus during the service reforms of the 1960s when underserved populations, often in an identifiable geographic area such as the inner cities, were saturated with all known health services that could be well defended for promoting health and preventing disease. Since that time, comprehensive care has been characterized as available, continuous, responsive, and family oriented. Private medical practice as provided by the family doctor is promoted by some as a desirable form of comprehensive care.

Most forms of comprehensive care, including both the practitioner model and the community clinics that originated in the 1960s, carry the burden of limited availability. Large sectors of the population that would benefit from these services have not been reached; efforts to extend such endeavors beyond the islands of successful demonstration have not been extensive. When comprehensive services have been tried, as with community health centers and rural clinics, economic restraints force the programs to be pruned and to become less than comprehensive.

The concept of medical care as comprehensive, continuous, and available from a single source is much cherished, but its support rests only partly on sound evidence. Some intuitions are involved. Supportive studies show that people who have a regular source of medical care, when compared with those who do not, make more extensive use of preventive services (Lave, Lave, Leinhardt & Nagin, 1979). That counts as an important benefit. On the other hand, some studies (e.g., Roos, Roos, Gilbert, & Nicol 1980) show that children who are involved with a continuous and regular source of medical care are not necessarily protected from procedures of dubious benefit, such as tonsillectomy. In fact, Roos et al. (1980) suggest that continuity of care from a single source may, in fact, contribute to the perpetuation of the same mistakes. Dutton and Silber (1980) compare anticipated disease rates among groups of children participating in a variety of ambulatory care systems. They found that children using multiple providers were not disadvantaged when compared with those who used a single source of care. When comparing different systems of care, they found that fee-for-service practice with solo practitioners provided the least protective benefit and prepaid group practice provided the most. Public clinics sponsored either by hospitals or by health departments fell at intermediate levels of protective benefit.

A recent survey of medical services sponsored by health departments selected for their favorable reputation interviewed clients in the waiting room (Miller, Moos, Kotch, Brown, & Brainard, 1981). Clients often said that an aspect of health department care they enjoyed most was having all services available under one roof—a practice which they saw as an advantage over previous piecemeal care obtained from private practitioners having consultants and laboratory services scattered at various sites. This observation contradicts the widespread perception that only public clinics foment fragmentation of services.

Emergency rooms are ordinarily regarded as sites of expensive, poor-quality care for many ambulatory services. Yet the proportion of children who make emergency room visits is not very different when comparing children from high- and low-income families (15% and 19%, respectively), even though the two groups differ strikingly in the proportions having a regular source of medical care (Kovar, 1978, p. 57). This circumstance may arise from changes in traditional medical practice which have minimized the availability of usual sources of medical care, either public or private, during evenings and weekends.

The record of accomplishment for categorical services on behalf of specific age groups deserves attention. Evidence can be cited to suggest that unless special efforts are made to reach children, they may get crowded out when competing with older people in the same provider system. These experiences tend to contradict the widespread bias in favor of comprehensive care for all age groups provided in the same system of care. A number of observers have reported that when medical care in Quebec became free, all population groups except children seemed to benefit. The number of physician visits for children declined, a phenomenon widely interpreted as an example of crowding out (Enterline, Salter, McDonald, & McDonald, 1973).

Wagner (1978) describes an experience in Denmark where children's clinics were converted to family clinics so that all members of a household could be served in the same setting. One outcome of this change was that elderly people with chronic disease tended to take over available services, thereby diminishing the care for children dramatically. Similarly, the 1974 administrative reorganization of health services in the United Kingdom phased out neighborhood maternal and child health clinics and placed their personnel in general practitioners' offices. Once again this was a well-intentioned effort to provide a single door of entry to medical services for all household members. Some years later, it was found that personnel who previously had been devoting all their time and effort to children were now spending half their time attending the elderly; for the first time in many decades, important indicators of child health—such as immunization rates—began to decline dangerously (Committee on Child Health Services, 1976). In our own country, Medicaid—the financing system for medical care for poor people—has demonstrated a pronounced tendency to allocate an increasing proportion of its resources to domiciliary care for the elderly at the expense of benefits for children. Diminishing dental benefits for children and deficient coverage for prenatal care (especially for first pregnancies) are examples of such neglect (Taft, 1976).

The record is strong that some services such as family planning, mental health, well child care, and possible pre- and postnatal care are rendered effectively in neighborhood settings close to clients, and it may be advantageous to separate services for the healthy from the complete spectrum of care for all age groups and for all kinds of morbidity. Few people would speak against incorporating the health maintenance services in comprehensive care. Nonetheless, the evidence reviewed above suggests that categorical, freestanding services are advantageous for promoting children's health.

Finally, the record is persuasive that the family doctor, the most cherished symbol of comprehensive care, provides services which are not always comprehensive and that public clinics, stigmatized as a symbol of fragmented services, can, in fact, render care which is both comprehensive and sensitive to client circumstances (Miller, et al., 1981). Categorical services allow for priorities to be set, for specified objectives to be achieved, and for the interests of underserved people to be addressed. Nevertheless, the current medical fashion strongly favors approaches that can be designated comprehensive and tends to minimize the possible advantages of categorical care even when strenuous efforts are made to link those categorical services with a full spectrum of other provider systems.

BEHAVIOR AND HEALTH: INDIVIDUAL CHOICE OR IMPOSED PATTERNS

Many experts agree that personal behavior and the quality of life are important determinants of health (Knowles, 1977). Perceptions begin to diverge when experts are asked how to improve either the quality of life or health-related behavior. Education may be part of the answer. If people are instructed about health-promoting behavior, they may change the way they eat, exercise, drink, smoke, and drive their automobiles. Some exhortations for improved personal behavior carry the implication that people who perversely persist in behavior that is counterproductive to good health may well deserve the consequences of disease and disability.

Other experts speak with a different emphasis. These people see poverty, racism, sexism, and even advertising as such potent determinants of life style and personal behavior that exhortations for improvements directed at individuals become meaningless. The potent and often adverse health messages emanating from advertising and television programs are seen as powerful determinants which overshadow more modestly supported efforts of public health education.

Education to change life styles holds the greatest promise for people who command resources sufficient to permit choices of life options. Are there people so dispirited by lack of options and so devoid of resources to change their living circumstances that appeals for them to improve themselves are a mockery? I think so, but the case is by no means clearcut. The divergence of views on this matter is further complicated by the widespread use of pejorative labels, such as blaming the victim and social engineering.

FEDERAL, STATE, AND LOCAL GOVERNMENT: PARTNERS OR ADVERSARIES?

Confusion over functional linkages among different levels of government works to confound whatever degree of public responsibility may exist to protect the health of children. On a theoretical basis, a governmental chain of responsibility can be conceptualized with implementation of public programs at local and state levels in accordance with national standards of performance established at the federal level. This concept sees higher levels of government providing funds, standards, and guarantees to make up for deficiencies or gaps in performance at lower levels.

Although state and local governments have increased expenditures for health services over the past decade to maintain at least a constant proportional share of the total outlay, the private share has declined so that the federal government emerges as the major and growing source of financing. Federal financing mechanisms include an elaborate system of grants to state and local governments and to private and voluntary agencies, revenue sharing to local governments, and reimbursements to provider systems with varying degrees of administration through state governments.

The concept of a chain of responsibility linking different levels of government breaks down most dramatically when applied to the grant programs. The staffs of federal agencies are apt to regard their state and local counterparts as contenders vying for funds and privilege along with all the other applicants. The large amount of federal money granted to private and voluntary agencies in fulfillment of public responsibilities to render medical care has resulted in the growth of a "third world" of medical politics. It is a world neither public nor private, but made up of independent agencies which spend public money to promote public service policies. Planning agencies and a thousand community health centers fall under this rubric. These domestic "third world" agencies enjoy the benefits of federal funding but escape much of the accountability required of official public agencies.

Confusion about state and federal roles is further confounded by inconsistencies written into much legislation. The Social Security Act of 1935 established old age security as a federal program at the same time that maternal and child health were established as state programs under limited federal financing. Confusion persisted with the amendments of the 1960s. Title XVIII, a health insurance program for the elderly, is largely a federal program with precise national uniform definitions of eligibility and benefits. Title XIX, a program of financing and providing medical care for the poor, makes use of federal money but with a wide range of state discretion—including the decision by one state not to participate. Inconsistencies persist even within the same program. Title V of the Social Security Act makes provision for maternal and child health services. The Special Projects under that Act were established during the 1960s as federal demonstrations of improved services for children and pregnant women at the same time that formula grants were being given to the states for the baseline support of maternal and child health services. The situation was further confused by President Nixon's new federalism which removed the Special Projects from federal authority and designated them as a state responsibility. The states were given no obligation to expand the projects to all populations who would benefit. Rather, each state was required only to continue one of each kind of project as a kind of perpetual demonstration of what might be done for underserved women and children.

Health planning authorizations represent another confusing and inconsistent treatment of federal and state responsibility. The Regional Medical Program of 1965 was intended to bring the newest technology for the treatment of heart disease, cancer, and strokes to all persons in need. It was a federal project implemented through "third world" agencies. It was soon joined by Comprehensive Health Planning which was designed as a partnership between federal and state governments. That partnership suffered from the serious limitation of a mandate for orderly planning to improve health services without changing usual and customary practice. The program was subsequently replaced by the National Health Planning Act of 1974 which was first proposed to be implemented by bypassing the official state and local health agencies and was later allowed to be implemented through a mix of state and federal responsibility at the discretion of the governors.

The domestic reforms of the 1960s, backsliding on these reforms in favor of commitment to the war in Vietnam, election of President Nixon and implementation of his new federalism, the mixed messages in the administration of Jimmy Carter, and the more recent election of Ronald Reagan all have been associated with pendulum swings of public policy on both the degree of public responsibility for the health of children and on how that responsibility should be exercised. These vacillations have caused many promising programs to be blighted by limited funding, limited support, and temporary commitment.

Some serious issues about federal–state relationships simply will not go away when contemplating new programs for the future. One of these issues has to do with minority populations. In important respects, the federal government has been the focus of reform to correct racist practices in relation to voting, education, public accommodations, and employment. Glaring racial inequities in health and health services persist, and in the view of many people they can be corrected only by force of federal action. Historically, the states have been allowed wide discretion in the use of federal funds for development of children's health programs. But that discretion has resulted in less than vigorous efforts to fill unmet needs and to correct inequities. If the states are relied on to implement expanded children's health programs, the record suggests that a degree of national standard setting, monitoring, and regulation will be required.

Policy analysts not willing to entrust the health futures of minority children to the states are left with the dilemma of how action at the federal level can do better. There simply is no national infrastructure of health services, except through state and local agencies. And these offer uneven prospects at best. The alternative leads federal government into efforts to persuade and pay private and voluntary providers to cope with unmet needs. To date, this has been an expensive and only marginally successful approach which creates ideological inconsistencies by setting client protection in opposition to provider prerogative not to participate.

Neither a federal nor state focus of responsibility for protecting children's health is entirely satisfactory. Formulations for improving the interdependence of different levels of government escape current political reality.

SELECTED OR UNIVERSAL SERVICES

The last dilemma weighs the comparative advantages of selected services of high technological sophistication against universal involvement in basic services. The American perspective has long favored the former approach. We have exported it to developing countries and we have relied on it in developing major medical centers in this country. In support of this bias favoring technologically sophisticated health care centers, many people have argued that such centers of excellence have an elevating effect on the level of medical care for entire surrounding populations. A diffusion of services and benefits is presumed to reach out to all underserved populations. In developing countries, the experience is strong that such an approach is expensive and that diffusion of benefits, if it does occur, is slow and by no means assured. Similarly, experience in this country has shown that some of the most neglected populations live adjacent to islands of medical excellence.

The World Health Organization and many experts in this country have in recent years taken a different approach. This approach urges the universal involvement of all persons in basic services with clear definition of benefits and an obligation over time to upgrade and increase those benefits. Michigan recently took this approach with its new health code. This code requires state government to provide, through official health agencies as may be necessary, a package of medical benefits to the entire population. The package is periodically redefined after assessment of needs and resources.

The issue of selected vs. universal services becomes urgent when considering regionalized programs of care. Current attention focuses on regionalized perinatal care. In some states, perinatal care features elaborate centers of tertiary care, particularly for low birth-weight infants.

That emphasis seems at times to preempt efforts to involve all pregnant women in early and continuous prenatal care which might contribute to the prevention of low birth weight. Reason urges that preventive care and tertiary care are not mutually exclusive. Cannot assurances be given for universal participation in basic services at the same time that provision is made for more elaborate care, when required? More than a simple affirmative answer is required. Deliberate provision for such a dual approach seems mandatory; it has not just happened, not even under two decades of various organized forms of health planning.

No prudent policy analyst urges that prevailing systems of medical care for this country be set aside in favor of a new grand design. Clearly, pluralism among providers will prevail, and among those providers private and voluntary systems will predominate. To the extent that universal participation in basic health care is defensible, the question may be raised as to whether some provider system needs to assure that participation. The only valid measure of adequacy of access is utilization. Even when the doors to medical care are open, we know that not all needy clients will enter those doors. If clients decide not to enter, then some provider system needs to assume responsibility for examining the circumstances and to improve them in a fashion that will enhance utilization until we approach the point of universal involvement. Abundant demonstrations confirm that such an achievement is possible without threat of coercion or compulsory participation.

The typology of controversies about children's health services presented here is not necessarily complete. But such a formulation of issues may suffice to confirm the fact that profound disagreements persist on the extent to which there is a public responsibility for children's health. Disagreements are further confounded by different perspectives among people of good conscience on how that responsibility should be fulfilled. These disagreements are not always openly argued when children's health programs are under debate. The issues may instead be represented in the unstated attitudes which influence operational policy and programs. Nominal policy—what we say we do—may be argued on quite a different basis. For example, opposition to health initiatives may find overt expression as a caution about costs or a request for better data on costs and benefits. Such data are appropriate but not always politically persuasive even when available. The situation is paradoxical because even the most ambitious programs for children's health cost a pittance when compared with other expenditures which are assumed almost by inadvertence without question and often without sound justification; witness, for example, the recent dramatic increase in public expenditures to finance the rise in caesarian section rates (Shy, LoGerfo, & Karp,

1981). Persistent and unwarranted caution about the cost of children's health programs invites speculation that sensitivities other than fiscal ones are involved.

The public's commitment to children's health is in a weakened and deficient state. For at least 40 years, the country has tinkered with token programs, token commitment, and token support. None of the approaches taken thus far has been sufficiently well supported to marshal a persuasive prospect, if dramatically expanded, either for success or failure. In this confusion the health of children has been slighted. Confirmation of those slights includes a high proportion of low birth-weight infants, a high proportion of unattended disabilities and handicapping conditions, a high rate of growth-stunting particularly among poor children, a poor record of prenatal care, and all of the emotional, intellectual, and physical frailties that attend these circumstances. This record is well documented in the report of the Select Panel.

New recommendations to address children's health needs must cope with both the silent and overt policy controversies and make progress toward resolving them in one way or another. Some approaches offer little promise of success. Few people argue persuasively that our country should do less than we are doing now for maternal and child health. Many analysts urge an approach which can be monitored and measured against predetermined outcome objectives. Otherwise noble rhetoric invoking the cause of children's health can be used to distribute resources on behalf of many causes, not all of them either explicit or worthy. Although political feasibility must characterize any public program, safeguards must be put in place to protect children's interests over those of special agencies or special provider systems. The children's cause can be argued in ways that benefit interests other than those of children.

Most analysts would argue for an approach which promises permanence. Policy hopscotch among a variety of defensible approaches has weakened the public commitment to children's health. A negotiated health policy offers many advantages in a democratic society, but it risks negotiating away the interests of vulnerable and politically weak populations. New policy must promise widespread agreement that some issues of children's health are not negotiable. Most analysts would also argue that approaches which promise more resources and more efforts on both sides of every controversy will risk perpetuating confusion, high expense, and further neglect of children. Our society places a high value on compromise. In matters of children's health, best approaches may not be found in a middle position which trades away potential benefits of either extreme. In health care financing, the golden mean of public policy has come to characterize the price tag rather than the health benefits.

The Select Panel's Report is the most complete document available on the status of children's health and on the condition of public programs to improve it. That achievement by itself assures long-term influence for the report in deliberations on health policy. But the report offers much more. The analysis and recommendations from the report address in both direct and indirect ways all of the controversies identified in this chapter. The extent to which those controversies are resolved is a proper matter for careful deliberation in the months and years ahead. In this volume, some of the critical issues of child health will be discussed in great detail by a group of our nation's foremost authorities on these topics. Whatever the outcomes of these and similar discussions provoked by the Select Panel Report, the promise is great that the report will elevate to a high plane of informed consideration all of the salient issues of maternal and child health. For it will be clear to all who study this report that its authors have carefully examined the policy alternatives and have made recommendations which carry strong credentials both for political feasibility and for improvement of children's health.

Some considerations of the report are so striking that they deserve early recognition even at risk of anticipating their more detailed analysis elsewhere in this volume. Highlighting certain contributions may be desirable because their implications are not all explicitly emphasized in the report. The report is a committee effort; in some places it dilates on themes presumably of special interest to individual committee members. These passages do not contradict final recommendations, but may dilute their impact.

Although the scholarship of the report is of a high order, it is essentially a political document. That realization may offend some readers and gratify others. Our nation is not far removed from an ethic which erroneously held that health services are a professional matter, aloof from politics. The report treats with respectful attention nearly all possible interpretations and courses of action. No slates are wiped clean to allow for utopian formulations. Deference to political reality, and caution not to arouse opposition unnecessarily may invite criticisms that the report lacks bravado or fresh inspiration. Such criticisms are ill-founded. The report is both inspired and courageous in its recommendations, but the reader who seeks those qualities must strip away some elaborations that were designed for other audiences.

The report makes a strong declaration in support of the social value of protecting children. The family is extolled, but not narrowly defined; strong emphasis emerges on organized community efforts to protect the health of children, whenever possible by means of supporting and strengthening the family. Health is recognized as a state which is subject to many influences. Improved nutrition, home improvement, and accident prevention are given highest priority. Helpless people are not abandoned with an exhortation to improve and protect themselves in these matters; societal initiatives are accepted and defined. Critics who sense political expediency in the Select Panel's Report should give special attention to the recommendation on hand guns. It is strong, forthright, and—regrettably enough—unpopular.

With respect to personal health services, the report makes the strongest statement yet available on the assured universal participation of women and children in a defined cluster of essential basic services. Multiple provider systems are recognized as appropriate to this participation, but substantial reforms for both public and private systems are defined. The case is made for organized, community-based, personal health services. If there are still advocates for maintaining the status quo for publicly-subsidized, solo private medical practice on a take-it-or-leave-it basis, they will find little comfort from this report.

The Panel's recommendations for restructuring the health system are not simplistic, and neither is the structure they address. The proposed changes set a direction and chart a course of action. It is a more constructive approach than some others which have portrayed Oz but not the yellow brick road.

Present political uncertainties make predictions premature on the aspects of the Panel's Report which may be implemented. Caution should attend the interpretation that recent elections represent an expression of the public will against government sponsorship of essential human support services. The public's will in this regard is both fickle and difficult to interpret. The present administration was placed in office by little more than a quarter of the electorate. Such a vote can scarcely be interpreted as repudiation of any recent strong governmental commitment to improve the health of children. Such efforts have not been strong during any of the past three administrations.

The Select Panel deserves a sense of accomplishment for having contributed more than any effort in many decades to enhance and improve consideration of the public's commitment to children's health. The Select Panel, including its staff and leadership, has served the nation's children very well indeed. The recommendations with supporting analysis and documentation will determine the national agenda for children's health policy for many years to come. It is a promising prospect.

REFERENCES

Bremner, R. (Ed.). *Children and youth in America.* Cambridge: Harvard Univ. Press, 1971.

Caldwell, B. M. Balancing children's rights and parents' rights. In R. Haskins & James J. Gallagher (Eds.), *Care and education of young children in America: Policy, politics, and social science.* Norwood, N.J.: Ablex, 1980.

Committee on Child Health Services. *Fit for the future* (Vol. I). London: Her Majesty's Stationery Office, 1976.

Dutton, D. B., & Silber, R. S. Children health outcomes in six different ambulatory care delivery systems. *Medical Care,* 1980, *18,* 693–714.

Enterline, P. E., Salter, V., McDonald, A. D., & McDonald, J. C. The distribution of medical services before and after "free" medical care—the Quebec experience. *New England Journal of Medicine,* 1973, *289,* 1174–1178.

Feshbach, N. D., & Feshbach, S. Toward an historical, social, and developmental perspective on children's rights. *Journal of Social Issues,* 1978, *34,* 1–8.

Helfer, R. E., & Kempe, C. H. *Child abuse and neglect: The family and the community.* Cambridge: Ballinger, 1976.

Knowles, J. H. The responsibility of the individual. *Daedalus,* 1977, *106,* 57–80.

Kotch, J. B., & Johnson, K. A. The fate of joint public-private planning for child health in North Carolina. *Journal of Public Health Policy,* 1981, *2,* 136–152.

Kovar, M. G. *Health, United States, 1978.* [DHEW Pub. No. (DHS) #78–1232]. Washington, D.C.: U.S. Gov. Printing Office, 1978.

Lave, J. R., Lave, L. B., Leinhardt, S., & Nagin, D. Characteristics of individuals who identify a regular source of medical care. *American Journal of Public Health,* 1979, *69,* 261–267.

37

Ludington, T. *John Dos Passos: A twentieth century odyssey.* New York: Dutton, 1980.

Miller, C. A., Moos, M. K., Kotch, J. B., Brown, M. L., & Brainard, M. P. Role of local health departments in the delivery of ambulatory care. *American Journal of Public Health,* 1981, *71,* 15–27.

Pasternack, S. A. The American connection: Handguns and homicide. *Medical Annals of the District of Columbia,* 1973, *42,* 369–374.

Roos, L. L., Roos, N. P., Gilbert, P., & Nicol, J. P. Continuity of care: Does it contribute to quality of care? *Medical Care,* 1980, *18,* 174–184.

Shy, K. K., LoGerfo, J. P., & Karp, L. E. Evaluation of elective repeat caesarean section as a standard of care: An application of decision analysis. *American Journal of Obstetrics and Gynecology,* 1981, *139,* 123–129.

Taft, J. States put scalpel to Medicaid in budget-cutting operation. *National Journal,* 1976, *8,* 581–586.

Takanishi, R. Childhood as a social issue: Historical roots of contemporary child advocacy movements. *Journal of Social Issues,* 1978, *34,* 8–28.

Wagner, M. *Denmark's National Family Guidance Program: A preventive mental health program for children and families* (DHEW Publication No. ADM 77-512). Rockville, Maryland: U.S. Dept. of Health, Education, and Welfare, 1978.

THREE

INTERGOVERNMENTAL RELATIONS IN CHILD HEALTH: A CRITIQUE OF THE SELECT PANEL'S REPORT

BEVERLEE A. MYERS AND
DAVID E. HAYES-BAUTISTA

INTRODUCTION

Policy Making for Maternal and Child Health

The policy-making process is both difficult and thankless. The ideal is that we develop policies today to guide our actions tomorrow. This presumes that the world of tomorrow is the same as the world of today. But tomorrow's world seems nearly impossible to predict; events half-way around the world create problems for our economic and political process, while internal events shape our modern culture and social structure in ways not easily foreseen. Trying to develop policy in this situation is most unsettling.

The plight of the policymaker may be summed up in this aphorism: "There are too many givens and too few knowns" (Hayes-Bautista,

1980). The report of the Select Panel for the Promotion of Child Health is a comprehensive statement of Maternal and Child Health (MCH) policy. Like many policy efforts, this one suffers from starting with too many givens and possessing too few knowns. Some of its conclusions and recommendations are not in step with current economic and political situations. This lack of concordance might blunt an attempt to improve maternal and child health policies.

Stasis vs. Change: Parmenides and Heraclitus

In ancient Greek philosophy, two major schools of thought were epitomized by two individual philosophers. Parmenides, with a jaded eye, believed that the world was basically static and unchanging. According to him, the way things were was the way they had been and the way they were to be forever.

Heraclitus, on the other hand, was fascinated by the world, intrigued by the constantly changing nature of things, and felt that the only constancy was change. He illustrated this by the example of wading across a stream. The first step is taken into a stream—a concatenation of water, pebbles, sand, plant, and animal life. By the time the second step is taken, the concatenation has changed somewhat—a fish has moved, a tadpole hatched, a plant eaten, a pebble dislodged. By the third step, it had changed again. In essence, one never steps into the same stream twice.

These two schools of thought have managed to persist through the centuries, and they may be seen in health and medical care efforts in general, and MCH efforts in particular. Those who follow Parmenides feel that there is no hope for change; indeed, that there is no need for change. The way programs have been done in the past is the way they will be done in the future. The Select Panel (1981) Report appears to be taking a similar stance toward MCH: what the country's MCH policy needs is "more of the same." There are, however, Heraclitean approaches to MCH policy that are built upon change and uncertainty. This chapter is based on such an approach in its attempt to provide a framework for the development of policy and programs in a constantly changing society.

Objectives

There are four objectives in this chapter:

1. To provide a brief description of the way in which our American socio–economic–political stream has changed and some analysis of those changes;

2. To present an overview of how changes in the stream have created new imperatives and constraints for MCH policy;

3. To offer a perspective on how a change in federal–state relations may be used creatively to bring MCH efforts into harmony with the changed stream;

4. To emphasize the importance of change and development in MCH thinking and political efforts in order to survive in the constantly changing socio–economic–political stream.

Our intention is less to produce substantive answers than to ask appropriate questions. Answers still lie somewhere beyond either the Select Panel's report or this critique. Rather, both the report and this critique should provide a basis for further, more intense, MCH policy development.

CONDITIONS AND CONSTRAINTS FOR MCH POLICY MAKING

If we examine American society, we can notice some recent major changes that impose two principal constraints upon MCH policy. These constraints, however, received only passing consideration in the Select Panel's Report, perhaps because these changes became more apparent after the report first appeared in December, 1980.

Economic Constraints

The first constraint is economic. It is quite apparent that this country is experiencing some economic difficulties. These difficulties have had many symptoms, such as Kemp–Roth, Proposition 13, and many other tax revolt measures. Productivity is falling and with it tax revenues. For some officials, an immediate scapegoat is the human services portion of budgets at federal, state, and local levels. There simply will be less money available for maintenance of MCH and other health and medical care efforts in the future. In many states, one must already talk of where and how to make cuts in services, not if such cuts should be made. This means that if past MCH efforts have not met their goals, a simple application of the principle of "more of the same" not only will not get us any closer to reaching those goals, but will not even be a fiscally viable approach.

Political Constraints

The second constraint is political. From the days of the New Deal to the days of the Great Society, there was usually a sufficient legislative constituency behind social legislation to guarantee its passage and implementation. Today, that legislative constituency has shrunk, in power and cohesion, as well as in numbers. Political parties do not seem to be as effective as they once were. The old legislative leadership, a point of considerable leverage for the MCH constituency, has been considerably reduced. New interests and interest groups have been emerging. As a result, once-sacred cows are being closely scrutinized.

This current political and economic dilemma is well summarized in Lester Thurow's (1980) recent book, *The Zero Sum Society:*

> Our economic problems are solvable. For most of our problems there are several solutions. But all these solutions have the characteristic that some-one must suffer large economic losses. No one wants to volunteer for this role, and we have a political process that is incapable of forcing anyone to shoulder this burden. Everyone wants someone else to suffer the nec-essary economic losses, and as a consequence none of the possible solu-tions can be adopted. (p. 11)

These two constraints—economic and political—will exert a major influence on health policy in the future. Yet, their effect seems to be ignored by the Select Panel Report, both in the aforementioned fiscal sense and in terms of constituency changes. It is of utmost importance that people understand that MCH policy making cannot, and must not, take place in a vacuum, insulated from the harsh realities of economic and political life. Yet, one often gets the feeling from the Select Panel Report that policy making is insulated from changes in the economic–political stream. A model might help to understand how MCH policy is bound by changes in the economic–political stream.

The Relation of the MCH Programs to Society-at-Large: The Iceberg Analogy

In the spirit of the aqueous analogy of Heraclitus's stream, let us freeze a portion of it into ice to form a related "iceberg analogy." At the tip of the iceberg are the categorical programs in maternal and child care. Viewed from the ocean's surface, these programs stick up separately and appear to be operating independently of one another, perhaps even competing for funds. However, if we move down into the iceberg be-neath the ocean's surface, we find that, in fact, these seemingly separate MCH programs stem from a base in general policies affecting overall health and medical care efforts. Thus, general trends in medical care policy will influence subsequent trends in MCH programs. However, health and medical care policy rest upon the constantly changing eco-nomic and political situation of American society. Events in society in-fluence medical care policy and eventually, MCH policy. Or, put another way, no MCH policy should be made without remembering that it stems from the larger societal condition, and all the stresses, strains, woes, tensions, and cleavages in society will be felt in MCH policy at some point.

The economic and political constraints upon MCH programs are not temporary, nor are they easily avoided. Since these constraints stem from changes, it is necessary that the process of change be understood for better policy making.

IMPERATIVES FOR MCH POLICY

The Humanitarian Imperative

It is time to examine some of the imperatives for an MCH policy. In the recent past, MCH policy was based on a humanitarian imperative: suffering was bad and had to be alleviated (Ginzberg, 1977). The vision of thin, emaciated children with running sores emerged from the discovery of poverty and provided impetus for the creation of many MCH and other social programs.

But humanitarianism is no longer very popular; it is supposedly neither cost-effective nor efficient. In some quarters, there is talk of a "lifeboat ethic" under which those who already are in the boat survive, and those who are not lucky enough to get in the boat early on, perish. The alleviation of suffering and pain makes little fiscal sense to those who hold this ethic.

However, there are many other reasons, in addition to humanitarianism, which can be put forth as the rationale for strong MCH programs. Part of the process of defining a national MCH policy should include the definition of new imperatives that can be the basis for MCH policy. The Select Panel Report does not develop these new imperatives. Developing a complete list of these imperatives is beyond the scope of this paper, but we would like to define and discuss one imperative that makes sense in today's policy climate.

A New Imperative:
An Age/Ethnic-Stratified Society

The imperative we have in mind could be called the economic self-interest imperative for a strong MCH effort. The age pyramid in the nation is changing from one with a large base of young persons and a small cap of older persons to one with a smaller base of young and a larger cap of older persons. Moreover, the younger population is increasingly a minority population. Some projections indicate that in California by the years 2010–2020, a majority of the state's population will be minorities[1]; in the United States as a whole, this landmark is projected to occur by 2050–2080.

What are the likely consequences of an age/ethnic stratified society? Consider the situation in California in about one more generation. There will be an elderly, primarily Anglo population (the one now graduating from college) which has benefited from public education, public health services, medical research, and other public services, just entering retirement. As they will be a much larger proportion of the total population than is now the case, they will place greater demands upon Social Security funds, pension funds, Medicare, and other forms of insurance that require a larger pay-in than pay-out. Already many of these funds are severely strained. The younger, productive (in an economic sense) population will be overwhelmingly composed of minorities, largely Hispanic in California. If that younger force is in poor health and poorly educated, it will simply have less productive capability. That lowered productivity will lessen inputs to social insurances, pension plans, and retirement funds, just at the time greater demands are being placed upon them. There will be, then, a polarized society; elderly Anglo and younger minority—with the elderly asking the younger to sacrifice.

A grim scenario, but quite possible. Already, the short-range impulse of tax-slashing measures is to cut deeply into health and education efforts, setting up precisely this sort of situation. Even should the younger minority generation of 2010 wish to support the elderly, it might not be able to.

And who is to say that the younger population will want to shoulder that burden? With the growing rise in ethnic identity (coupled with a growing sense of nationalism in third world countries such as Mexico) and with minorities now being asked to bear the brunt of budget cuts, can they be expected to sacrifice again in the future so that the elderly might continue to live in the style to which they have become accustomed? Just as today there is an attitude of benign neglect—a conscious lack of will to provide social services to the young—there could just as easily (and just as wrongly) develop by 2010 an attitude of benign neglect toward the elderly. This is the epitome of Thurow's zero sum game: any game where losses exactly equal winnings and where some have to lose if others win.

Such a scenario is potentially avoidable by the regeneration of a strong MCH effort. Thus, one imperative for MCH efforts is a generational economic self-interest. The young who are given good health services and a good education now will have the capacity (and, one hopes, the will) to support the elderly when the time comes.

A MODEL FOR STATE-LEVEL POLICY INITIATIVE

Much of MCH programs and policy has been generated at the federal level. One result has been that federally mandated programs and activities are not always the most appropriate or adequate for a given state or locality. States have not been given sufficient flexibility to develop, adapt, or create health activities which are most amenable to the local situation (Advisory Commission, 1980).

Yet, for all this reliance on federal policy, there is no identifiable federal initiative in health. Talk of national health insurance is dead. Major new health initiatives are not forthcoming. Indeed, it appears that currently the major policy consists of a grim determination to hang on to what has been developed in the past. In spite of this lack of policy initiative from the federal level, the states are not being encouraged to develop their own policy initiatives. Innovation and flexibility are discouraged, if not actually prohibited, as the federal level preempts the state's role in many areas. Yet, at the state level, such occurrences as the taxpayers' revolt and declining tax bases create situations which require innovative and imaginative approaches to old problems. It simply will not be possible for MCH policymakers to adopt a "more of the same" approach.

How do federal–state relations fit into this paradox? As long as the federal–state relationship is one in which states serve as managers of federal programs, the directors of state health departments are, in truth, not directors at all (Myers, 1978). States, then, are tied into the same categorical way of viewing the world of health and MCH that characterizes the federal perspective. As a result, the lack of a federal initiative is passed on to create a lack of state initiative.

As pointed out by the Advisory Commission on Intergovernmental Relations (1980, pp. 26–27), state administrators often are caught up in a federal funding system which has two characteristics:

1. Complexity, which refers to the number of types of funds an agency receives, such as the many types of categorical funds; and
2. Diversity, which is caused by federal funds coming from a number of federal agencies.

The inflexibilities and the administrative burdens created by this complexity and diversity lead to feelings of federal interference, intrusion, and skewing of local priorities (Advisory Commission, 1980, pp. 48–50). Although the Select Panel Report recognizes this situation, the report does not develop it in detail and does not discuss its implications.

There is a model for federal–state relations which could break this policy initiative impasse (California Department of Health Services, 1980; Myers, 1977). This model is based upon a shift in policy responsibility and program management that will allow states to develop the service mix that best fits their local situation. Such a shift in federal–state relations is one which gives policy initiative to the state while building upon the goals of public accountability, equity, and expenditure control.

These goals could be achieved through a rediscovery of governance based upon: (1) a clear statutory policy mandate, periodically reviewed; (2) a decentralized governmental structure with the roles of each level clearly specified and the interrelationships among levels negotiated through a contractual arrangement; and (3) an intense and open political process that produces policy and decisions at each level.

In this model, the federal role and authority encompass national planning and evaluation, the major financing functions, and establishing and monitoring performance standards for states. These are the most appropriate and relevant roles for the federal government, and they are consistent with the federalist form of government and the ability of a central government to manage complex social programs which must adapt to local conditions (Elazar, 1966; Lowi, 1969; Rivlin, 1971).

The federal government could contract with the states to carry out the functions of regulating the health care system; promoting capital investment; establishing political processes in local health service areas; negotiating and monitoring contracts and performance standards with local health service areas; transmitting federal and state funds to local areas; collecting, analyzing, and evaluating data on program performance and reporting to the federal level; and participating in local negotiations concerning funding, priorities, and delivery systems. In addition, states could share in service and subsidy costs.

Thus, states are the most active and important level of government in the model. State governments may well be the "most manageable civil societies in the nation," for not only do they capitalize on essential regional differences, they can also experiment and innovate (Elazar, 1966, p. 226). Moreover, they form a competent and capable administrative level between the federal and local governments (Bice & Kerwin, 1975; Elazar, 1966).

Given the circumstances described above, a contracting model to establish and monitor intergovernmental relationships would seem more appropriate then the utility regulation model favored by the Select Panel. The contracting model allows greater flexibility to adapt to local and state conditions and capabilities, creates incentives for efficiency, encourages adaptation to technological change, permits better control of administrative costs, and allows support of local as well as national priorities and social values (Capron, 1971; Elazar, 1966; Vladeck, 1975).

The role of a local health governmental body is central to the contracting model. This body would establish local goals and priorities; decide on the allocation of funds based on a negotiation process; request and manage funds for experimentation and special needs; and assure performance of the delivery system in terms of access, quality, and efficiency (Blendon, 1981).

Note that this model does not give complete flexibility to states and localities since the federal government must establish both national goals and the standards for achieving those goals. While the level of standards and the timing for achieving them could be negotiated with states and localities, the model does support national goals and standards. Under the contractual model, if a state or locality is either unable or unwilling to meet established goals or standards, then the federal government has clear responsibility to use other means for accomplishing those goals. These alternative means could include carrying out the programs directly or contracting with agents other than state government.

A limited application of this model has been accomplished in California. As a result of Proposition 13, county tax revenues were slashed. Because county property taxes had been a primary means of funding county health efforts, a coalition of state, county, and consumer health interests combined to secure enactment by the California legislature of a program for shared financing of local health services. A County Health Services fund, administered by the State Health Services Department, was established initially at a level based on county funding efforts during the year immediately preceding Proposition 13. Each county's allocation from the County Health Services fund is based upon that county's level of effort during the base year, thus creating a maintenance of effort incentive. Counties receive a $3 per capita grant plus matching of county health costs, potentially up to 50%. If a county is able to reduce its costs, provided that it demonstrates through a public hearing that such reductions are not detrimental to its health effort, it does not automatically lose the extra matched state funds. Rather, the county may retain them up to a 60/40% state/county match. Counties have substantial discretion in assigning priorities in using the County Health Services funds, since these funds are not categorically linked and the state Department of Health Services does not have authority to approve or disapprove program decisions or funding levels. Any savings that occur in the County Health Services fund can be reallocated by the state or other counties for special needs and priorities, but must still be matched on a 50/50 basis. Annual cost-of-living increases are also part of the County Health Services fund appropriation.

Thus, in California the three principles of health governance described earlier–clear statutory policy providing the basic framework for programs, decentralized government structure tied together through negotiated contracts, and policy decisions resulting from an intense and open political process—form the basis of a new state-county system of health care. So far, most parties are quite pleased. The counties have more flexibility, various constituencies have their input, and the state can see progress being made toward a more rational system.

It is only with this kind of flexibility in intergovernmental process that we will be able to adapt and adopt the new Medi-Cal pluralism to our MCH efforts. We should, therefore, turn toward a discussion of this new medical pluralism.

TOWARD A MEDICAL PLURALISM

Neither Conservative nor Liberal

In these politically touchy times, there are probably those who would claim that such a "state's rights" model is a conservative one. Definite political shifts are going on, but they do not easily fit into such simple categories as "right" or "left," "conservative" or "liberal." What is needed is a new political vocabulary to adequately express recent developments. The rise of single-issue interest groups, the decline of political parties, the use of media in politics, the emergence of new identities, and the changing ethnic composition of the population have all combined to alter the old recognizable political processes. We do ourselves a disservice to view these new events with the old conceptual lenses of conservative and liberal.

The Health-Based Social Movement in California

The new medical pluralism is a perfect example of how the old dichotomy can be misleading. In California, a social movement is afoot which some have labeled the "health-based social movement" (Hayes-Bautista & Harveston, 1977). Welling up from many different consumer and community groups, this movement has left an institutional "residue" which we may use as an indicator that something is indeed going on out there. Hundreds of community clinics have been established, scores of advocacy and consumer groups organized, and a tremendous interest has developed in "nonmedical model" paradigms for healing and maintaining wellness. Furthermore, there are many developments initiated by women's groups, which should be given serious consideration by MCH policymakers. These include client participation in the examination room, informed consent, alternative birthing practices including home births, use of midwives, and increased use of nurse practitioners. Problems previously viewed simply as an individual woman's bad luck are being redefined as society's health problems by this health-based social movement: rape, sexual harrassment, battered spouses, DES-induced defects[2], and others.

Women's groups have not been thinking only of themselves. They also raise issues regarding childrearing and the role of nonstandard family structures (e.g., single parents, working parents, unmarried parents, extended families of current and former spouses), as well as gay and lesbian parenting to name two permutations. Thus, both the "M" and the "C" in MCH policy have been taken to task by these groups. It is quite interesting and quite telling to note that much of the health-based social movement is a reaction—a reaction to inflexible, long-distance federal policy, a reaction to out-of-date state policies, and even a reaction to county policies which are viewed by some as being built on a "more of the same" approach (Millman, 1981).

Although the health-based social movement is very heterogeneous and quite amorphous in a normal political sense, there are some definite goals toward which it strives (Hayes-Bautista, 1977). These goals include:

1. Consumer empowerment. Much activity, in the form of education and lawsuits, seeks to make the consumer a better informed, more powerful decision-maker and participant in the healing process. Some groups say they wish to return the consumer's body back to herself or himself (Boston Women's Health Book Collective, 1971).
2. Decentralization. This has been sought by various consumer groups and community clinics. As outlined earlier, California contracts with counties for the delivery of services and, in turn, some counties contract with community groups. At each level of contractual arrangement, service delivery policy is decentralized to provide the freedom to develop and use a mix and style of services most appropriate for that level and that locale.
3. Creation of new delivery systems. Today in California, as a result of the health-based social movement, many health options are available to patients. The option may be by type of delivery organization, from standard fee-for-service private practitioner to exciting mixes of prepaid, public, private, and community-sector systems. One may also choose between different types of healing paradigms: the medical model and the many nonmedical model paradigms.
4. Decreased reliance on professional autonomy. This is the other side of the coin of consumer empowerment. Many groups seek to make professionals more responsible and accountable for their decisions and actions.

5. Decreased reliance on expensive, technologically based care. One of the major themes of the health-based social movement is that overreliance on hospital care and surgery is expensive, not always needed, and may at times be downright hazardous to one's health. The high rate of hysterectomies performed on American women provides one base for these criticisms.
6. Wellness orientation. Wellness is considered to be much more than the simple absence of physical illness. It is a state that requires constant, active effort to achieve and maintain, including efforts in prevention, diet, exercise, mental health, and style of life (Hayes-Bautista & Harveston, 1977).

These, then, are some of the major goals of the health-based social movement. One could make a liberal interpretation of these goals. After all, the goals are based on ideas such as power to the patient, community involvement, consumer control, increased freedom of choice, and increased service for currently underserved groups. On the other hand, one could also make a conservative interpretation of these goals because they are also based on self-reliance, suspicion of outside government, and entrepreneurship. Indeed, looking at the range of options available to patients in California, one might even suggest that a limited scale, supply-side economics is beginning to dictate practice.

The example of the health-based social movement should serve to illustrate the ultimate futility of reading current developments in health policy as either inherently liberal or conservative. A shift of health policy initiative from the federal level to the state and local levels should be seen as another of those modern service sector events which defy simplistic analysis.

An Analytic Model of Medical Pluralism

Figure 1 depicts a model of medical pluralism. Here, there are two axes which yield 12 different cells. Three types of health providers are listed on the vertical axis. Private and public sector providers need no introduction. A third type of provider, the community provider, requires further comment. These providers, stimulated initially by the health-based social movement, are private, nonprofit corporations. They usually have significant involvement of consumers and lay people in governance and often have a target population that includes those normally served by public sector programs or those who receive irregular or inadequate care from private providers. Such providers include community clinics, neighborhood health programs, and counseling and advocacy programs.

Figure 1
A model of medical pluralism

	tertiary and secondary care	primary care	prevention and wellness	non-medical model paradigms
private sector				
community sector				
public sector				

The horizontal axis is a continuum of levels of care: tertiary and secondary, primary, prevention and wellness, and non-medical model paradigms. Each of the 12 cells represents two things simultaneously: a field of activity and a focus for policy efforts.

In overall medical care policy, the vast majority of resources is poured into the private sector, tertiary and secondary care cell. In fact, most of the money spent on health education, personnel, research, construction, and insurance rewards and reinforces activity in this cell. A much lower level of health resources is invested in public sector, tertiary and secondary care, an even lower level in prevention and wellness within the private, community, and public sectors, and virtually none in non-medical model paradigms.

It is apparent that private sector providers of tertiary and secondary care have fared quite well under current health care policies. Yet, there is activity in other cells. In California, the health-based social movement has welled up, without much attention to normal policy channels, to create activity in each cell that has been previously ignored.

The model portrayed in Fig. 1 may help us understand that changes in federal–state relationships are not necessarily a movement backward, or to the right, or in whatever direction might be currently considered retrograde. For example, under current federal–state relations, the federal government regulates the states as if they were public utilities, in effect making the state a manager of federal programs. Federal emphasis has been on two or three of the cells, with a studied ignorance of the others. Thus, states have been more or less locked into the federal emphasis on these cells and have not been able to explore other options with federal funds (Myers, 1978). As a result, a policy and activity vacuum developed into which other groups have moved. A shift in policy initiative from the federal to the state level could allow states to foster a competitive climate beyond that suggested by Enthoven (1978). Our model suggests that not only should there be competition among providers in one or two cells, but also between different types of providers inhabiting different cells. Not only should physician groups compete against one another, but also against nurse practitioners, midwives, alternative birthing centers, publicly-owned facilities and programs, community clinics, and other types of providers. This is a more comprehensive competition. Shifting the policy initiative to the states allows them to become flexible and to encourage and prudently stimulate this type of competition, which ultimately places more responsibility and control in the hands of consumers. Thus, there should be pluralism regarding types of providers within a state.

There should also be a federal cognizance of the need for pluralism among the states. Different states will have to respond differently to their local conditions, such that no two will be exactly the same.

For any given state, the actual number of cells which are necessary or possible will vary. For example, in one state there might be a great demand for non-medical paradigms, whereas the demand in other states may be very low. Or there could be a large number of community sector providers in one state and none in another.

The message is that, whereas each state should explore that combination of cells best suited to its particular situation, the current federal–state relationship based on the utility regulation model makes such an outcome very difficult to achieve.

LESSONS FOR THE SELECT PANEL

Most recent policy efforts, and the Select Panel Report is no exception, do little to redirect resources from the two or three cells currently receiving the most attention to those that have the least. While the panel emphasizes primary care and prevention, it is still in the context of categorical funding.

The time has arrived for the development of new epistemological bases for MCH activities and efforts. As society continues to change, programs must change. We are facing a period in which community–county–state–federal relationships are being reevaluated and redefined. New imperatives for service are emerging simultaneously with new limitations and constraints. While the report is a marvelous document, it is already seriously out of date. The socio–political–economic stream of Heraclitus is changing rapidly, yet those changes are seldom reflected in the report's thinking.

In one context, reading the report of the Select Panel is like viewing a finely crafted, exquisitely detailed blueprint with each structural member, each point of reinforcement, each nut and bolt drawn to perfect scale. However, we are witness to the failings of the categorical approach to the health of mothers and children envisioned by the blueprint. None of the major programs considered by the Panel—Title V, EPSDT, WIC, P.L. 94-142, or Community Mental Health—has met its goals. Collectively, these programs have introduced a problem of general magnitude which could be called system design, coordination, or integration—a problem of making the pieces in the blueprint fit together. The Panel favors an approach which would augment each of the pieces through increased appropriation, greater federal regulatory and enforcement powers, and expanded eligibility, while providing coordination through a rejuvenated maternal and child health authority with "responsibility for planning, advocacy, quality assurance, and other activities including the use of grant funds to support needed services." These approaches are meant to achieve "the goal of a comprehensive and coordinated system that will assure women and children access to the services most essential to their health and development" (Select Panel, 1981, p. 19).

Concurrent with the work of the Select Panel, a distinguished group of Californians was convened by the Department of Health Services to advise the director on how to improve maternal and child health services. This Child Health Initiative Task Force presented a report early in October, 1981 which to a great extent, albeit more briefly, mirrors both the old problems and the need for new solutions described by the Select Panel.

However, the report by the California task force has a bottom–up, rather than top-down orientation. In conformance with the Panel's observation that "only at the levels of government closest to children and families can health care needs be assessed in detail, and services organized to meet these needs," the California report stresses the need for flexibility at the local level where innovation, initiative, and invention must be allowed expression. In order for the Department of Health Services to enter into a contractual relationship with county government based on fixed dollar subsidies and consistent rules, the counties and the state must be free to organize in a way that will actually foster competition and allow multiple choices of service delivery among consumers. The recommendations of the Select Panel, however, do not allow the necessary latitude for this to occur.

From the perspective of the California Department of Health Services, one senses a dissonance between the current political–social–economic context and the context in which the recommendations of the Panel could be enacted into legislation and implemented. In California, decisions must now be made about where to cut program budgets, not augment them; how to reduce the onerous burden of federal and state regulations, not increase them; and how to divest agencies of responsibilities which overlap one another, not add to the confusion.

SUMMARY

We have made five main points. First, the stream into which we all step—the stream of American society—is constantly changing. The global geopolitical and economic balance is shifting and will never again be the way it was in the fifties, sixties, and seventies. We must adapt to some fundamentally different economic and political realities. These changes affect the way in which we provide MCH services.

Second, new constraints, largely economic and political, threaten to jeopardize levels of funding for MCH efforts. Yet, new imperatives make continuing provision of MCH services an absolute must for humanitarian reasons, as well as reasons of economic self-interest.

Third, there appears to be no federal health policy developing. Either old answers are being continued or no answers are forthcoming–a policy level benign neglect.

Fourth, a change in federal–state relations can break this policy impasse. We propose that states contract with the federal government to provide the type of services most appropriate to their needs. This shift of policy initiative to the state is neither a conservative nor a liberal phenomenon. It is, instead, part of the growth of a new medical pluralism.

Fifth, MCH policy and program people will have to become enthusiastic and aggressive in meeting change and questioning MCH conventional wisdom.

As public health professionals deeply committed to the health of mothers and children, we are obligated to see the report of the Select Panel in the context of global, national, state, and local political and economic realities. Those realities are not conducive to the enactment of many of the Panel's recommendations vis-à-vis increased appropriations for categorical problems, increased regulatory and enforcement powers designed to cast state and local government into a federal mold, and the designation of state Title V agencies as responsible for coordinating the categorical system of health services for mothers and children.

Rather, we should take one of the basic assumptions of the Select Panel literally, namely, "that only at the levels of government closest to children and families—the nation's towns, cities, and counties—can health care needs be assessed in detail and services organized to meet these needs." If pluralism in provider resources is to be accepted and encouraged, then pluralism in federal–state–local relationships must also be accepted.

At a time when the old analyses do not lead us to new solutions, it is time to clear the way for fresh approaches to emerge. This time of uncertainty clearly provokes professional insecurity. It will take courage to accept insecurity and uncertainty in the delivery of health services to mothers and children, but from precisely such a condition will arise the new paradigm for solving the problem.

FOOTNOTES

[1] Some projections indicate that in California by the turn of the century or shortly thereafter, the majority of Californians will consist of members of current minorities. This trend is particularly evident in the minority birth rate which was 27% in 1960, 35% in 1970, and 46% in 1978. Those data coupled with significant immigrations to California from Southeast Asia, South and Central America, and particularly, Mexico, lead us to this conclusion. We might argue the exact dates and percentages, but for the policy purposes here, the trend is clear enough.

[2] DES (diethylstilbestrol) is an estrogenic compound taken to treat vaginitis, suppressed lactation, and menopausal symptoms, as well as to prevent miscarriages. After DES had been widely used for decades for these purposes, it was found to be associated with an increased risk of uterine cancer in daughters of women who took the drug.

References

Advisory Commission on Intergovernmental Relations. *1980 State Administrators' Opinions on Administrative Change, Federal Aid, Federal Relationships.* Washington, D.C.: ACIR, 1980.

Bice, T. W., & Kerwin, C. *Governance of regional health systems.* Paper presented at the meeting of the Milbank Memorial Fund Roundtable on Regionalization, 1975.

Blendon, R. J. The prospects for state and local government playing a broader role in the 1980's. *American Journal of Public Health,* 1981, *71,* 9–14.

Boston Women's Health Book Collective. *Our bodies, ourselves.* New York: Simon & Schuster, 1971.

California Department of Health Services. *County health services report.* Sacramento: Author, 1980.

Capron, W. M. *Technological change in regulated industries.* Washington, D.C.: Brookings Institution, 1971.

Elazar, D. J. *American federalism: A view from the states.* New York: Crowell, 1966.

Enthoven, A. The consumer choice approach to national health insurance: Equity, the marketplace and the legitimacy of the decisionmaking process. In W. Roy (Ed.), *Effects of the payment mechanism on the health care delivery system.* Hyattsville, Md.: National Center for Health Services Research, 1978.

Enthoven, A. The competition strategy. *New England Journal of Medicine,* 1980, *304,* 109–112.

Ginzberg, E. *The limits of health reform.* New York: Basic Books, 1977.

Hayes-Bautista, D. E. Marginal patients, marginal delivery systems and health systems plans. *American Journal of Health Planning*, 1977, *1*, 36–44.

Hayes-Bautista, D. E. *The sociology of health policy*. Unpublished manuscript, Univ. of California at Berkeley, 1980.

Hayes-Bautista, D. E., & Harveston, D. S. Holistic health. *Social Policy*, 1977, *7*, 7–13.

Lowi, T. J. *The end of liberalism*. New York: Norton, 1969.

Myers, B. A. *Organizing the health care system to allocate limited resources: A public equity model*. Paper presented at the 25th annual meeting of the National Health Forum, New York City, March, 1977.

Myers, B. A. *The future of the state's role in health care*. Unpublished manuscript, 1978.

Millman, M. The role of city government in personal health services. *American Journal of Public Health*, 1981, *71*, 47–56.

Rivlin, A. *Systematic thinking for social action*. Washington, D.C.: Brookings Institution, 1971.

Select Panel for the Promotion of Child Health. *Better health for our children: A national strategy* (4 vols.). Washington, D.C.: U.S. Gov. Printing Office, 1981.

Thurow, L. *The zero sum society*. New York: Basic Books, 1980.

Vladeck, B. C. *The limits of regulation: Implications of alternative models for the health sector*. American Political Science Association, Panel on Government Regulations, 1975.

Four

Promoting the Health of Children: Assessing the Case for Regulatory Change

Theodore R. Marmor and Julie Greenberg

The topics of both regulatory reform, which now generally implies loosening government regulation, and of increased regulation of certain industries, environments, or actions are very much on our political agenda. In many economic sectors, specification of the class of regulations to which political attention is being addressed is not necessary. For example, regulation of transportation networks is clearly assigned to the Interstate Commerce Commission (ICC) or the Civil Aeronautics Board (CAB), and is codified in the rules that those agencies promulgate. Regulation of communication networks is similarly assigned to the Federal Communications Commission (FCC). When reference is made to regulatory change in these areas, the agencies and their rules are implicitly considered.

But when considering regulation as it affects health in general and children's health in particular, the regulations at issue cannot be so automatically inferred. Distinctions must be made between, on the one hand, government rules that determine need, eligibility, coverage, and so on, in categorical grant programs such as Title V or welfare programs such as Medicaid, and on the other hand, regulations that are divorced from health care financing programs. Rules accompanying health care financing programs can indeed have dramatic health effects, but evaluating the need for change in that regulatory arena involves detailed analyses of the programs' goals and the effect of regulatory change on the likelihood of meeting those goals. No analysis of the desirability of those programs relative to others is obligatory. Yet we know that no conceivable reforms of existing health care financing programs alone will ensure that our children will be born healthy and mature into healthy adults. Anyone seriously considering the task of promoting the health of children must look beyond health financing programs to broader regulatory issues, primarily those regarding hazard reduction.

With the exception of discussion in Chapter 2 of *Better Health for Our Children* (Select Panel, 1981, Vol. I), entitled "Reducing Environmental Risks," the report indicates that regulatory change was definitely a subordinate concern of the Select Panel for the Promotion of Child Health. The bulk of the discussion and recommendations pertains to provision of medical care services. But in Chapter 2 and elsewhere, the report does recommend a number of regulatory changes that, with rare exception, focus on hazard reduction.

These recommendations can be categorized any number of ways for purposes of analysis. They could be divided into those that advocate regulation closely linked with existing regulatory authority and apparatus, and those that would require legislative action in significantly new areas. Or they could be divided into those implemented through a single administrative fiat and those requiring continual agency review, adjudication, and monitoring. One potentially useful way to review the political implications of the Panel's recommendations for regulatory changes is to divide them into those aimed specifically at safeguarding children and mothers and those affecting the health of the entire population, children and mothers included.

The following are Panel recommendations for regulatory changes aimed specifically at safeguarding children and mothers:

1. Cars should be made safer for children through special performance standards for child passenger safety (Vol. I, pp. 77–79), and car rental and leasing agencies should provide child car seats to customers free of charge (p. 82).

2. Homes should be made safer for children by requiring childproof caps on containers of dangerous household substances (p. 86).
3. Children's television entertainment should be made "adequate" and TV advertisements aimed at children should be made "fair" through (1) use of programming criteria for TV station license renewal (p. 135), and (2) reestablishment of the Federal Trade Commission's authority to investigate program content and TV ads (p. 135).
4. Day care centers and schools should be more healthful and health-giving, respectively. Federal regulations should require that specific health services be provided and safe facilities and procedures should be adopted for the former (pp. 110–111); state laws enabling auxiliary health personnel to provide services to students are desirable in the case of the latter (p. 250).
5. Pregnant women and children should be protected from ingesting unsafe (or unsafe levels of) prescription and nonprescription drugs. Appropriate labeling and consideration of the special physical characteristics of pregnant women and children in establishing drug standards are recommended (p. 98).
6. Lastly, our present health regulatory structure, including Health Systems Agencies (HSAs), Certificate of Need (CON) Agencies, and State Health Planning and Development Agencies (SHPDAs), should establish "criteria of need" reflecting concern for the adequacy of medical care services for children and mothers (p. 362).

Recommendations for regulatory changes that would affect the health of the entire population, children and mothers included, are as follows:

1. Cars, motorcycles, mopeds, and minibikes should be made safer through regulations requiring passive passenger restraints for cars (p. 79), better design of vehicles and roadsides (pp. 79–80), a 55 mph speed limit (p. 80), licensed use of cycles and bikes (p. 81), and helmet use by cycle and bike drivers (p. 81).
2. Fire hazards in homes should be reduced by upgrading construction and housing codes (p. 86).
3. The safety of water-based recreation should be increased by strengthening laws on use of pools and boats (p. 88).
4. Handguns should be very strictly controlled (p. 87).
5. Levels of lead in our air and water should be reduced, presumably by Environmental Protection Agency regulation (p. 92).

Several other recommendations can be placed in this second category (measures that affect the entire population) despite the fact that as written, they imply focused concern on health of mothers and children. It seems likely that the following recommendations could not be implemented in the absence of a regulatory framework or program that would benefit the entire population:

1. The recommendation that special pesticide exposure and ingestion standards (p. 94), and x-ray exposure standards for infants and pregnant women be established (p. 95).
2. The recommendation that a coherent national policy be established regarding food dyes and additives as these affect pregnant women, infants, and children (p. 98).

Leaving aside issues of environmental hazards, where the list of possible regulatory changes could be nearly endless, a number of other possible regulatory reforms not discussed in the report come to mind in the first category defined above. Two of these—establishing fluoride standards for public drinking water supplies and requiring a warning label on alcoholic beverage bottles about fetal alcohol syndrome—are quite compatible with the report's discussion. The neglect of two others—public policy on abortion and regulation of midwifery—is almost glaringly obvious. The former is, of course, controversial. But the Panel did take a firm position on the controversial topic of handgun control, an issue more distant from the focus of its concerns. The latter would seem to fit in naturally with recommendations favoring increased use of other auxiliary health professionals, as well as the general discussion of issues in obstetrical care.

Discussion of two other issues in regulation could arguably have been included. The first, and the one most directly relevant to the Panel's concerns, pertains to state laws on child custody after divorce and in cases of foster care. The second involves teenage employment. Evidence from a recent survey conducted by Greenberger and Steinberg (1980), social psychologists at the University of California, Irvine, suggests that working minors are more likely than their peers to use marijuana and alcohol. Considering recent suggestions that the minimum wage for that age group be eliminated to encourage employment, some discussion of health implications, and especially the differential implications for black and white teenagers, seems appropriate.

In the category of regulation with broader public impact, the report does not comment on the need for state prohibitions of smoking in public places. Other than this obvious area of neglect, the Select Panel might also have considered issues related to decriminalization of marijuana use, or policies on flex-time and part-time work arrangements in federal and state civil services.

With what criteria can we assess the case for implementing any one of these possible regulatory measures? In reading the Panel's recommendations, a somewhat nonhierarchical set of criteria for assessing their desirability came to mind. The most obvious one—health impact—may also be the easiest to analyze. Although data are not as complete as we might hope in studies of the health implications of various hazards, in most cases the relative magnitude of health effects can be determined. For example, accidents of all kinds are the greatest single cause of death and disability among children. Thus, regulations to reduce hazards to children in the car and home must be ranked as highly desirable, while the suggested reform in procedures of Health Service Agencies and other components of the health regulatory structure must rank low.

The second criterion might allow the selection of practicable regulations from among all those that would have a large beneficial impact on health were it possible for them to be successfully implemented. Here analysis is more difficult. Implementation analysis is in its infancy and predictions about the forms of regulation that will work are fairly primitive and promise to remain so for some time. Again, however, some distinctions can be drawn among recommendations with sensitivity to the match between complexity of the regulatory task and the competence of any regulator. For example, using feasibility criteria, requiring the use of childproof caps on containers of dangerous household substances would be ranked more desirable than increased FTC regulation of children's programming and ads.

Another criterion that could be applied to those regulatory changes with large beneficial impacts on health is whether health is really the pivotal concern of public policy in that area. To the extent that everything can be demonstrated (and sometimes very concretely demonstrated) to affect health, broadly construed, health impact can be an attractive gauge for the desirability of a public policy. But that gauge should not be employed indiscriminately. It is not "healthy" for example, for handgun-toting criminals to stalk victims or for children to shoot themselves or others with handguns secreted at homes, in cupboards or drawers; statistics on the carnage that results are clear enough. But to categorize this issue as a health issue is to trivialize it.

On the other hand, sometimes health impact criteria should be paramount and they are not, or they are applied in the wrong part of issue analysis. For example, it could be argued that abortion policy, often construed as complexly interwoven with ethical values, should be evaluated primarily on health criteria, because abortion policy may have a minor effect on the incidence of abortion but a major effect on abortion outcomes. Of course, the question of whether the incidence of abortion is sufficiently high to generate concern about the state of the nation's "moral fabric" is divorced from health criteria and, as with the issue of handgun control, would be trivialized by placement in the health context.

A final criterion, related to feasibility but a bit more slippery, pertains to the indirect or secondary effects of some forms of regulation. There are numerous difficulties that might arise from regulations segregating children and pregnant women as a protected class, as is recommended in the case of setting standards for their exposure to various drugs, chemicals, and radiation. First, despite our ignorance of the physiological effects of many potentially harmful substances, it is probable that there is a range in sensitivity among the population as a whole and that many adults are as sensitive or nearly as sensitive as children and pregnant women. Does this imply that all standards for exposure to environmental hazards or drugs should be set at levels to protect the most sensitive class?

Second, if exposure standards are set separately for children and pregnant women, to what use are such standards to be put? In the case of x-ray exposure or drug labeling, standards inform personal choice. But in the case of exposure to chemicals found in occupational settings, standards could be a force for occupational discrimination. And a third, much more subtle difficulty is the potential intimation of patronage in a regulatory system established and administered primarily by men for the protection of vulnerable women, fetuses, or infants (and especially for the protection of fetuses and infants from "irresponsible" women).

Beyond the question of desirability of regulatory changes is the equally important question of political feasibility. The feasibility of each regulatory change depends on a combination of factors, but, in fact, none appears imminent. While the service-related recommendations are probably more expensive—or will at least figure larger in federal or state budgets—and therefore less politically acceptable, the relative cheapness of some regulatory changes in this era of skepticism at the value or efficacy of government regulation is not a compelling characteristic. Were concern for children an exceptionally potent political force, the recommended regulatory changes of the first category (policies specifically for mothers and children) might be relatively more politically feasible. Conversely, if the children's lobby could easily align itself with other interest groups, changes in the second category (policies for the general population that affect mothers and children) might be more feasible. Such easy differentiation between policies addressed exclusively to children and mothers and policies addressed to the general population seems impossible, although advocates should be sensitive to this distinction and its political implications, particularly in light of two features of the politics of children's policies.

The first feature is that political advocates for children have historically been weaker than those representing, for example, labor or the aged. Child advocates have not bound together social altruism and economic self-interest in the mix that has characterized other more successful political lobbying groups. That children are not the focus of a durable congressional standing committee both reflects this weakness and aggravates it. The result is a double liability: relatively weak institutional mechanisms both for producing legislative changes when coalitions do develop and congressional sponsors are enlisted, and for subsequently overseeing agency action on children's programs that are enacted and implemented.

The second special feature of the politics of children's policies bears on the American consensus on the site of responsibility for children's welfare. Though the suggestion that Americans are a child-loving people is arguable, the view that the public is responsible for some children in some circumstances is widespread. That consensus could change, however, with important political implications. Over the next decade or two, the very problems that incite gravest concern (e.g., the use of drugs, alcohol, and cigarettes by children and adolescents, teenage sex, pregnancy, and the incidence of venereal disease, abortion, juvenile crime, and uncertain relations between children and step-parents or single parents) could change the distribution and character of American attitudes toward child policies. Coupled with the blurring boundary between childhood and adulthood, the environment of child policy could substantially shift. One effect might be public hostility or resignation sufficient to cause a renunciation of some forms of public responsibility toward children.

We would now like to address a few comments to the report's overall adequacy in presenting regulatory issues. A major deficiency lies in the absence of any mention of regulations enacted or rejected in other countries, as well as lessons that can be learned from these experiences. Just as information on the health services provided to children in other nations informs us of potential improvements in our own services, so, too, information on regulatory policies elsewhere can inform our own initiatives.

However, overall, the Panel must be given credit for giving attention to the health hazards posed by environmental pollutants and accidents. These hazards have been given less attention than their due in the past, especially in view of the fact that they affect all of us as much as they affect children and pregnant women.

Looking at the Select Panel Report as a whole, and stepping away from a focus on regulation, additional comments can be made. First, the report is both overly defensive in its repeated denunciations of cost–benefit analysis and confused in its criticism of such analysis. Cost–benefit analysis is assuredly defective, but does have value and, moreover, *will* be used despite the Panel's protests. This denunciation is peculiar, because in both the regulatory and service spheres good cost–benefit analyses of Panel recommendations seem apt to be generally favorable. Even considering the implications of analysis of long-term costs and benefits, such as the need to discount the value of future benefits and to incorporate effects of confounding unrelated life experience, most important steps to maintaining the health of children will be cost-effective. For example, the report states that vision screening may not be cost-effective, since "it is undeniably cheaper to have a generation of children in which 15 percent cannot see well than to rectify this problem, even if national productivity suffers as a result" (Select Panel, 1981, Vol. I, p. 33). If national productivity suffers from a population with vision difficulties, it would seem that screening *would* be cost-effective. Contrary to the report's assertions, the burden of proof on programs and policies for children appears lower than for other groups.

Second, little is said about the role of community initiatives in improving child health, although consumer awareness and activity will probably be very significant in prevention programs.

However, it must also be said that the Panel was correct in emphasizing the family rather than the individual child in its analyses and should be praised for that effort.

Viewed as policy suggestions for the early 1980s, the Select Panel's Report is unlikely to be widely used. It presumes an activist, expansionist role for government, hardly the most accurate estimate of the agenda for the 1980s. Yet viewed as a collection of materials relevant to an expanded government role concerning child health, it is both a useful compendium of information and a prod to imaginative selection among possible policies.

REFERENCES

Greenberger, E., & Steinberg, L. D. Part-time employment of in-school youth: A preliminary assessment of costs and benefits. In Vice President's Task Force on Youth Employment, *A review of youth employment problems, programs, and policies* (Vol. 1). Washington, D.C.: U.S. Dept. of Labor, 1980.

Select Panel for the Promotion of Child Health. *Better health for our children: A national strategy* (4 vols.). Washington, D.C.: U.S. Govt. Printing Office, 1981.

FIVE

CHILD HEALTH: WHOSE RESPONSIBILITY?

ELI H. NEWBERGER, MICHAEL ST. LOUIS,
AND CAROLYN MOORE NEWBERGER

INTRODUCTION

Had the Select Panel for the Promotion of Child Health (1981) waited another 6 months before bringing out its report, their conception of children's health and the view of who is responsible for it might have changed dramatically. The political climate for social programs and the sense of responsibility for dependent members of our society appear to have been profoundly altered by the 1981 presidential election, the national taxpayer revolt, and the election to Congress of an unprecedented number of fiscal and social conservatives.

The Select Panel Report, read in the light of current political developments, seems very much a product of its time: a cautious expansion of medical services for children is proposed, with gradual increases in the eligibility of less affluent children for services supported by or delivered by the government, and a gradual, incremental increase in the amount of public responsibility for children's health.

The essential reasoning is found in the first two paragraphs of the Prologue to the report:

It is a biological fact that human infants and children depend upon others to an extent not found in any other species. In tacit recognition of this fact, all human societies, ancient and modern, have developed elaborate systems of shared family and community responsibility for the young. The makeup of such systems and the precise division of duties within them have varied from one culture to another and from one generation to the next. But the central theme of shared responsibility for the young endures.

In the United States today, our system of shared responsibility has contributed much to ensuring the healthy growth of our children. But despite great achievements, we are still falling short of doing what we believe most Americans want to see done to promote the health of all our children. In recognition of this fact, the Congress created a Select Panel for the Promotion of Child Health to assess the status of maternal and child health and to develop, for the first time, "a comprehensive plan to promote the health of children and pregnant women in the United States." (Select Panel, 1981, Vol. I, p. 1)

It is now clear, perhaps more than ever, that our country is even less concerned with assuring community responsibility for the young. The new administration's proposed dismantling of programs which are vital for the health of millions of American children (e.g., drastic reductions in child nutrition, Medicaid, services to pregnant women, and childhood immunizations) suggests a need to gradually make more effective the existing array of programs. For the moment has changed, and it seems apparent that well-intended and intelligent efforts to better children's health through government action may no longer be welcomed.

The challenge now for those concerned with children's health is threefold. First, at a conceptual level, we must define what we mean by "child health." Child health is not simply the absence of definable medical problems. If each child is understood as a naturally developing being with an inherent right to develop his qualities and potentials to their full extent, then child health must be defined as the unfolding of such development reasonably free of impediments to growth. In that perspective, the focus of medical responsibility must include factors in the child's environment, as well as in the child, which are necessary to facilitate development. These include nutrition, family well-being, environmental safety, mental health, and dental health. When our definition of child health is more explicit, our understanding of what needs to be done to promote it and to prevent and treat disease will be clearer.

Second, at a practical level, we must define which health service is needed, who receives it, and how to get it to children efficiently and economically. No longer can we tolerate redundancy and overlap in such situations as this:

> Consumers participating in both the WIC [Special Supplemental Food Program for Women, Infants, and Children] and EPSDT [Early and Periodic Screening, Diagnosis, and Treatment] programs, for example, described the amount of work and school time that is lost because they must appear at clinics several times in order to receive the WIC nutritional assessment, an EPSDT screening, and routine obstetric or pediatric care, and appear on other days for treatment services. Service providers commented on the wasted time and resources. (Select Panel, 1981, Vol. II, p. 5)

Third, at a political level, we must fight to save what we can in order to prevent harm to the most vulnerable. This is a matter of personal values and responsibility; for most of us, it falls outside the domain of our professional lives.

The present situation with regard to children's health in the United States can be characterized as a crisis. A Chinese ideogram for crisis is a superimposition of the words "danger" and "opportunity"—and both are apparent in the current situation. The signs of danger are clearly before us: falling immunization rates could lead to epidemics of polio and measles, the human and financial costs of which will be enormous; major nutritional deficits, unfamiliar since the initiation of the War on Hunger during the Nixon administration, may return, with serious consequences for children's abilities to withstand infection, to learn, and to become productive adults; and a rising toll of neonatal morbidity associated with low birth weight as a consequence of inadequate prenatal care, which could result in neurological and psychological handicaps to be paid for by all of us for years to come.

Not so immediately apparent is the opportunity latent in the current crisis. The next few years will provide a chance to review in a critical and rigorous fashion what we know and what we can do about children's health. Knowledge produced by such a review can help us improve our program models and invent new program ideas against the day when federal health initiatives will once again be feasible.

This chapter addresses issues of responsibility for children's health from a different vantage point from that chosen by the Select Panel. Rather than to look at existing programs with occasional references to available data, the issues of responsibility are addressed here from the perspective of the child.

Readers of the Select Panel Report (1981) will be impressed that, notwithstanding the huge amount of careful work on the part of the Panel and its staff, it was not possible to assemble a series of recommendations based on data about children's health or about the impact of various programs. This problem is a consequence both of the heterogeneity of our system for delivering children's health services and of the fact that such data-gathering organizations as the National Center for Health Statistics do not focus on children's health problems. An additional problem with available data on children's health is that our nation has relied nearly exclusively on superficial indicators, such as infant mortality. Budgetary constraints have played a role in this lack of health outcome data, but more important has been poor understanding of the developing child's health needs and the consequent inability to translate such understanding into data-gathering on the actual content of child health. (In some ways the most useful volume of the Select Panel Report is the third, *A Statistical Profile*. It is unquestionably the most comprehensive summary of data relating to the health of children ever amassed, and the analysis is lucid.)

Yet the recommendations of the Select Panel do not seem so much to flow from a reckoning with the data and with the needs of children as from a contemplation of what already exists in preventive and therapeutic services for children in the private and public sectors. The Panel's approaches to change seem more focused on what providers can provide, rather than on what children need.

Issues of responsibility for children's health needs are not clearly defined in the report of the Select Panel. Through the following clinical cases and commentary, several principles will emerge which will display what is needed and how better to assure that needs are met. In reflecting on these cases, the reader will find it useful to keep in mind two questions: "What is the need?" and "Who is responsible?" These questions have different implications for individual children at particular ages, living in distinct cultures with their own parents. The cases are representative of infancy, early childhood, middle childhood, and adolescence, and the families come from different ethnic and socioeconomic groups. Table 1 provides a framework for thinking about these questions at three levels: social, familial, and individual.

FOUR CASE STUDIES

Case 1

A 10-month old black female entered the hospital for the second time. Her first admission 2 months earlier was for evaluation of weight loss. The second admission was for physical neglect and continued low weight.

TABLE 1:   CHILD HEALTH NEEDS AND RESPONSIBILITY

What is the need?	How can the need be met?	Who is responsible?
Level 1: Social & environmental context		
To support the family's efforts physically to sustain and emotionally to nurture its members	Reduction or elimination of poverty	Federal and state governments
	Guaranteed system of payment for health care for all family members	
	Education for employment and universal employment for all eligible workers	
Level 2: Family context		
To provide direct stimulus for growth and remove direct impediments to health of the child	Child rearing supports	Community health, mental, health, and social service institutions
	Education for parenthood	
	Access to physical and mental health care	Schools and community organizations
Level 3: Individual child		
To optimize the child's personal, physical, and psychological qualities	Adequate nutrition	The child
	Preventive and curative pediatric and dental care	The parents
	Cognitive and emotional stimulation, stability and affection	Individual health, mental health, and social service practitioners and their organizations and institutions
		The schools

The child was born at term, and weighed 2.85 kg. Delivery and the perinatal period were unremarkable. At home, the child was said to be a quiet baby, and her mother reported that she was worried at first that the baby did not move her legs enough. She said, "I was sure

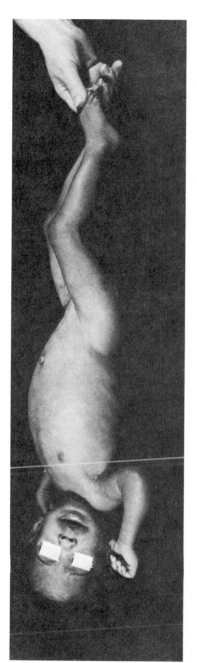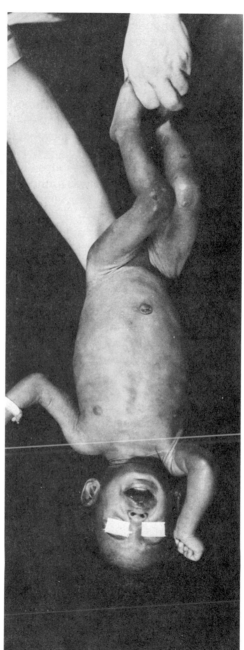

Figure 1
Ten-month-old infant admitted to hospital for low weight and physical neglect

there was something wrong with her." Reports of early vomiting and poor sucking led to a change from a prepared formula to an evaporated milk–corn syrup preparation which was tolerated well. Cereal and canned juices were added at about 1 month; mashed beef, vegetables, banana, and potato at 3 months. At the time of admission the mother said the infant was being offered food three times daily and taking chicken, noodles, peaches, vegetables, and other table foods. The child had no history of vomiting or diarrhea. Developmental milestones were delayed: she could neither sit up nor maintain a sitting position. She was said not to vocalize in response to social stimulation.

On examination, she was found to be a small, emaciated child who did not respond to play. Her length was 62 cm, weight 3.95 kg, and head circumference, 38.5 cm. These growth measures were well below the third percentile of the normal distributions for children her age. Physical neglect was suggested by a general maculo–papular rash over her upper chest, hands, and arms; scaly skin with cracks over the knuckles and between the fingers, which she sucked constantly; and moderate hip and elbow contractures. Skeletal x-rays showed a bone age of 5 months, but all laboratory analyses were normal.

The family did not have a history of short stature. The mother was unmarried, and this was the third child of a third father. The mother was one of seven children born and raised in North Carolina. Both her parents were seriously ill. She first came to Boston in her early twenties with a cousin and worked for a year as a domestic. She then left work, due in part to pregnancy with her first child, who was 4 years old at the time of the patient's admission. In Boston, the family had few friends or relatives, and the mother suffered from constantly aching teeth.

The mother and her children were supported by public welfare, with approximately half ($115) the monthly stipend going for rent. Although a home visit revealed a spacious, clean, and well-kept apartment, the mother described a life pattern consistent with family disorganization: all household members slept until noon and stayed up until 1 a.m. or 2 a.m.; meals were at irregular times.

While at first the mother appeared slow to grasp instructions, on further contact it became clear that she had adequate intellectual understanding of her problems. Yet she could muster little energy to care for her children. Although the mother was thought to be depressed and isolated, treatment was focused on the child.

The baby, while being kept in the hospital, was given a regular diet with an average daily intake of 250 calories/kg. She promptly gained weight, started to smile, and demonstrated interest in people who played with her. Physical therapy mobilized her stiff elbows and hips. At the outset, the hospital identified the needs of this child only in terms of her immediate physical needs, and responsibility thus focused on the success of the hospital staff in resolving her immediate symptoms. The family context in which the child's symptoms were expressed was not considered. She was soon sent home with only routine follow up in the medical outpatient department.

On readmission 2 months later, she was a small, dirty, smelly infant, with restless movements in her hands, and again underweight.

While the child again responded to refeeding, there was a clear recognition that the child's symptoms reflected not only nutritional inadequacy, but also problems in the family context which made the mother unable to provide the physical and emotional support necessary for the child's development. Appreciation of the mother's depression and her many problems—including untreated health problems (carious teeth and chronic urinary tract infections)—led to a different understanding of responsibility and a different form of intervention. She was seen as one overwhelmed by stress and unable to provide for her baby's needs. Practical and emotional support were offered: dental and medical care, regular counseling with a social worker, and child care for the older two children. As her depression lifted and her capacity to provide for the child's needs for stimulation, love, and care appeared to improve, the child was sent home for progressively longer visits. After discharge, in addition to the efforts already underway, follow-up care included a homemaker and a public health nurse for day-to-day support. Four years later at the age of 5, the child's physical and psychological growth are in the normal range.

From this history one can recognize that all three levels of need—social, familial, and individual—were involved in the etiology of this child's illness. Events in the social and environmental context, on the national, state, and city level shaped the mother's move from North Carolina to Boston, the difficult material circumstances of the family, and the irregularity of their medical care. Similarly, on the family level, the mother's own early experiences, limited education, social and personal isolation, and susceptibility to depression impeded her ability to care for the child. Her feelings toward the pregnancy and the child she feared could not be normal remained unexplored. And within the child, the possibilities that constitutional activity level contributed to a "temperamental mismatch" between child and parent or that she brought with her some particular vulnerability cannot be excluded.

But medical care in this case focused on both an intermediate variable—a family which was not functioning well—and on the immediate nutritional needs of the child. Intervention included providing social supports to help the family and was gratifyingly effective. By acting on the causes of the mother's despair—the loneliness, the aching teeth, the failing baby—and so demonstrating that solutions exist for troubles, the clinicians helped the family begin to cope. The mother is now able to manage the tasks of living and provides nurture for her children despite the fact that her own early history could not be changed, and the hospital was not able to assume responsibility for changing the larger social and economic reality. All these levels of family need, and the lines of responsibility for meeting those needs, are summarized in Table 2.

It is well to underline certain clinical features of this case. There were early symptoms of trouble in the mother–child dyad, manifest both in the parent's concern about whether the child was normal and in the neonatal feeding difficulties. Klaus and Kennell (1976) have drawn attention to the critical importance of the newborn period in establishing an enduring maternal–infant bond. On the first hospital admission for failure to thrive, there were both physical and developmental signs of inadequate care as shown by the child's weight, length, social behavior, hygiene, and hip and elbow immobility. The child's discharge from the hospital was, in retrospect, premature. But the discharge was premature not because the child's symptoms had not been cured, because they had, but rather because of a failure to recognize the level of need from which the symptoms derived. When the child was admitted the second time bearing signs of neglect, there was a more comprehensive understanding and response from the medical staff.

Although it is easier in many such cases to separate the child from its family, the psychological cost for the child and the financial burden for society are considerable (Fanshel & Shinn, 1978). The anger aroused by such cases, however, often leads clinicians to look for someone to blame. A punitive approach to parents is implied by simple diagnostic formulations such as "parental failure," "maternal deprivation," and the "battered child syndrome." Ryan (1971) has aptly characterized such an approach to parental problems as "blaming the victim." Identifying those aspects of the mother's social, physical, and psychological context which undermined her ability to care for her children, and which could be addressed by the individuals in the setting to which she came for help, was the primary task to inform intervention; judgment and blame, as well as superficial approaches to symptom reduction in the child, would prove of little value in cases such as this.

Such cases demand flexibility, understanding, and creativity in clinical diagnosis and treatment, and they frequently pose formidable ethical, technical, and organizational changes.

TABLE 2:   CASE 1: NEEDS AND RESPONSIBILITIES

What is the need?	How can the need be met?	Who is responsible?
Level 1: Social & environmental context		
A health program with guaranteed payments and availability Adequate income	Accessible and available universal health care Income support through guaranteed income and/or training and employment with adequate wages	Federal and state programs which will guarantee a minimum level of health and income supports to enable families to care for their children's needs
Level 2: Family context		
Relief for maternal depression Treatment for dental and physical health problems Enhancing knowledge about the child's needs	Counseling and advocacy Dental and medical care for the mother Parent education Public health Nursing and social services	Hospital medical, psychiatric, and social service personnel Practitioners in the community
Level 3: Individual child		
Adequate nutrition Health care and physical therapy Emotional stimulation and care Cognitive stimulation	Individualized feeding programs Provision of care in hospital and at home Enhancement of the ability to trust caregivers	Hospital with transfer of responsibility to community practitioners and parent

Further insight into the issues of responsibility for child health in this case is provided by a physician's response to the photograph shown in Fig. 2. The case was presented as an example of the successful management of the "failure to thrive" syndrome at a refresher course for family practitioners who were studying for their family practice board examinations in 1977. When the photograph—which was taken at the 5-year follow-up visit—was shown, a physician in the audience exclaimed: "Doctor, what did you let her have that other baby for?"

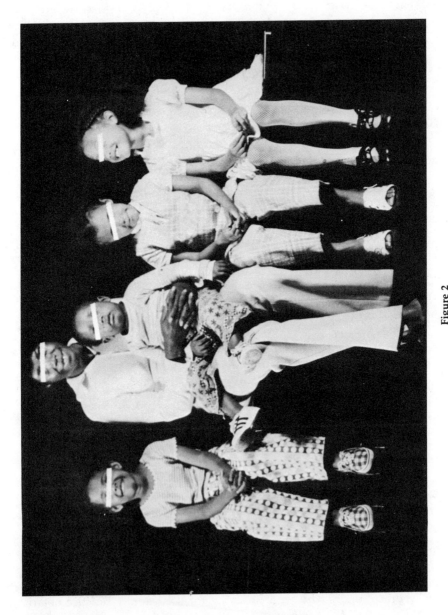

Figure 2
Previously neglected and underweight infant and family

The question provoked a review of the issues of professional responsibility for child health and maternal responsibilities for sexuality and procreation. Implicit in the question were values about black mothers on welfare: the physician who posed it would not have thought himself sexist or racist, but he might have been willing openly to assert the doctor's right to assure that dependency on the public dole was limited. In addition to suggesting that physicians—no more or less frequently in the Boston area than elsewhere—have their values and prejudices which often translate to the actions of practice, this case demonstrates that there were, and remain, many opportunities for expressions of anger by the medical community toward low-income and minority mothers and children.

More profoundly, perhaps, the doctor's question taps a fundamental ethical and personal issue which is rarely acknowledged and imperfectly understood by professionals who care for children. Do we indeed arrogate to ourselves others' rights and responsibilities? Or more modestly, do we try to make available to children and families the tools with which they can make their own decisions and which enable them more adequately to cope with the realities of their lives?

This issue of personal responsibility for others underpins much confusion with regard to who bears responsibility for children's health. It is confused with our conflicting feelings about people (including children) who are dependent in a society which values independence and autonomy.

Although it should be clear from the case study presented above that the health, if not the survival, of at least one child in the family depended on nonmedical services, the Select Panel degrades these vital supports for child health by referring to them as "boundary" services (Select Panel, 1981, Vol. I, pp. 50–51). For many families, social services are indispensable for child health. Viewed from a clinical perspective, they are not at the boundary but at the center of professional action. Without them, the necessary preventive and therapeutic medical interventions are of little use, a point demonstrated by the first hospitalization of the child with failure to thrive.

In addition to factors at the levels of family and individual child, it is clear that poverty was a major contributing factor to this family's dysfunction and to the child's failing to thrive. The report of the Select Panel draws attention to the significance of poverty in determining the health of children. Curiously, the Panel stops short of recommending any initiatives to address poverty:

> While the implications of these demographic changes for the health of mothers and children cannot always be pinpointed with precision, some are fairly apparent. In particular, it seems evident that the increase in

single-parent families has some ominous implications for child health since
such families generally have low incomes and poverty is the single biggest
predictor of poor health in this country. Further, the unrelenting stress
experienced by a woman trying to raise a family by herself on severely
limited resources can have a detrimental impact on her own health and
that of her children. The same is, of course, true of a single father, although
he is less likely to be poor. (Select Panel, Vol. I, pp. 56, 58)

This passage contrasts sharply with the forthright recommendation
of the Advisory Committee on Child Development of the National Academy of Sciences which concluded 5 years before the Select Panel:

There is need for a system of a guaranteed minimum income to bring poor
families—in which nearly one-sixth of America's children live—within
striking distance of the income levels of the majority.
    The emphasis in this chapter on income support must not be taken
for an argument that it would in itself be enough to achieve what we
regard as reasonable goals for our nation's children. It is rather that nothing else will work very well without it. If the family—the front-line institution in child development—is not enabled to use all its considerable
strength, the task of raising children is too big and too difficult for any
forces outside the family to cope with. (National Academy of Sciences,
1976, p. 54)

Case 2

A 3-week-old boy was brought to the emergency room by his
mother, who promptly informed the staff that the child had received
his injury, a hand-shaped bruise over the left temple, at the hands of
his father, a professional person who worked in another hospital in the
Boston area (Figure 3).

The father was associated in a religious fellowship with the family's
private pediatrician who was on the hospital's staff—and who was reluctant to report the case (as mandated by law) to the Department of
Public Welfare. The father was seen by a social worker and a psychiatrist,
who noted a severe personality disorder, with paranoid features and
poor impulse control. He associated the birth of his child with a sense
of abandonment by his wife. Ultimately, the attending physician agreed
that a child abuse case report was appropriate, and he explained the
concerns of the staff to the family and prepared them for the visit of a
protective services social worker. They were angry with the plan as they
saw no need to have a stigmatizing report made to a public agency when
they could, and would, purchase privately the recommended counseling
services for themselves. After a visit from the social worker, which followed the legally mandated case report, the child was discharged to
their care and the parents engaged in therapy for themselves. There
were no further injuries.

Figure 3
Infant of professional family admitted to hospital for physical abuse

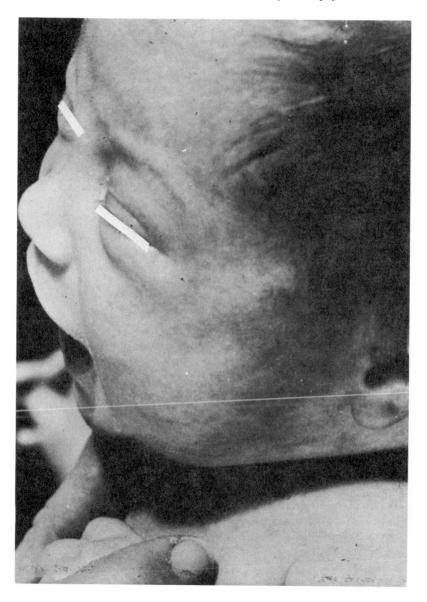

This infant, from an affluent family, nearly missed receiving attention to his family's urgent problems. Although a hand-shaped bruise would not have been easy to classify as accidental, such misclassifications are often made when affluent families are involved. Frequently, it is the context in which services are delivered and to whom they are delivered—rather than the nature of the injury or the relationship of the family to the child—that defines which cases of traumatic injury are identified as accidents and which cases are identified as abuse. More affluent families receive their care from private practitioners, for whom the ethics of payment and the nature of confidential relationships often interfere with value judgments about the parents' ability to fulfill their protective and nurturing responsibilities. Private practitioners are reluctant to assign the terms "child abuse," "child neglect," and "the battered child," to the injuries of their young patients since these terms all strongly suggest fault on the part of caregivers, whereas the term "accidents" implies no fault or need for intervention.

The under-reporting of child abuse cases in middle- and upper-class families is now reasonably well defined, although as the Select Panel points out, the data are still inadequate (Select Panel, Vol. III, p. 39). Poor, socially marginal, and minority families are more likely to attract to their problems the more unattractive labels. This has, in large part, to do with the fact that they receive care for their children at public clinics, where personnel are not paid on a fee-for-service basis, where there is great social distance between provider and patient, and where care is unlikely to be given over a period of time by the same personnel.

With regard to responsibility for care of the child described in Case 2, neither the parents nor the attending physician in the private sector was able to assure the protection this child needed. In fact, both had failed: the father's actions could have killed the baby, and the physician's initial refusal to consider the possibility of child abuse as a clinical diagnosis could also have been threatening to the child's life. In this case, the government clearly had a major and lifesaving role to play by mandating reporting and investigation as a matter of law. Such reporting and investigation would require the family to acknowledge its potential for violence, and to receive treatment enabling the parents, and especially the father, to protect the child from the consequences of parental anger.

As with Case 1, treatment for the child's symptoms alone would not have been sufficient to address the child's health needs. In order for this child to have an opportunity to develop normally and in safety, the family context had to be addressed. In this case, the parents' relationship and the father's pathology became the focus of intervention.

From the clinical perspective, as indicated by this case, children's

TABLE 3:   CASE 2: NEEDS AND RESPONSIBILITIES

What is the need?	How can the need be met?	Who is responsible?
Level 1: Social & environmental context		
A universal system of rules and values about children's rights independent of their parents'	Rules to limit violence in schools, homes, and in the media	Federal and state legislatures and executive departments
To address the acceptability of violent methods of resolving conflict in the home and in society	Laws mandating reporting of possible abuse or neglect	Advertisers, citizens, and producers of media
	A system for responding promptly and effectively to case reports of abuse and neglect	Parents
	Gun control	
Level 2: Family context		
Channels for anger and resolution of its source in family relationships	Marital and individual therapy	Health, social service, and mental health providers
	Social services	Parents
Level 3: Individual child		
Protection from harm	Neurologic evaluation	Pediatrician and other health providers
	Documentation of bruises	Parents
	Mandated reporting to social services	Social services
	Parental control of anger and impulses	

needs are not always perceived by parents as congruent with their own. Thus, responsibility for child health cannot be left to parents alone. This is especially critical for infants and preschool children, who may not be in regular contact with any care providers except their families. In fact, children can be lost from public view between birth and the start of school.

Childhood immunization patterns can be a useful marker of which preschool children are in contact with services outside their homes. By and large, immunizations, which are the easiest health service to deliver to children, are provided when children are in contact with health organizations. Despite recent government efforts to achieve higher levels of immunization, the Select Panel points to serious lags:

> Achieving high levels of immunization for preschool children appears to remain a major problem. In 1978, of the 12.2 million children 1–4 years of age, only about 6 out of 10 had received full protection for measles, rubella, and polio; the proportion for diphtheria was somewhat higher; for mumps, somewhat lower. The best estimates available indicate that preschool minority children and those in poverty areas of central cities are the least likely to be immunized; even though those children, often living in crowded housing, are at great risk of contagion. Problems of access may partially account for the low levels of immunization for these children but parental beliefs are also important. In 1978–79, 22 percent of the minority parents in contrast with 12 percent of all parents believed that most children's diseases had been conquered and there was no need to immunize against them; 44 percent of the minority parents in contrast with 28 percent of all parents believed that it was the responsibility of the government and the schools—as opposed to the parents—to immunize children against childhood diseases. (Select Panel, 1980, Vol. III, p. 35)

Clearly, there is a disparity between the perceptions of minority and majority parents concerning who bears responsibility for children's immunizations. This must be held in mind as immunization programs are improved. It also suggests a need to involve families more consistently in the planning of health programs for children. When considered along with Case 2, such findings point to the need for some universal system of health contact and health care for children of all ages.

Case 3

An 8-year-old white male was admitted to the hospital for evaluation of short stature and an unusual feeding disorder; i.e., a craving—unmanageable in the home—for foods to which he was thought to be allergic.

His history included an unremarkable pregnancy and delivery, with birth weight of 3.3 kg, an apparent milk allergy from early infancy which led to his being fed a milk-free formula, and retarded growth, both in height and weight, from the second year. Parents were of average height. His motor and linguistic development were unremarkable. Clinical investigation at two hospitals did not support the parents' continuing belief that food allergy in this "sickly" child accounted for his stature; physicians could point to no specific cause for the growth failure. Oppositional behavior in the home about his eating habits seemed a more likely factor. He picked at meals (while parents tried to make him eat), then made nightly raids on the refrigerator (which the parents tried, ineffectively, to lock), gorged on foods such as mustard and chocolate, and then awakened his mother and vomited. It was the way he ate (in a larger sense, the way the family fed him and he ate), rather than what he ate, that was stunting his growth. He had become a babyish child, scapegoated by his peers.

On admission the patient's height and weight were appropriate for an average 4½-year-old; he had not gained any weight in a year, nor any height in six months. Aside from his stature, he lacked physical and biochemical stigmata of malnutrition. Behaviorally, he alternated between the clinging and whining associated with younger children and subtle provocation of other children, resulting in his being scapegoated. At meals he dawdled, took large portions, did not eat them, and got up and walked around the dining room. In his play and fantasy he showed fears of his own assertiveness. Frustrated in developing autonomy, he seemed always to be looking for outer controls, but in self-defeating ways. His family's responses (such as dictating what he could eat or locking the refrigerator) only confirmed his unconscious identity as one incapable of inner controls.

Play therapy and treatment in an inpatient therapeutic milieu where he lived with other children offered him a chance to experiment with his own assertiveness and to see that he could make choices autonomously, without endangering himself or others. His parents had the opportunity in social casework to review the issues in their lives which had made this child hard to care for and to appreciate the ways in which they could foster, rather than fight, his attempts to do things for himself.

During a 2½-months' hospitalization, he began eating appropriately and even (for the first time in his life) with gusto, and resumed growth. He eventually closed between one third and one half of the large gap between his retarded growth progression and the third percentile for his age. This pattern continued after discharge. There was no vomiting, regardless of what he ate. Marked gains occurred in peer relations and in school behavior and work.

The parents were particularly pleased to be able to enjoy activities with this child, rather than finding themselves always engaged in an oppositional struggle with him. The major casualties of that struggle had been his growth and their mutual enjoyment of each other.

In this case, as in Case 1, an initial, medically focused investigation, including two hospitalizations, was inadequate to point the way toward understanding of and effective intervention for the child's severe health problems (Table 4). Frequently the concern of physicians and parents is to identify organic, as opposed to familial or psychological, determi-

TABLE 4:   CASE 3: NEEDS AND RESPONSIBILITIES

What is the need?	How can the need be met?	Who is responsible?
Level 1: Social & environmental context		
Availability of specialized services for child mental health	Interdisciplinary, hospital-based psychosomatic, in-patient unit	Federal and state laws and executive departments to assure the availability of specialized services
		Private health insurers
Level 2: Family context		
Mutual pleasure as a family rather than oppositional struggles	Medical diagnostic and therapeutic services with a rich psychiatric content	The child's physician
		The hospital-based treatment program
	Social casework with a psychiatric emphasis	
Level 3: Individual child		
Adequate nutrition	Hospitalization	Parents
Resolution of emotional and relational issues interfering with the eating process	Individual milieu and family therapy	Pediatrician and other health and mental health care providers
		The child

nants of a child's symptoms. This can lead to costly and unhelpful diagnostic studies. Furthermore, it can obscure attention to what is really important, such as a child's relationship to his parents.

Physicians who care for children are frequently poorly educated in understanding child development and in the psychological concomitants of illness. In this case, it was the active intercession of a concerned physician which led to the child's successful treatment.

The availability of such specialized services for child mental health was a matter of urgent concern to the Select Panel:

Current estimates indicate that at most, only 20 percent of the children who need mental health services are, in fact, receiving them. This low proportion is even more disturbing in light of the fact that there are approximately 70,000 chronically mentally ill children under the age of 18 in the United States today, and 50 to 80 percent of them will retain their disabilities into adulthood. (Select Panel, 1981, Vol. II, p. 90)

The current frenzy of budget-trimming in social service systems throughout the country augurs ominously for children with developmental disabilities and psychological problems. There are implications for health, although not nearly so dramatic as in this case. Increasingly, physicians and members of affiliated disciplines who deliver health care to children must have the skills to diagnose and treat many mental health and psychosomatic disorders. Indeed, such affiliations constitute, as the Panel points out, much of the "new morbidity of" childhood:

> In a recent study of seven primary care facilities, the proportion of children recognized as having behavioral, educational, or social problems ranged from 5 to 15 percent, and was substantially higher among low-income children. Similarly, it has been estimated that 25 percent of physician referrals for children today are related to psychosocial or behavioral problems. Other manifestations of such problems, which some have termed "the new morbidity," include the following:
>
> - Although mortality rates for all other age groups have declined steadily since 1900, death rates for adolescents and young adults aged 15 to 24 have actually gone up since 1960, largely as a result of the growing toll from accidents, homicide, and suicide.
> - Suicide is the third leading cause of death among teenagers and young adults aged 15–24; homicide is the leading cause of death among black teenagers and young adults, accounting for 30 percent of deaths in this age group.
> - Up to 1 million children each year are the victims of child abuse and neglect. Between 2,000 and 5,000 die annually at the hands of their parents or caretakers.
> - Approximately 11,000 girls under age 15 give birth each year, incurring significant medical, psychological, and economic risks.
> - Between 1975 and 1979, the proportion of high school seniors reporting alcohol use within the past month climbed from 68 to 72 percent; marijuana use, from 27 to 36 percent; and cocaine, from 2 to 6 percent.
> - In 1979 almost 13 percent of women aged 12–18 were regular cigarette smokers as compared to 8 percent in 1968. (Select Panel, 1981, Vol. I, pp. 45–46)

Because psychological disabilities of the types just cited are stigmatizing to many American adults, it is difficult both for parents and for health providers to acknowledge the importance of dealing with psychological factors in children's illnesses. Thus, an educational effort should be made both for parents and for health workers. Specifically, parents and health workers need to understand that it is proper to have feelings and to talk about them in the medical office. Simply to identify the presence or absence of an organic component of illness is not sufficient for the health provider; and, conversely, a parent should be reluctant to take a prescription, say, for a stimulant drug because a child is having problems controlling restlessness in school.

But inasmuch as medical schools, postgraduate training programs, and many institutions in which children spend long periods are unresponsive to approaching children as human beings, an aggressive effort to establish standards for child health care and training shall have to be made. Initially, this can best be done by formalizing a conception of child health which includes the child's emotional and familial experience as well as biological threats to health. Responsibility for this must be shared by medical workers, professional schools, specialty-certifying organizations, as well as the private and governmental units that pay for services. For example, the fee schedules which prevail in medical practice "offer physicians excessively strong incentives to furnish technical services and insufficient encouragement to perform as the patient's advisor, counselor, and health advocate" (Almy, 1981, p. 225).

Pediatricians surveyed in private offices spend, on the average, less than 1 minute per visit in counseling their patients on prevention (Hoekelman, 1980). When the time spent advising about specific measures such as immunizations and car seats was deducted from the total, an average of only 6 seconds remained for anticipatory guidance to parents about the developmental tasks facing them and their children. On average, adolescents received 7 seconds of counsel. By contrast, pediatric nurse practitioners working in physicians' offices elicited and discussed more descriptive information about the child, discovered a greater number of mothers' concerns, and provided more directives to the mother than did pediatricians (Foye, Chamberlin, & Charney, 1971).

Case 4

A 13-year-old girl was interviewed by journalist Pamela Blafer Lack (1979):

Question: Do you know, Ernestine, that this is the International Year of the Child?
Answer: No.
Q: What do you think that means?
A: I don't know.
Q: Well, it means that grownups all over the world are taking time out this year to think about what can be done to help children. Now, can you tell me which children you think could use some help? Are there any kids you feel sorry for?
A: My friends.
Q: Your friends? Why?
A: 'Cause their mothers abuse them.
Q: Abuse them? In what way?
A: Extension cords. Sticks. And tree branches.
Q: What do your friends do to deserve this? Are they so bad?
A: When their mother gets angry she takes it out on them.
Q: What makes the mother angry?

A: The girl's mother and father gets in a argument.
Q: And she gets it?
A: Yeah—Yeah.
Q: Is there anything else that really bothers you about grownups?
A: First thing is that they abuse too many children. That's what I don't like. I like nice—nice things.
Q: Do you like where you're living?
A: No—too many things be goin' on around there.
Q: What's going on?
A: Shootin' trouble.
Q: What do you mean?
A: Well, my friend—her mother told her to go to the store about 10 o'clock at night and they were shootin' out—and she went outside and they shot her.
Q: Who shot her?
A: Some gangsters.
Q: Is she all right?
A: No—she got killed.
Q: When did this happen?
A: Couple of weeks ago.
Q: What was her name?
A: Christina.
Q: How old was she?
A: Thirteen.
Q: Why do you think there's so much trouble?
A: Really, if they would break up the gangsters there wouldn't be no trouble around where I live.
Q: What kind of life do kids want to have?
A: A nice life.
Q: What's a nice life to you, Ernestine?
A: When you don't get killed. You could go outside and don't be abused by your parents.

The impact on child health of the social acceptance of violence is imperfectly understood, but clearly many children are victims of a violent social milieu. Ernestine's friend, Christine, was 13 when shot by "gangsters" in her neighborhood. Other friends were beaten in their homes, and Ernestine's conception of a nice life was one in which children would simply be permitted to survive.

Between the ages of 5 and 15, the average American child views the killings of more than 13,000 persons on television (Somers, 1976). Our children are surrounded by metaphors of violence, and the implements of destruction are readily available as well. But in contemplating the impact of handguns on children, the Select Panel stumbled on the politics:

Easy access to firearms appears to be a prime contributor to the appalling U.S. murder rate. From 1960 to 1974, handgun sales in this country quadrupled to more than 6 million a year. During that same period, the hom-

TABLE 5:   CASE 4: NEEDS AND RESPONSIBILITIES

What is the need?	How can the need be met?	Who is responsible?
Level 1: Social & environmental context		
A universal system of rules and values about children's rights independent of their parents'	Rules to limit violence in schools, homes, and in the media	Federal and state legislatures and executive departments
To address the acceptability of violent methods of resolving conflict in the home and in society	Laws mandating reporting of possible abuse or neglect of children	Advertisers, citizens, and producers of media
		Parents
	Gun control	
Level 2: Family context		
Interpersonal relationships free of violence	Economic, psychological, and medical support for parent	Social work, medical and mental health service providers
		Parents
Level 3: Individual child		
Survival	Outreach program addressing the safety of the child's environment	Social work and health care providers
		Parents
	Mandated reporting to social services	
	Parental control of violence toward child	

icide rate jumped from 4.7 per 100,000 to 10.2 for the population as a whole, and from 5.9 per 100,000 to 14.2 for young people aged 15–24.

Evidence from England and elsewhere shows that prohibiting the possession of handguns dramatically reduces the number of shooting deaths and injuries, especially those unrelated to criminal assaults. The Panel is aware of fierce political controversy in this country about any form of gun control, and recognizes the strength of the organized firearms lobby. Nonetheless, the stakes for the nation's children are so high that nothing short of a total ban on the sale of handguns, with exemptions for persons such as police, military personnel, and pistol clubs, seems reasonable. We realize such a ban is not likely to prove politically feasible in the short term. One useful, less controversial step would be to mandate the development of child and youth protection standards relating to gun safety. These standards might be jointly developed by a variety of interest groups, including the National Rifle Association, U.S. Conference of Mayors, gun manufacturers, and others. The effects of such a safety campaign on child and adolescent death rates should be carefully assessed. Failure to reduce the incidence of youthful handgun deaths by more than half should be regarded as further impetus for an overall ban. (Select Panel, 1981, Vol. I, pp. 85–86)

The political feasibility of handgun control appears even smaller now than when the Select Panel drafted its report. This should not, however, deter action. Violence accounts for an extraordinary amount of childhood death and suffering, with a considerable impact on children's families as well. It must be checked.

Adolescents require a special framework of health services. These are summarized well in Volume I of the Select Panel Report. It is gratifying to see the unflinching support for family planning services, although the Select Panel skittered away from abortion, which is not even mentioned in the service compendium. This omission is unfortunate as members of the Select Panel apparently know well:

From 1967 through 1978, 6.3 million women obtained 7.9 million legal abortions; about one in eight U.S. women of reproductive age has had a legal abortion. Since the 1973 Supreme Court decisions that declared restrictive abortion laws unconstitutional, the annual number of legal abortions has increased by 85 percent, but the rate of increase has been smaller each year. In every year since 1972, women who obtained legal abortions were mainly young, white, unmarried, and childless; for many this was their first abortion. Teenagers have nearly one-third of all abortions, but the percentage decreased slightly between 1972 and 1977. In each year since 1973, women obtained abortions at earlier, and thus safer, gestational ages. (Select Panel, 1981, Vol. III, p. 12)

CONCLUSIONS

Given the complexity and heterogeneity of child health—including nonmedical—services and the persistent confusion about their context, one cannot help but be concerned about the usefulness of the Select Panel's discrete program-by-program approach. George Silver (1978), who favors a substantial revision of the organization for child health promotion, notes:

A variety of bureaucratic hazards undermine the accomplishment of the basic national child health objectives: the elimination of unnecessary morbidity and mortality in childhood. The legislative and executive branches of the federal government and of the state governments, by reasons of their inter- and intra-agency rivalries and conflicts, obstruct effective performance even when sufficient resources are available. For the most part, however, sufficient resources are not made available because the necessary information about the exact nature of the gaps is neither asked for nor collected. The fact that so little demand for information is made on the states tends to confirm the theory that the federal government really gives the states funds for state programs rather than for national programs to be implemented in the states. (p. 94)

Silver concludes from his review of European systems of child health care, and the problems in our own system, that a wholly revised program is in order:

1. An umbrella of social protection for children, which includes,
   a. money, or the equivalent, to offset the added costs of child rearing and allow for decent housing, nutrition, and clothing;
   b. special housing subsidy and nutritional programs for children, especially free school lunch;
   c. special treatment for the pregnant woman—maternity leave if she works, home help before and after childbirth.
2. Health (preventive) services, including:
   a. prenatal care;
   b. infancy and preschool supervision;
   c. school health services.
3. Comprehensive, prepaid medical care services for all children.
4. Organizational innovations, including:
   a. separate child health services in (2) above;
   b. emphasis on nurses with pediatric training and on midwives;
   c. local organizational control;
   d. private sector involvement in public sector activities.
5. Financing preventive services separately through family and local community contributions along with state and federal funds.
6. Social and legal protection for the child against abuse and neglect by parents, schools, and society in general.
7. A vigorous children's advocacy program, including (4) and (6) above—a separate, national program, publicly funded. (Silver, 1978, pp. 235–236).

The Select Panel Report (1981) provides an ambiguous basis for the definition of responsibility for children's health. Unless and until a concept of children's health is defined which can guide the development of a national policy, it will be difficult to delineate who is responsible for what aspects of child health.

Certainly, responsibility will continue to be shared, but it would be well to specify those components of responsibility which belong primarily to child, parent, professional, and society. As our case reports suggest, the child is not always in a position to protect, or to speak for, himself. Nor, frequently, are parents. Professionals may mete out harm in the guise of help as they try in a blundering way to take responsibility.

The following four principles, which could serve as the basis for framing questions of responsibility, were insufficiently understood by the Select Panel:

1. Where possible, the child should be empowered, and when, because of age, handicap, or social status, the child cannot speak for himself, his needs should be addressed by an advocate who will be accountable to the child over time.
2. Services and money should follow the child and accommodate his needs, and not the other way around.
3. Programs for child health should be constructed from the child up, and not from the government down.
4. The causes, not only the symptoms, of childhood morbidity and mortality should be addressed in child health practice, even if this means focusing on uncomfortable familial and social issues, such as poverty, violence, and racism. To the extent that these are allowed to persist, we will have forsaken our responsibility for children's health.

Times are hard for many children in this land, and those concerned for them must now speak out, facing forthrightly the politics of the day, as the Select Panel was constrained not to do. The late Billie Holliday, whose short and deprived childhood did not keep in check a powerful artistic vision, sounded a note of reality with regard to child health in the present day in her song, "God Bless the Child."

Them that's got shall get
Them that's not shall lose
So the Bible Said
And it still is News:
Mama may have. Papa may have.
But God Bless the Child that's got his own! That's got his own.
Yes, the strong gets more
While the weak ones fade
Empty pockets don't even make the grade:
Mama may have. Papa may have
But God Bless the Child that's got his own! That's got his own.
Money, you got lots o' friends
Crowdin' round the door;
When you're gone and spendin' ends,
They don't come no more.
Rich relations give crust of bread, and such.
You can help yourself, But don't take too much!
Mama may have. Papa may have.
But God Bless the Child that's got his own! That's got his own.

REFERENCES

Almy, T. P. The role of the primary physician in the health-care industry. *New England Journal of Medicine*, 1981, *304*, 225–228.

Fanshel, D., & Shinn, E. B. *Children in foster care: A longitudinal investigation*. New York: Columbia Univ. Press, 1978.

Foye, H., Chamberlin, R., & Charney, E. Content and emphasis of well-child visits: Experienced nurse practitioners vs. pediatrician. *American Journal of Diseases of Children*, 1971, *122*, 483.

Hoekelman, R. A. Got a minute? *Pediatrics*, 1980, *66*, 1013–1014.

Klaus, M. H., & Kennell, J. H. *Maternal-infant bonding*. St. Louis: Mosby, 1976.

Lack, P. B. For Bushwick kids, 'Year of the Child'? Ha. *New York Times*, October 13, 1979.

National Academy of Sciences. *Toward a national policy for children and families*. Washington, D.C.: Author, 1976.

Ryan, W. *Blaming the victim*. New York: Random House, 1971.

Select Panel for the Promotion of Child Health. *Better health for our children: A national strategy* (4 Vols.). Washington, D.C.: U.S. Govt. Printing Office, 1981.

Silver, G. A. *Child health: America's future*. Germantown, Md.: Aspen Systems Corp., 1978.

Somers, A. R. Violence, television, and the health of American youth. *New England Journal of Medicine*, 1976, *15*, 811–817.

Six

HEALTH MANPOWER NEEDS AS PROJECTED BY THE SELECT PANEL FOR THE PROMOTION OF CHILD HEALTH

FERNANDO A. GUERRA

INTRODUCTION

The purpose of this chapter is to examine the health manpower needs recommended by the Select Panel for the Promotion of Child Health. In so doing, I would like to suggest some mechanisms for delivering health services that might be effective in meeting some of the deficiencies in supply and distribution of health manpower. I will not deal with the specific projections and statistical data that are found in the third volume of the Select Panel Report (1981), or with those published in the Graduate Medical Education National Advisory Committee (GMENAC; *Summary Report,* 1980). However, there are some discrepancies in the manpower data and projections published by the Select Panel, GMENAC, and most recently, the American Academy of Pediatrics (1981) Manpower Committee report. These discrepancies in data, of course, raise some dilemmas that should be addressed. It would have been helpful for the Select Panel to have had access to the data, conclusions, and recommendations of both GMENAC and the Academy of Pediatrics Report.

The document representing the work of the Panel and its consultants and reviewers leaves me with considerable respect and admiration. I feel confident that, with time, the work of the Select Panel should have a profound effect in protecting and promoting the health and well-being of children, families, and young parents. At the same time, however, I have some disappointments which I will discuss after stating two caveats.

These caveats are, first, that there is a disadvantage inherent in reviewing and reacting to such a voluminous document that, as complete as it might be, does not necessarily reflect all of the lengthy discussions and comments that took place before the Panel arrived at each particular conclusion or recommendation. For the critic of the report, the disadvantage is that something of relevancy may have been omitted—perhaps for good reason—that would clarify the Panel's reasoning. The other caveat has to do with the format used by the Panel. In particular, their discussions and recommendations about health manpower are not conveniently located in one place in the report. Rather, they are buried in chapters dealing with "Needed Services," "Improving the Organization of Health Services," "Delivery Problems," "Special Populations," "Financing," and so on. It is at times difficult to select specific manpower issues, although the Panel did express definite concerns with manpower issues.

PRODUCTIVITY

An effective indicator of adequate manpower in whatever work, discipline, or profession is productivity. My major disappointment with the Panel's Report is that in its almost idealistic hope for improving the quantity and quality of health services and care for children and mothers, it did not clearly deal with those issues affecting productivity. There is no mention of the waste, abuses, duplication, confusion, and inappropriate health care utilization for which the present system rewards both consumers and producers. The abilities, experience, and skills needed by providers are dealt with only in an indirect way. All these issues should have significant impact on discussions of health manpower needs, and especially for planning future manpower needs.

In providing services to children, especially young children, we must recognize that the system is mostly a "third party interpretative" one that brings the supervising or responsible adult (parent) to an interface with the provider. Although I am sure the Panel recognizes the critical role of parents in our health system, some of their recommendations fail to reflect this understanding. In such a third-party interpretative system, the interested adult brings certain attitudes, preconceived notions, needs, knowledge, and skills to the health care setting, and these impact significantly on the health provider's role. Depending on the relationship that develops between parent and provider, the provider may or may not be successful in responding to the child's needs. This characteristic of our health delivery system also affects such manpower issues as distribution, utilization, economics, and efficiency. If, for example, parents cancel appointments at the last minute or bring in their children as "walk-ins," the schedule of the doctor's office or clinic is thrown into chaos—with obvious implications for cost and efficiency. To take this further, a development already occurring in some communities—either as a fad, because of economic hard times, or because of disenchantment with the system—is that some adults and parents are assuming more personal responsibility for their own and their children's health. I suggest that the "holistic health movement," home deliveries, and self-care concepts are examples of trends that may have an effect on health manpower (Gordon, 1980).

Another concern with the report's manpower is that the Panel seems to assume that health professionals with needed skills and abilities are interested in, and waiting to take care of, patients as long as there is some method of remuneration. From experience with both the public and private sectors, I would assert that this is often not the case. Some physicians prefer to exercise selectivity in deciding which patients they will care for. I have noticed with alarm, for example, that many recent graduates of medical training programs prefer not to accept Title XIX recipients into their practices. Even fewer doctors are willing to treat medically indigent patients, unless it is a dire emergency. Thus, in projecting health manpower needs, or in calculating the adequacy of service providers for particular geographical areas, it is essential to consider "effective" providers as well as total number of providers per total population.

In calculating the total number of providers in given communities, a number of other complicating factors must also be considered. Women physicians, women nurse practitioners, and women physician extenders, for example, often have serious constraints on their time because of family responsibilities. I do not say this as a criticism, because historically, women physicians have contributed greatly; rather these differences between male and female providers should be noted. Other considerations that affect manpower are the life-styles of physicians (and especially the desire by many physicians to have better control of their time), job satisfaction, support systems, and "burn out." Of interest here is that informal discussions with health practitioners seem to in-dicate a significant level of job dissatisfaction and "burn out" in the specialties of pediatrics and obstetrics–gynecology (Palfrey, 1981).

Another problem with the report pertains to the recommendation for increasing the number of trainees in primary care specialties, in-cluding nonphysician providers, and the failure to distinguish "need-based" from "demand-based" manpower requirements. Some of these differences have been alluded to above, but they require further com-ment. The need-based manpower requirement is the estimated number of physicians needed to respond appropriately to the incidence of health problems in a given population. On the other hand, the demand-based manpower requirement is the felt need by consumers and interpretative third parties to see a physician—for whatever reason. Without question, demand-based manpower estimates are difficult to ascertain. Nonethe-less, an adjusted manpower estimate derived from both the need-based and the demand-based requirements would serve to more accurately make manpower recommendations for the primary care specialties.

The Select Panel recognized the need for increasing the number of providers in smaller communities and rural settings and expressed hope that such an increase will occur as more individuals enter primary care specialties and the National Health Service Corps continues to at-tract young physicians. Again, this seems too much to hope for, at least in the immediate future. However, with 20 million children already living in rural America, some urgency is needed here (U.S. Bureau of the Census, 1980). Thus, the Select Panel should have more clearly and realistically developed a strategy to increase the number of health care providers in rural areas.

Finally, I am concerned with the recommendation that occurs re-peatedly in several chapters for an expanded role by health providers in the areas of psychological, environmental, and behavioral problems, e.g., in dealing with the so-called "new morbidity." In making this recommendation, the Select Panel also calls for new linkages between health care providers and community agencies, schools, social workers, and outreach programs. Despite the importance the Select Panel attached to these issues of the new morbidity, the report provided few details of how this expanded role for health care providers is to be carried out. To take just one example of the need for specific details in this area, unless such a system is well coordinated there is bound to be great inefficiency. Think of the confusion and duplication of effort that occurs when school personnel or social workers initiate referrals without coordinating with the primary physician.

To be sure, the new morbidity represents an important new di-mension of health care as well as a set of services that are sorely needed by American families. But to recognize a need is not enough. If health care providers are to provide these services, we need to know how many new providers will be needed, what training will be required, and how they will coordinate their efforts with those of agencies and professionals already addressing these problems.

THERAPEUTIC ALLIANCES

So much for the problems and disappointments. At this point, I would like to review a few recommendations that might serve to enhance the productivity of providers of health care to children and families. In this context, I would like to introduce the term "therapeutic alliances." The term is not a new one and generally means a good relationship between physician and patient that ultimately leads to a favorable health outcome. If this concept could be expanded to include not only physician and patient, but all individuals involved in providing services to a particular child or family, and to imply ongoing communication for treatment plans and desired goals among all these individuals, health care in America could be much improved. Within such an alliance, a contractor must act on behalf of the patient. From experience, I have found primary physicians or their delegated substitutes to be well-suited for this role. Such a system of cooperative planning and treatment enables providers to do much more for particular children and families than could be accomplished by individual professionals working alone. As members of the alliance work together over a period of time, they can more effectively use their combined prior experience in case management to expedite new cases. This approach works especially well with abused children, children with chronic illness, school problems, or handicapping conditions that often require many evaluations as well as assistance from community agencies and rehabilitative programs. Such an alliance may not even require formal meetings or staffing conferences; a phone call or dictated note to the members coordinated by the contractor may be all that is necessary. In my own experience, I have found that this approach works well within my office practice, a neighborhood health center, and an inpatient hospital setting.

As health professionals, we must recognize that we have considerable latitude—and considerable responsibility—for being innovative in order to respond aggressively to health needs that exist in our communities, especially when there seems never to be enough doctors or dollars to take care of everyone. To cite a few examples of possible innovations, group practices or even solo-practitioners could reorganize their office schedules to comply with their patients' schedules. Extending office hours a few days a week or holding office hours in the early evening would more easily allow working parents and single parents to avail themselves of health services for their children, either on a scheduled or walk-in basis. Extended office hours would curtail early evening phone calls and visits to the emergency room for minor illness, as well as promote better record-keeping, health maintenance, and continuity of care. Training programs for primary care physicians should introduce trainees to innovative concepts such as this to demonstrate their effectiveness in responding to demand as well as need.

In our Barrio Family Health Center in San Antonio, we have used both National Health Service Corps physicians and a cadre of part-time primary care providers (who are all in private practice) to provide early evening clinic sessions for low-income, minority, and working families. In many instances, these physicians have followed the same group of patients for the entire 10-year life of the clinic, almost as they would in their own practices. Such an arrangement has greatly enhanced the productivity of the clinic, and the providers as well. I might mention also that we currently have a waiting list of physicians who have expressed an interest in working with the clinic as slots become available.

I turn now to a consideration of health manpower needs for special population groups. I prefer to limit the term "special population groups" to migrants, seasonal farm workers, refugees, and aliens, rather than the broader use suggested by the Panel which also includes children with chronic diseases, handicapping conditions, and learning disabilities. The reason for limiting the groups to which this term applies is that, from a health manpower standpoint, the economic, political, cultural, and practical needs of those included in the Select Panel definition are strikingly different from the needs of those included in the more restricted definition. Furthermore, it would seem that the health delivery system that can best meet the needs of special populations included in the more restrictive definition is quite different than our traditional delivery system. More specifically, such a delivery system must have sufficient flexibility to permit the use of indigenous, preprimary-care health workers, i.e., "barefoot doctors" and *"consejeros"* (health advisers), to provide a link with the traditional delivery system. Moreover, because of the extreme mobility of this special population an effective delivery system must have the capability to relay information back and forth between various providers, whether by computer, phone, or special mailing forms. I might mention that the Academy of Pediatrics, together with the Academy of Family Physicians, has recently identified a network of providers and health care facilities with interest and capabilities for serving migrant families during the time they are "in stream." It is too soon to know about the effectiveness of this effort, but initial impressions from last season are that it has helped clinics and providers at the migrant's "home base" to get information "up stream" and thereby assure follow-up care for patients in need. For aliens, serious problems remain from the health provider standpoint, although, at least for aliens from Mexico, early attempts are being made in the area of maternal and child health. Such attempts are especially important—even critical—in view of the fact that almost 50% of this population is under 15 years of age. For health providers on either side of the U.S./Mexico border, the provision of health care to pregnant mothers and children must be the paramount concern in planning for health manpower.

In closing, I reiterate my praise for the Select Panel and the dedication to its work during the past 18 months. It has given all of us hope that we can provide better health services to America's children, their mothers, and young families. I feel confident that we, as providers and health professionals, can respond to this challenge as never before.

REFERENCES

American Academy of Pediatrics, Committee on Pediatric Manpower. Critique of the final report of the Graduate Medical Education National Advisory Committee. *Pediatrics,* 1981, *67,* 585–596.

Gordon, J. S. Holistic health centers. In A. Hastings, J. Fadiman, & J. Gordon (Eds.), *Health for the whole person.* Boulder, Colo.: Westview Crafts, 1980.

Graduate Medical Education National Advisory Committee. *Summary report* (Vol. I). [DHHS Publ. No. (HRA) 81-656]. Washington, D.C.: Dept. of Health and Human Services, 1980.

Palfrey, J. S. *Maternal and child health research: Health of preschool children.* Paper presented at the Conference on Research Priorities in Maternal and Child Health, Brandeis University, Waltham, Mass., June, 1981.

Select Panel for the Promotion of Child Health. *Better health for our children: A national strategy* (4 Vols.). Washington, D.C.: U.S. Govt. Printing Office, 1981.

U.S. Bureau of the Census. Estimates of population of the states by age. *Current Population Reports,* Series P-25, No. 875. Washington, D.C.: U.S. Govt. Printing Office, 1980.

Seven

Primary Care and the Cost Dilemma: A Case for Nurse Practitioners

CAROLYN A. WILLIAMS

INTRODUCTION

To provide a context for discussion of the Select Panel's Report and nurse practitioners, I will first provide some general background on the nurse practitioner movement, with which we have had approximately a decade and a half of experience. Second, I will review briefly the current status of the nurse practitioner movement with particular attention to projections of the Graduate Medical Education National Advisory Committee (1980), better known as GMENAC.

Emergence of the nurse practitioner movement can be traced to a number of factors, not the least of which was the felt need on the part of many nurses in ambulatory settings for more meaningful roles in patient care—roles which would allow for increased levels of autonomy and responsibility in decision-making, which would enhance the care provided to patients, and which would legitimize such practice by significant groups. These aspirations represented a necessary condition for the development of the present pool of approximately 20,300 graduates of nurse practitioner programs, including midwives.[1] However, since such aspirations predated the development of the first formalized program to prepare nurse practitioners, it can be argued that they were a necessary, but not sufficient, condition to explain the momentum and vitality of the nurse practitioner movement. Clearly, it will be the task of future historians to put the various determinants of the practitioner movement into a more formal perspective. However, in a more general sense, I think it is defensible to suggest that in the late 1960s and early 1970s, there was a significant subset of nurses, physicians, others associated with the health care system, and the public who shared the notion that the nurse practitioner was an "idea whose time had come." Factors frequently commented upon as influencing the development of early training programs and the demand for services by nurse practitioners were: (1) an increased awareness of the importance of primary care by the public and policymakers; (2) a concomitant awareness of gaps in the accessibility to, and quality of, primary care services, due in part to geographic and specialty maldistribution of medical personnel; (3) a national interest in making primary care accessible to underserved segments of the population, particularly in rural and inner city locations; and (4) the potential for contributing to cost containment. Since development of the first training program in an academic institution in 1965 (the pediatric nurse practitioner program at the University of Colorado in Denver), preparation for nurse practitioner roles has moved from its initial location in short-term, continuing education offerings into the mainstream of nursing education. In short, nurse practitioner training has now been institutionalized in academic settings.

At this point, clarification of the term "nurse practitioner" is in order. In one sense, it is simplistic to use the term since a variety of practitioner roles have developed. These range from caring for individuals in specific age groups (pediatric nurse practitioners, adult nurse practitioners, geriatric nurse practitioners) or patients representing particular needs (e.g., family-planning nurse practitioners, OB/GYN nurse practitioners, and nurse midwives), to the generalized family nurse practitioner whose concerns cut across groupings by age and care problems. However, the term "nurse practitioner" is used there to refer to nurses who, in addition to basic nursing education, have received further formal preparation enabling them to increase the scope of their services to include selected assessment and management decisions formerly reserved for physicians. It is important to point out that assumption of such decision-making, which usually occurs in a framework of guidelines mutually agreed upon by medical and nursing personnel, places the nurse practitioner in a new relationship to consumers and physician colleagues.

EFFICACY OF THE NURSE PRACTITIONER ROLE

In the 15 years since the beginning of the nurse practitioner move-ment, a considerable amount of favorable evidence has accumulated regarding the efficacy of nurse practitioners. Efficacy has been examined from a variety of perspectives: the extent to which the envisioned role is practiced (do graduates of educational programs actually practice in primary care roles?); the extent to which nurse practitioners provide care in rural or other underserved areas; the extent to which nurse practi-tioners are accepted by patients and physicians; the extent to which quality of care is maintained or enhanced; and the extent to which the practice is considered economically viable. At this point I will briefly comment on data concerning two areas of efficacy considered particu-larly important in this discussion; namely, quality of care and acceptance and satisfaction by other patients and providers.

Impact on Quality of Care

Since 1974, five comprehensive reviews or studies have examined the quality of care provided by nurse practitioners (Cohen, 1974; Health Resources Administration, 1977; Lawrence, 1978; Prescott & Driscoll, 1980; Sox, 1979). Cohen (1974) reported that numerous small studies supported the conclusion that nurse practitioners and physicians' as-sistants "performed as well as physicians, judged by standards devel-oped within practice settings" (p. 128). After reviewing a variety of studies available by 1977, authors of the Health Resources Administra-tion's (1977) Physician Extender Work Group *Report* concluded that within the limits of current methods for measuring quality of care: "The performance of the nurse practitioner/physician's assistant has compared favorably with that of the physician on both process and outcome meas-ures" (p. 51). They went on to argue that "until better methods are developed to measure quality of care, this issue needs no further re-search" (p. 51). In a 1978 review, Lawrence concluded that there was little evidence that quality declines when nonphysician health providers are used to render routine services. In fact, he pointed to indications that in certain cases, nonphysician health providers obtained somewhat better outcomes, especially in the level of patient compliance and in behavioral outcomes for patients suffering from selected chronic dis-eases.

Sox (1979) analyzed 21 studies published between 1967 and 1977 in which care provided by nurse practitioners or physician's assistants was compared with that given by physicians. He concluded that the "quality of primary ambulatory care given by nurse practitioners and physicians's assistants was indistinguishable from that given by physicians" (p. 465). However, Sox found a number of limitations in the studies. For example, only a few investigators used detailed quality of care measures or patient groups that had been adequately characterized or appeared comparable. Moreover, a number of the studies dealt with a very narrow range of patient groups or measures of performance. Additional criticisms included the sparcity of information on care given in emergency rooms and nursing homes and the lack of stratification for the difficulty of the patient's problems. Thus, the care of patients with serious medical problems may have been overlooked. Finally, Sox pointed out that since nurse practitioners who participated in such studies might have been unusually cooperative and above average in their effectiveness some caution was necessary in generalizing to the broader practice community. Despite these limitations, Sox (1979) stated that:

> The primary care physician has enough information to predict the impact of a nurse practitioner or physician's assistant on the quality of care in a practice. A nurse practitioner or physician's assistant should be well accepted by patients, and provide the average office patient with primary care that compares very favorably with care given by the physician. (p. 467)

In a recently published review of 26 studies comparing nurse practitioner performance to that of physicians, Prescott and Driscoll (1980) reported that the predominant finding was that "no difference" existed between the two provider groups. However, they further noted that findings which showed nurse practitioners with better scores than physicians (e.g., in areas such as the amount and depth of discussion regarding child care, therapeutic listening, support offered the patient, preventive care, completeness of history, physical exams, and patient's knowledge about the management plan) were frequently overlooked or played down in the conclusions of those preparing the reports.

Patient and Physician Acceptance/Satisfaction

The vast majority of published data dealing with questions of consumer acceptance and satisfaction with nurse practitioners and physician's assistants is positive, i.e., satisfaction with services provided by nurse practitioners is found to be equal to, or greater than, satisfaction with physician care. To some extent the results may be influenced by a methodological problem inherent in most studies of patient satisfaction—the selective nature of the population surveyed. Such studies are conducted in practice settings in which patients are willing to see nurse practitioners. Those with doubts may choose not to go to such settings or the dissatisfied may choose not to return. Another limitation of these studies is the potential for bias on the part of investigators, many of whom have been associated with training programs. Despite these potential limitations, the consistently positive nature of the data gathered from many groups and in a wide variety of settings must be acknowledged.

In a review of studies on patient satisfaction prepared as a background paper for the Institute of Medicine's Primary Care Study, Ruby (1977) noted that "high acceptance is reported for nurse practitioners and physician assistants functioning at all levels of independence, delivering many types of care (well baby care, care for chronic disease, care for broad range problems), functioning in all settings and performing varied activities" (p. 23).

Investigators from System Sciences (1980) have pointed out that direct questioning of patients about their satisfaction with providers and the care received invariably results in positive responses. Thus, it would be desirable to have complementary data on patient satisfaction from other sources, such as the physician colleague or the employer of nurse practitioners. In System Sciences's analysis of nine national studies dealing with either nurse practitioners or physician's assistants, it was found that 90% of the responding employers (some of whom were physicians) reported that nurse practitioners were well, or fairly well, accepted by patients. The System Sciences study concluded that:

> . . . patient satisfaction with physician extender [this term was used to refer to both nurse practitioners and physician assistants] service was not directly addressed by any of the nine studies included in this evaluation analysis. However, several of the nine studies inquired about patient satisfaction from responding providers. Physicians and physician extenders had the same positive view of patient satisfaction, i.e., that patients were satisfied with and accepted the physician extender. (System Sciences, 1980, pp. 60–61)

NURSE PRACTITIONERS AND THE REPORT OF THE GRADUATE MEDICAL EDUCATION NATIONAL ADVISORY COMMITTEE

Despite what generally appears in the evaluation literature as an overall positive picture, within the last few years there has been a growing impression that all is not well and there may be some retrenchment in the utilization of nurse practitioners. Unfortunately, I cannot document this phenomenon with systematic data. However, comments are beginning to appear in the professional literature which refer to this pattern of retrenchment (Kahn, 1979; Edmunds, 1981). And my own impression, based on conversations with nurse practitioners in practice and others associated with training programs, suggests a trend in some settings for nurse practitioners to be replaced by physicians when physicians are available. Although distressing, the situation is not surprising. From the beginning of the nurse practitioner movement there were those who argued that the increased involvement of nurses in primary care was only a stopgap measure, accepted by medicine and the public as an interim circumstance while the training and deployment of primary care physicians was stepped up. From the perspective of supply and demand, and in view of the relative positions of nursing and medicine in the politics of health care delivery, a reasonable question to ask is: Will the nurse practitioner fade from the scene if the problem of physician distribution is resolved? It has been suggested that the answer "may depend in large part on whether the nurse practitioner is conceptualized, prepared for, and practiced only as a physician substitute role or whether it is seen as a role which is complementary to the physician's" (Williams, 1978, p. 208).

The recent release of the Graduate Medical Education National Advisory Committee (GMENAC) *Summary Report* has brought to center attention the question of the nurse practitioner's future in primary care. GMENAC was established in 1976 by the secretary of the then Department of Health, Education, and Welfare to advise the secretary on health planning objectives that pertain particularly to physicians. The core of GMENAC's work was to estimate the number of physicians required in each specialty in order to meet health care needs for the future; the time frame for focus was 1990. In order to make these estimates, a series of mathematic models was developed. A Nonphysician Health Care Provider Technical Panel (NPHCP) was developed as part of the overall GMENAC methodology. This panel was asked to provide recommendations to GMENAC regarding the impact of nonphysician providers on physician requirements. The panel focused on those nonphysicians who were formally prepared to provide services for which the physician is currently perceived as the usual provider. Since primary care was the area the panel felt offered the greatest potential for nonphysician utilization, their work focused on nurse practitioners, nurse midwives, and physician's assistants. In the following paragraphs, I will mention several of the key recommendations pertaining both to physicians and nonphysician care providers.

GMENAC concluded that in 1990 there will be 70,000 more physicians than required to provide physician services (Graduate Medical Education, 1980, Vol. I). In order to deal with this oversupply, GMENAC recommended that by 1984 all allopathic and osteopathic medical schools reduce entering class size by at least 10% relative to 1978–79 enrollment or 17% relative to the 1980–81 entering class. An additional recommendation was to severely restrict the number of graduates from foreign medical schools entering the U.S. If immigration by foreign doctors cannot be restricted, GMENAC recommended a further decrease in the number of entrants into medical schools.

A second major conclusion of the GMENAC report was that by 1990 shortages will exist in some specialties and surpluses in others. Of particular concern to this discussion are the GMENAC estimates for various primary care physician groups. The surplus estimated in three primary care disciplines combined (general pediatricians, general internists, and family physicians) was counted as trivial in overall percentage (about 7%). In fact, GMENAC suggested that 7% was probably within error range for the estimation models they used. Based on these estimates, the committee made the following recommendation:

> In view of the inevitable aggregate surplus of physicians in 1990, GMENAC recommends that the surplus be encouraged to enter the three primary care fields for training purposes once the shortages in other specialties have been corrected as much as possible. Therefore, although the models estimate a small surplus in the three primary care disciplines, GMENAC recommends that a larger surplus be created deliberately in the 1980s as an interim measure so an aggregate balance can be achieved in the 1990s. (Graduate Medical Education, 1980, Vol. I, p. 27)

A third major conclusion of the GMENAC study was that requirements for nonphysician health care providers should be integrated into physician manpower planning. In the Panel's consideration of nonphysician personnel, several important points surfaced. First, consistent with data cited previously in this chapter regarding the efficacy of nurse practitioners, the Panel made the following statement:

> GMENAC concluded that nurse practitioners (NPs), physician assistants (PAs), and nurse midwives (NMWs) make positive contributions to the health care system when working in close alliance with physicians. The committee supports the practice of nonphysician providers under the supervision of physicians but does not endorse the concept of their practicing independently. Nonphysician providers can enhance patient access to services, decrease costs and provide a broader range of services. Certain consumers prefer the nonphysician provider. (Graduate Medical Education, 1980, Vol. I, p. 28).

Second, GMENAC made a series of seven major recommendations pertaining to nonphysician personnel. These ranged across recommendations concerning training levels, needed changes in state laws and regulations, requirements and suggestions regarding third-party reimbursement, and structuring of graduate medical education to include experience for residents in working with nurse practitioners. In general, one could say that the recommendations support continued involvement in primary care by nonphysician personnel.

The fundamental issue which underlies GMENAC's discussion of nonphysician providers and which influenced their recommendations is the dilemma created by an acknowledgment, on the one hand, of the success achieved by nurse practitioners, nurse midwives, and physician assistants in selected aspects of medical care, and on the other hand, an awareness of the expected physician surpluses. The task of making projections is further complicated by the recognition that each nonphysician provider gives services in addition to medical visits. Thus, in the words of GMENAC, "A public policy dilemma occurs in an era of physician surplus because we do not know how simultaneously to preserve or extend the nonmedical services of nonphysician providers without simultaneously extending their contribution to the medical surplus" (Graduate Medical Education, 1980, Vol. VI, p. 28). The report continued: "At the current rate of training nurse practitioners, physicians' assistants, and nurse midwives the supply will double by 1990. The approximately 20,000 nonphysician providers in 1978, and 40,000 in 1990, will add further to the surplus capability" (Graduate Medical Education, 1980, Vol. VI, p. 28).

GMENAC's initial response to this dilemma was to suggest that a rather extensive research program of the requirements for nurse practitioners, physicians' assistants, nurse midwives, and other nonphysician providers be undertaken as soon as possible. Areas which should be researched include: the effect of a physician excess on nonphysician utilization; the relative cost and expenditures of using nonphysicians in place of physicians for selected medical care services, especially in underserved areas; the distinctive features, if any, of care given by nonphysicians and the relationship to patient outcome; the upper limit of delegation in the various specialties; the reasons for consumer acceptance of, and preference for, nonphysician providers; the minimal physician supervision needed to assure quality care provided by nurse practitioners and physicians' assistants; the content of care in nursing practice and its overlap with medicine and patient conditions seen; services given; outcomes and legal responsibility—the list of research topics goes on to include approximately 13 or 14 additional items. Further, GMENAC suggested that until the recommended research is completed, the number of nurse practitioners and nurse midwives in preparation for child medical care, adult medical care, and obstetrical/gynecological care should remain at the present level.

I turn now to several observations on implications of the GMENAC report for nurse practitioners and for discussion of the Select Panel Report. First, one does not see the concept of nurse practitioner, nurse midwife, or physician's assistant questioned with regard to basic viability. Nor does one see recommendations that these roles be abandoned. But what one does see is some affirmation of the fear that once physician levels are increased, the preparation and utilization of nurse practitioners, nurse midwives, and physicians' assistants will be affected negatively.

The GMENAC report provides a clear example of this phenomenon. During the process of arriving at recommendations, a Delphi Process involving experts was used by the Modeling Panel. In all specialty areas examined, the experts concluded that nonphysician personnel could be delegated a higher percentage of the work load than was actually recommended in the final report. For example, the Modeling Panel suggested that nurse midwives should handle 7% of all deliveries for 1990. This was reduced to 5%, "to reflect the constraint which will be imposed by the excess of obstetricians expected in 1990" (Graduate Medical Education, 1980, Vol. VI, p. 28). At this point it should be mentioned that a surplus of approximately 10,450 is estimated for obstetrics–gynecology (Graduate Medical Education, 1980, Vol. I, p. 29). The Delphi Panel suggested that 34% of the ambulatory gynecological service requirements could be delegated to nonphysicians. This was reduced to 18% (Graduate Medical Education, 1980, Vol. VI, p. 28). With regard to child care, the Modeling Panel recommended that 27% of the total ambulatory work load be delegated to nonphysicians by 1990. This was reduced to 15% (Graduate Medical Education, 1980, Vol. VI, p. 33).

The clear message is that the future of the medical component of the nurse practitioner role seems to rest on the availability of physicians and not on evidence and experience regarding the competence or acceptability of nonphysicians. In one sense, such a situation could be viewed as a successful commentary on an important subset of the nurse practitioner role—the area of medical substitutability. However, the situation could foster the development of a more competitive atmosphere between physicians and nurse practitioners with negative cost implications for the public.

PRIMARY CARE AND THE NURSE PRACTITIONER IN THE SELECT PANEL REPORT

A large number of recommendations, all worthy of further comment, were made by the Select Panel. Here, attention will be directed to what I believe are some of the most important recommendations and their manpower implications. The recommendations on needed services presented in Chapter 5 are particularly impressive. The Panel made significant recommendations concerning the scope of services which should be made available to mothers and children, with emphasis given to the position "that the health services needed by this population will necessarily entail not only traditional medical care, but also a range of services such as counseling, anticipatory guidance, and various information and education activities that are oriented to psychosocial issues" (Select Panel, 1981, Vol. I, p. 178).

A second recommendation of central importance to our discussion

is the very strong statement the Panel made regarding the necessity of
health care coverage for certain populations:

> A finding of preeminent importance is the Panel's conclusion that there
> are three broad classes of services for which there is such a clear consensus
> regarding their effectiveness and their importance to good health, that it
> should no longer be considered acceptable that an individual is denied
> access to them for any reason, because of financial barriers; barrier resulting
> from the time, place or manner in which the services are provided; in-
> adequate personnel capacity; or other reasons. These services are:
>   (1)   prenatal, delivery and postnatal care
>   (2)   comprehensive health care for children from birth through age 5
>   (3)   family planning services
> The Panel has concluded that it is unconscionable for a society such as
> ours to have any of its members need these services yet not obtain them,
> particularly because the components of these services are well understood
> and essentially noncontroversial, their lifelong beneficial impact on health
> status is indisputable, and they are of virtually equal value and necessity
> to all segments of the population irrespective of income, geographic lo-
> cation or other variables. (Select Panel, 1981, Vol. I, p. 192)

The report continues with the suggestion "that the Federal Government
and the States develop new and clear assumptions of responsibility for
assuring the availability of these services" (Select Panel, 1981, Vol. I, p.
192).

In considering these recommendations, several points are relevant.
First, I would emphasize the clear philosophical consistency between
what has historically been a focus for nursing in the area of maternal
and child health and the nature and scope of services which the Select
Panel thinks must be provided to mothers and children. Indeed, some
recognition of this consistency was mentioned in Volume I of the Select
Panel's Report where it stated that "the training and practice of nurses
engaged in maternal and child health care have long emphasized precisely those concerns the Panel sees as central" (p. 394).

A second observation is that the model lists of health and health-
related services which the Panel recommends be made available and
accessible to women in the reproductive age span, infants in the first
year of life, preschool, and school-aged children and adolescents (see
Vol. I, pp. 181–191) demonstrate a high level of congruence with contemporary programs for preparing nurse practitioners to work with
mothers and children.

In view of the two preceding points, it is somewhat disappointing
that the Select Panel Report was relatively passive in their comments
regarding the involvement of nurse practitioners in implementing these
and other recommendations. This is not to say that the report failed to

acknowledge the desirability of involving nurse practitioners and other nonphysicians, but it does suggest that the recommendation was somewhat modest. Nonetheless, the report did pave the way for nurse practitioners by clearly speaking to the necessity of encouraging team practice in primary care so that primary care physicians are not isolated from other personnel whose expertise complements their own.

Other comments pretaining to personnel arrangements and nurse practitioners include:

- Primary care units should establish practice patterns involving collaboration among various health professionals which make possible the effective delivery of needed primary care services at reasonable cost . . . . Practice patterns should encourage primary care practitioners to work closely with other personnel whose talents and expertise complement their own. Primary care units which are organized to provide for substantial collaboration among various types of health professionals can provide better and more cost effective care. (Select Panel, 1980, Vol. I, p. 228)
- We believe that the broad spectrum of health needs of children and pregnant women, and the attributes of delivery arrangements most likely to meet these needs, implies that for the future, groups of health professionals, especially when nurse practitioners and other health personnel are included, are preferable to physicians working alone, and that public policy should be designed to promote a closer relationship between office-based practitioners and other sources of care and service. (Select Panel, 1980, Vol. I, pp. 232)
- The Panel therefore recommends that, over the long term, individual primary care physicians be encouraged to join in practice with other physicians and with other health professionals. (Select Panel, 1980, Vol. I, p. 232)

It is interesting that the only recommendations in the entire report that actually mentioned nurse practitioners by name were as follows:

- Federal support for the development of nurse practitioner and nurse midwife clinics in sparsely populated areas should be increased. (Select Panel, 1981, Vol. I, p. 241)
- The adoption of State laws and policies to permit full use of nurse practitioners, dental auxiliaries and other qualified personnel in the schools in offering a wide range of educational, preventive and primary care services to children. (Select Panel, 1981, Vol. I, p. 250)
- We . . . urge that training and use of midlevel practitioners be supported and expanded. Steps toward this end include continuing support of training programs for such personnel, encouragement of team training with physicians, incentives for public programs and private practitioners to hire these health professionals, and the development of organized practice settings which allow appropriate modes of team practice to flourish. (Select Panel, Vol. I, p. 398)

One wonders if the recommendations about nurse practitioners would have been more definite had the report been prepared 10 years earlier when the notion of the nurse practitioners was still in its ascendancy—and before the projection of a physician surplus. Even in the absence of data regarding efficacy of nurse practitioners, would there have been much stronger recommendations regarding the need to have such providers complement physicians in making recommended services available, and in dealing with the problems of coverage identified by the Panel? One can only wonder. On the other hand, one could argue that the philosophical congruence between the thrust of the report and the nurse practitioner movement would have compelled a stronger recommendation by the Panel.

Today, I think one can argue that the philosophical compatibility remains. In addition, we have the efficacy data cited earlier, and last but not least, we have some important economic realities.

Considerable interest has focused on the economic viability of nurse practitioners. In 1977, economist Jane Record headed a team of investigators funded by DHEW to undertake a literature review on the issues of delegation, productivity, and cost of primary care by nonphysician personnel. Their search of the literature on these three topics yielded over 1,000 items (monographs, journal articles, research reports, etc.) About 400 of these documents merited intensive analysis and formed the basis of the report submitted to the Division of Medicine. One of the major conclusions which emerged from the analysis was:

> It seems reasonably clear from the empirical record that nonphysician health personnel, when well used, tend to substitute adequately for physicians in a high percentage of primary care services, and that, given supportive market conditions nonphysician providers can achieve the activity level that will assure their cost effectiveness; certainly the latter is true if the present differential in the cost of MDs and nonphysician health providers is maintained. (Record, 1979, p. 10)

The System Sciences's study (1980) mentioned above also addressed several economic issues. Their overall conclusion was that:

> Supervising physicians/employers were very satisfied with physician extender productivity and cost effectiveness; physician extenders increased the volume of patients seen at a lower cost increment than adding an equivalent half time position; and some of this cost saving was passed on to the consumer or the third-party payer. (System Sciences, 1980, p. 90)

The investigators cautioned, however, that generalized cost of care conclusions cannot be drawn from these data without additional information on hospitalization rates, laboratory costs, and referrals.

Overall, results of studies done to date appear to support a positive economic impact of nurse practitioners; however, it must be recognized that this impact is highly sensitive to practice setting variables and the role of the nurse practitioner (Freund & Overstreet, 1981). At this point it is important to mention that the generally favorable cost data prevail, in spite of the fact that nurse practitioners spend more time with patients. When estimated, substitution ratios for nurse practitioners and physician's assistants range from about .50 to .75. This suggests that one such provider can substitute for one half to three fourths of a physician (Record, McCally, Schweitzer, Blomquist, & Berger, 1980).

In closing, I would like to consider several possible futures for the health manpower recommendations in the Select Panel Report. First, there is one we have all thought of in the face of current economic and political pressures: the report could simply gather dust with very little movement on its recommendations. If this happens, we will all lose. A second scenario might go as follows: If the prediction of a physician surplus materializes, and if the Panel's recommendation that payment schedules and methods be revised to more adequately reflect the value of counseling and other time-intensive aspects of primary care, (see Select Panel, 1981, Vol. I, p. 322) were to be accepted by private third-party payers, but not public ones, and if there were no additional funds to expand services, the resulting outcomes might be predicted. First, physicians would concentrate their activities on private patients and receive reimbursement not only for medical functions but also for what some would see as nursing services. Second, nurse practitioners would probably be concentrated in publicly funded services, but due to financial constraints would have to confine their activities to very technical medical functions (care limited to the diagnosis and management of physical complaints)—as would those physicians who were so involved. Third, there would be a further widening of the gap in services between those with private sources of payment and those on public funds; specifically, the increased scope of services recommended by the Select Panel Report would be available only to those in the private sector and would not reach those on public funding. Finally, the cost of private services would go up.

Clearly, both scenarios are unacceptable. The challenge, then, is to find how, in a time of fiscal constraints, we can more closely approximate the ideal offered in the report; that is, increasing the scope of services and extending coverage to the targeted groups of mothers and children. As decision-makers consider the recommendations and the options available for implementation, I hope that much more attention will be given to a third scenario in which nurse practitioners would have more prominent and active roles both in the private and public sectors. Although I do support the Panel's recommendation that payment schedules and methods need to more adequately reflect the importance of counseling and other time-intensive aspects of primary care related to health promotion and prevention, I fear that reimbursement for such activities in a climate of physician surplus *without* strong incentives for involving nurse practitioners would serve to further increase the costs of primary care, as well as the discrepancies between various subgroups in the population. On the other hand, by actively involving nurse practitioners in these reimbursement schemes and other mechanisms for supporting their role as primary providers, I think the necessary health care could be rendered at a cost which is more acceptable. This is important for the private sector, but it is probably essential in the public sector if we are to move toward the ideals set forth in the report.

FOOTNOTE

The 1980 estimate for nurse practitioners is 18,100 based on the Division of Nursing's report of 16,000 nurse practitioners at the end of 1979 and the estimate of 2,100 graduated in 1980. The estimate for midwives for 1979 was 2,000 with about 175–200 added for 1980 (Graduate Medical Education, Vol. VI, pp. 17, 21, 26, 27).

REFERENCES

Cohen, E. D. *An evaluation of policy related research on new and expanded roles of health workers.* New Haven: Office of Regional Activities and Continuing Education, Yale Univ. School of Medicine, 1974.

Edmunds, M. Nurse practitioner–physician competition. *Nurse Practitioner,* 1981, *6*, 47; 49; 53–54.

Freund, C. M., & Overstreet, G. A., Jr. The economic potential of nurse practitioners. *Nurse Practitioner,* 1981, *6*, 28–29; 32.

Graduate Medical Education National Advisory Committee. *Summary report* (Vol. I). *Non-physician health care providers technical panel* (Vol. VI). [DHHS Publ. No. (HRA) 81-656] Washington, D.C.: Dept. of Health and Human Services, 1980.

Health Resources Administration. *Report of the physician extender work group to the Health Resources Administration's Policy Board* (HEW No. 017-022-00555-6). Washington, D.C.: U.S. Govt. Printing Office, 1977.

Kahn, L. The influence of funding on the future of pediatric nurse practitioner programs. *Pediatrics,* 1979, *64*, 106–109.

Lawrence, D. The impact of physician assistants and nurse practitioners on health care access, cost and quality: A review of the literature. *Health and Medical Care Services Review,* 1978, *1*, 1–12.

Prescott, P. A., & Driscoll, L. Evaluating nurse practitioner performance. *Nurse Practitioner,* 1980, *5*, 28–32.

Record, J. C. An overview. In J. C. Record (Ed.), *Final report on provider requirements, cost savings, and the new health practitioner in primary care: National estimates for 1990* (DHHS Contract No. 231-77-0077). Washington, D.C.: Division of Medicine, Bureau of Health Manpower, 1979.

Record, J. C., McCally, M., Schweitzer, S. O., Blomquist, R. M., & Berger, B. D. New health professionals after a decade and a half: Delegation, productivity and costs in primary care. *Journal of Health Politics, Policy and Law,* 1980, 5, 470–497.

Ruby, G. Consumer acceptance of nurse practitioners and physician assistants. Unpublished manuscript, Institute of Medicine, 1977.

Select Panel for the Promotion of Child Health. *Better health for our children: A national strategy* (4 Vols.). Washington, D.C.: U.S. Govt. Printing Office, 1981.

Sox, H. C. Quality of patient care by nurse practitioners and physician's assistants: A ten-year perspective. *Annals of Internal Medicine,* 1979, 91, 459–468.

System Sciences, Inc. *Final report on evaluation of findings for nurse practitioner and physician assistant studies* (NCHS Contract No. 233-78-3015). Washington, D.C.: National Center for Health Services, 1980.

Williams, C. A. Primary care: Contributions of nursing personnel. *Annals of the New York Academy of Sciences,* 1978, 310, 207–211.

Eight

The Effects of the Status Quo in Child Health Programs: A Look at Children in 1990

LEWIS H. MARGOLIS

> *Imagine that you are creating a fabric of human destiny with the object of making men happy in the end, giving them peace and rest at last, but that it was essential and inevitable to torture to death only one tiny creature—that baby beating its breast with its fist, for instance—and to found that edifice on its unavenged tears, would you consent to be the architect on those conditions?*
>
> Dostoevsky, *The Brothers Karamazov*

Projections by the U.S. Bureau of the Census (1977) estimate that 4 million babies will be born in 1985. Five years later, that cohort of children will enter kindergarten. For these children to benefit maximally from their schooling, they must enjoy good health (Birch & Gussow, 1970; Oski, 1979). It is appropriate, then, to ask the following question: If we maintain the status quo or diminish our investment in child health programs, what will be the health status of the entering kindergarten class of 1990? If recommendations proposed by the Select Panel (1981) and other groups (e.g., Children's Defense Fund, 1976; Silver, 1978) are implemented, how much ill health and its accompanying detrimental effects on educational ability and productivity can be averted?

In order to understand the data presented below, it is necessary first to understand my purpose in assembling these numbers. My goal is to provide a perspective on: (1) the mortality and morbidity that may be experienced by the class of 1990; and (2) the potentially avoidable death and illness. I have chosen to concentrate on case numbers rather than rates and proportions because numbers portray individual effects sometimes obscured by changing rates and proportions. For example, in a population of 1 million births, an infant mortality rate of 40/1,000 results in 40,000 actual deaths. An impressive halving of the rate to 20/1,000 results in 20,000 deaths. However, on a personal level such a reduction means that 20,000 infants who could not otherwise have done so will reach their first birthdays. The economic and psychological value of that year to those infants, not to mention their individual families, is substantial. This value can be obscured when subsumed as part of a trend.

Since data are not commonly available in one-year stratifications, rates for the 1- 4-year stratification have been used as an average for the entire cohort of infants over the 4-year period of 1986–1990. For example, the rate for a given disease may be 5/1,000 for the 1- 4-year-old stratum, but 10/1,000 in 1-year-olds and only 2/1,000 in 4-year-olds. Technically, a yearly recalculation is needed because each 1-year cohort declines in size by the end of the year. The total mortality is then derived by summing the yearly totals. Here, the overall rate of 5/1,000 has simply been applied to the total initial population. Although this procedure may overestimate death or illness in the "healthier" 4-year-olds, it underestimates the effects in 1-year-olds.

The data here are derived from a variety of sources, many of which provided background for the Select Panel Report (1981). The intent is not to determine exact estimates which can be used for projecting required hospital beds, classrooms, cribs, or other future needs. Rather, the purpose is to provide a perspective on how many individual children will die needlessly or suffer avoidable illness and associated effects.

Therefore, conservative estimates of future morbidity and mortality rates have been derived from extending current trends. Confidence intervals could be applied by planners or demographers, although such a procedure is not necessary for my purposes here.

Some may argue that simply extending current trends assumes that events such as child accidents or teenage pregnancy are somehow immutable. However, by 1985 it is unlikely that any major technological breakthrough—such as the newborn intensive care units which appeared in the middle 1960s (Lee, Paneth, Gartner, Pearlman, & Gruss, 1980)—will occur. In addition, since economic policy changes designed to improve living conditions by raising incomes through increased investment, reindustrialization, and improved productivity take time, newly implemented programs will not be effective on a wide scale soon enough to benefit markedly the babies born in 1985.

Let us begin, then, with a consideration of the potential members of the class of 1990 who will not make it to kindergarten because they die before the age of 5. If current trends in declining infant mortality continue, in 1985 the rate for white infants will be approximately 11 deaths per 1,000 live births; for all other groups, the rate will be 17 deaths per 1,000 live births. The proportion of all births attributable to nonwhite families has remained at approximately 20% for several years, and although the proportion of nonwhite births may increase slightly by 1985, I nonetheless will use the 1979 figures. Given these assumptions, 35,200 white infants and 13,600 nonwhite infants will die before they reach their first birthdays.

Among the factors which could contribute to declines in infant mortality are the availability and use of prenatal care. Impressive reductions in infant mortality have been reported by Maternal and Infant Care Projects in all sections of the country (Wallace, 1978). However, in 1974, fewer than 15% of eligible women were enrolled in such projects. Similarly, a 1979 study by the Guttmacher Institute found that 34.1% of the women at risk for unintended pregnancy and with incomes below 150% of the poverty level were unserved by either organized programs or private physicians (Torres, 1979).

Using 1978 proportions, 11% of white and 41% of black infants (352,000 and 328,000, respectively) will be born into poverty (U.S. Bureau of the Census, 1979). If two thirds of these mothers are unserved by prenatal care and the infant mortality rate for such unserved populations is 30/1,000 (Wallace, 1978), then 13,668 infants will die. If this rate were reduced by one third (Wallace, 1978), then a rate of 20/1,000 would result in 9,100 infant deaths. Thus, prenatal care alone could prevent the deaths of over 4,500 infants in 1985.

The mortality rate for children 1–4 years of age remained relatively stable during the latter 1970s (Select Panel, 1981, Vol. III, p. 120). In 1978, the rate was 69.2/100,000. Based on continuation of the recent trends, the mortality rate for 1– 4-year-old children will be approximately 62.3/100,000 in 1990. Since rates are available only for the 1– 4-year-old cohort and not single years, it is necessary to apply this rate to the entire cohort of 1-year-old children. Doing so indicates that 9,846 of 1-year-old children will die before reaching their fifth birthdays.

The three major causes of death for 1 to 4-year-olds are accidents, congenital anomalies, and malignancies with 1977 mortality rates per 100,000 of 27, 9, and 5, respectively (National Center for Health Statistics, 1980). Motor vehicle accidents are the largest single component of accidents, and the mortality rate has unfortunately remained virtually unchanged at 10–11/100,000 since 1955. Deaths from all other accidents have gradually declined from 22/100,000 in 1955, to 18.2/100,000 in 1978.

Given the probable repeal of the 55 mph speed limit and the growing prevalence of small cars, it is not unreasonable to expect the rate of motor vehicle deaths to remain at 10–11/100,000. That rate will result in the deaths of 1,738 of the children born in 1985 before they reach the age of 5 years. Of these, approximately 60% will die as passengers and 40% as pedestrians (Scherz, 1979).

Child safety restraints effectively reduce deaths from motor vehicle crashes. Yet restraints are routinely used for fewer than 10% of child passengers (Paulson, 1981). Since restraints are 90% effective in reducing the number of child deaths (Scherz, 1979), if all children born in 1985 were always put in safety restraints by their parents, then nearly 950 of the children who enter kindergarten in 1990 would be children who otherwise would have died in motor vehicle crashes.

The likelihood of universal safety restraint use is low. However, mandatory restraint laws have been effective in increasing the rate of use to a respectable 70–80% in Australia and New Zealand, and to 19% in Tennessee, which, although low, is at least twice the usual prevalence. If each state adopted a mandatory restraint law raising restraint usage to only 20%, then 82 deaths would be averted in the cohort that enters kindergarten in 1990.

The mortality rate for burns—the second most frequent type of accident—was 5/100,000 in 1980 (National Center for Health Statistics, 1980). Technology such as smoke detectors (Reisinger, 1980) and simple household practices, such as reducing the setting on hot water heaters (Feldman, Schaller, Feldman, & McMillon, 1978) are readily and inexpensively available. If such devices and practices were in widespread use by 1985, then a substantial proportion of the nearly 800 children who would die of burns before 1990 will have been spared this agonizing form of death.

Congenital anomalies, which rank just below accidents as a cause of child death, resulted in 9 deaths/100,000 in 1980 (National Center for Health Statistics, 1980). If that rate were to persist, 1,422 children born in 1985 would die before entering kindergarten.

In recent years, phenomenal progress has been made in prenatal diagnosis and treatment of genetic and metabolic disorders (Oakley, 1981). Extending from heterozygote screening programs which identify carriers of conditions such as sickle-cell anemia and Tay-Sachs disease, to amniocentesis for fluid sampling, and to fetal cell cultures and fetal blood sampling, current techniques offer prospective parents a variety of options. For example, Down's Syndrome, a leading cause of mental retardation, can be diagnosed prenatally. If all pregnant women over the age of 35 underwent amniocentesis for the diagnosis of Down's and agreed to abort a Down's fetus, it would be possible to reduce the incidence of this condition by 20%. Nevertheless, only 15% of older women have access to prenatal diagnosis.

It is apparent that a substantial proportion of the class of 1990 will die needlessly before the first day of school. However, more importantly, a substantial amount of morbidity will occur which can be averted. The Collaborative Perinatal Study (Niswander & Gordon, 1972) showed that the rate of handicapping malformations was 1.5 times higher than the mortality rate. Other investigators have suggested that the rate for morbidity resulting in lifelong deficits is more than 3 times the infant mortality rate (Bierman, Siegel, French, & Simonian, 1965). Figures cited earlier showed infant mortality rates per 1,000 live births of 11 and 17 for whites and nonwhites, respectively, which will result in 13,668 deaths in 1985. If the morbidity rate is 3 times the mortality rate, then 41,004 children born in 1985 will have handicapping conditions from birth—conditions which will impede their education and greatly reduce their ability to lead productive and comfortable lives in our society. Just as prenatal care conceivably could assure the survival of 4,500 infants, so it could probably free approximately 13,500 members of the class of 1990 from significant lifelong morbidity.

Motor vehicle crashes will contribute to handicapping conditions just as crashes will account for a sizable proportion of the deaths. Unfortunately, even though auto accidents are the major cause of accidental death, little data has been rigorously collected on the prevalence of disability among survivors. A 7-year study in Washington state found that of 31,602 children under the age of 5 years involved in crashes, 125 died and 716 suffered disabling injuries (Scherz, 1979). In another study of 63 children with motor vehicle injuries admitted to one hospital, 83% had head or neck injuries. These figures from Washington State indicate disabling injuries could have been reduced by 66% if all the child crash victims had been in safety restraints.

Based on the Washington data, we can assume that the ratio of disabling injuries to mortality is 5.7/1. Applying this to the previously calculated deaths for our potential kindergartners, we arrive at more than 5,900 disabling injuries, most notably head injuries. Universal safety restraint use could save 3,911 of these kindergartners from disabiling injuries.

In addition to salient deficits resulting from major insults (such as inadequate prenatal care or motor vehicle crashes) are subtle handicaps which are not preventable but easily treatable. Data from the Early and Periodic Screening, Diagnosis, and Treatment (EPSDT) Program suggest other deficiencies that we may find in these kindergarten children (Children's Defense Fund, 1977). Of the 659,000 children in poverty, 10%, or 65,960 individuals, will have visual problems and 3%, or nearly 20,000, children will have hearing deficits. Needless to say, both these problems diminish the educational abilities of the affected children.

In addition to direct medical conditions which impede schooling are indirect conditions such as inadequate nutrition. Nutrition was recognized as an important determinant of children's health by the 1935 National School Lunch Act, which had the stated purpose "to safeguard the health and wellbeing of the Nation's children . . . through . . . the establishment, maintenance, operation and expansion of non-profit school lunch programs." The Special Supplemental Food Program for Women, Infants, and Children (WIC) and the Food Stamp program also are designed to aid in raising the nutritional level of numerous American children.

HANES I (Health and Nutrition Examination Survey) documents some of the nutritional deficiencies which food aid programs are intended to ameliorate (Popkin, Akin, Kaufman, & McDonald, 1981). More than 85% of the preschoolers had substandard iron intakes: for children living below the poverty level, 4.9% of white and 8.3% of black preschoolers were found to have low hemoglobin levels, an indicator of iron deficiency. For children above the poverty level, the proportions were 1.3% and 7.7%, respectively. Low caloric intake (defined as fewer than 1,000 kcals daily) was found in 14% of white children and 23% of black children. Thirty-three percent of surveyed black preschoolers and 13% of white preschoolers had below standard calcium intakes. Despite these obvious nutritional deficiencies in American infants and children, in 1979 only about 15% of WIC-eligible children were actually enrolled.

Although much of WIC may survive Reagan administration cutbacks, it is unlikely that the proportion of enrollees will increase substantially if the WIC appropriation is not increased. If we apply the above figures to the class of 1990, the nutritional readiness for school will be inadequate. Focusing on the children below 150% of the poverty level, as shown above, 341,440 white infants and 318,160 black infants will survive the first year. Assuming 15% of these children who may enroll in WIC will achieve nutritional status similar to that of nonpoverty children, this still leaves over 36,000 nonenrollees who will experience low hemoglobin levels before the time of kindergarten entrance. For the children above the poverty level, more than 73,000 will be similarly affected. It would be naive to deny the complexity of the process from agricultural production, to distribution, to family purchase, to individual consumption, to improved nutritional status. Nutritionists, economists, and policymakers are studying and debating the most efficient points at which to intervene in this chain to better the nutritional status of children. Nevertheless, given the bountiful production of food in the U.S., it is difficult to justify even one case of iron-deficiency anemia, let alone over 100,000.

Being born to a teenage mother is another preventable condition which can detrimentally affect children's educational abilities. Of the children born in 1985, nearly 12%, or 474,712, will have mothers 19 years old or younger. Using regression techniques, Jacqueline Forrest of the Guttmacher Institute has derived figures indicating the success of organized family planning services in averting births in 1976 (Alan Guttmacher Institute, 1981). She concluded that for white and nonwhite, respectively, .107 and .090 births were averted for each program participant.[1] Unfortunately, in 1979, only 30–35% of adolescents had access to organized family planning services. Applying these figures to the 8,857,000 15– 19-year-old women in 1985, it is possible to estimate the number of births to unmarried teenagers which could be avoided if family planning services were universally available. If current trends continue, fewer than 8% of these young women will be married and 50% will be sexually active. As stated above, nearly 1.5 million 15– 19-year-old women will be in poverty and based on 1978 estimates (when family planning clinics were on the ascendancy in contrast to the threatened cutbacks of fiscal 1982), 34.1% will be unserved by either public or private family planning programs. Applying Forrest's estimates to this population shows that 23,531 births to impoverished teenage girls would be averted if family planning were universally available.

In summary, imagine a crisp, fall day in 1990. The peal of school bells beckons a new class of kindergartners. When the teachers call the roll, what will the class be like? Table 1 suggests the answer.

Sadly, more than 51,000 children are absent because they have died before their fifth birthday. Considering babies of all income levels,

TABLE 1:   PROJECTIONS OF CHILD MORTALITY AND MORBIDITY FOR 1990

	Projection of current trend	Projection with use of known, effective programs	Mortality/morbidity avoidable or treatable
Deaths			
Before 1 year of age	48,800	44,000	4,800
From 1-4 years of age:			
Motor vehicle crashes	1,738	788	950
Burns	800	200	600
Total	51,338	44,988	6,350
Handicapping conditions			
Birth-related	41,000	27,500	13,500
Motor vehicle-related	5,943	1,989	3,911
Iron deficiency	109,000	51,366	57,634
Total	155,943	80,855	75,045

if racial inequities had been completely eliminated and the infant mortality rate for all had been lowered to 11/1,000, then an additional 4,800 children would have been present. Motor vehicle crashes have killed another 1,738 members of the class, although over 900 of these could have been prevented easily by the use of child safety restraints. Indeed, at least one child died in a motor vehicle crash on the first day of school.

For those who have arrived at school safely, their health is not as good as it could have been if even rudimentary programs had been put into place. Over 5,900 have suffered disabling injuries in motor vehicle crashes, even though over 66% probably could have been prevented by the use of safety restraints. Over 100,000 children have nutritional deficiencies of one form or another. Over 85,000 children from poverty-stricken homes have visual or hearing deficits.

More than 470,000 class members have been sent off to school by a mother who was a teenager when they were born. These teenage mothers were at increased risk of poverty, failure to complete high school, and additional childbearing, all of which will impede the educational progress of their children. The fact that most of these children resulted from unintended pregnancies suggests that the availability of sex education and family planning (putting aside the charged issue of abortion) could have averted many of these pregnancies.

Across the political spectrum there is consensus that the most desirable solution to problems such as high infant mortality and poor nutrition is a robust economy which provides good jobs and an equitable society that assures opportunities for all. The Reagan administration contends that in order to achieve such goals the role of the federal government must be reduced. The 25% reduction in federal spending for child health would indeed diminish the federal role. This cutback will result in less federal support for services such as prenatal care and decreased federal leadership in areas such as child safety. As states, families, and individuals scramble to meet the health needs of children, programs which are known to decrease mortality and prevent morbidity will at least falter, if not disappear.

Ironically, these changes will occur even though economic arguments strongly favor preventive programs directed at children. The lost potential earnings of a child who dies far exceed the potential earnings of a 65-year-old coronary bypass recipient. Sound nutrition supports maximum productivity, which for children means full development of their educational potential. Widespread screening and prompt referral and treatment help to assure productive, well-educated students, who in turn become the productive workers and enlightened citizens of the future.

While the Reagan architects go about "creating a fabric of human destiny with the object of making men happy in the end," children will needlessly suffer. If, as a nation, we intend to place a higher value on political abstractions like "individual responsibility" or "less government" than we do on the concrete, immediate needs of children, then we must grapple with the question posed by Ivan in Dostoevsky's monumental novel:

> "And can you admit the idea that men for whom you are building [an ideal society] would agree to accept their happiness on the foundation of the unexpiated blood of a little victim? And accepting it would remain happy forever?"

FOOTNOTE

Access to a program is not the equivalent of contraceptive use. Forrest's figures refer to the accessibility of family planning. If all participants used contraceptives regularly the number of averted births would of course be much greater.

REFERENCES

Alan Guttmacher Institute. *Teenage Pregnancy: The problem that hasn't gone away.* New York: Author, 1981.

Bierman, J. M., Siegel, E., French, F., & Simonian, K. Analysis of the outcome of all pregnancies in a community. *American Journal of Obstetrics and Gynecology,* 1965, *91,* 37–45.

Birch, H. G., & Gussow, J. D. *Disadvantaged children: Health, nutrition, and school failure.* New York: Harcourt, Brace & World, 1970.

Children's Defense Fund. *Doctors and dollars are not enough.* Washington, D.C.: Author, 1976.

Children's Defense Fund. *EPSDT: Does it spell health care for poor children?* Washington, D.C.: Author, 1977.

Feldman, K. W., Schaller, R. T., Feldman, J. A., & McMillon, M. Tap water scald burns in children. *Pediatrics,* 1978, *62,* 1–7.

Lee, K-S., Paneth, N., Gartner, L., Pearlman, M., & Gruss, L. Neonatal mortality: An analysis of the recent improvement in the United States. *American Journal of Public Health,* 1980, *70,* 15–21.

National Center for Health Statistics. *Vital Statistics of the U.S.: 1976* (Office of Health Research, Statistics, and Technology, DHHS). Washington, D.C.: U.S. Govt. Printing Office, 1980.

Niswander, K. R., & Gordon, M. (Eds.) *The women and their pregnancies* (Public Health Service, DHEW). Washington, D.C.: U.S. Govt. Printing Office, 1972.

Oakley, G. P. Antenatal diagnosis: Potential for major reduction in pediatric morbidity. *Pediatric Annals,* 1981, *10,* 13–21.

Oski, F. The nonhematologic manifestations of iron deficiency. *American Journal of Diseases of Children*, 1979, *133*, 315–322.

Paulson, J. A. The case for mandatory seat restraint laws. *Clinical Pediatrics*, 1981, *20*, 285–290.

Popkin, B. M., Akin, J., Kaufman, M., & McDonald, M. Nutritional program options for maternal and child health: A summary. In Select Panel for the Promotion of Child Health, *Better health for our children: A national strategy* (Vol. IV). Washington, D.C.: U.S. Govt. Printing Office, 1981.

Reisinger, K. A. Smoke detectors: Reducing deaths and injuries due to fire. *Pediatrics*, 1980, *65*, 718–724.

Scherz, R. G. *Epidemiology of childhood motor vehicle related accidents.* Paper presented at the Twenty-Third Stapp Car Crash Conference, San Diego, October, 1979.

Select Panel for the Promotion of Child Health. *Better health for our children: A national strategy* (4 Vols.). Washington, D.C.: U.S. Govt. Printing Office, 1981.

Silver, G. *Child health: America's future.* Germantown, Md.: Aspen Systems, 1978.

Torres, A. Organized family planning services in the United States, 1976–1977. *Family Planning Perspectives*, 1979, *11*, 342–347.

U.S. Bureau of the Census. Projections of the population of the U.S.: 1977–2050. *Current Population Reports*, Series P-25, No. 704. Washington, D.C.: U.S. Govt. Printing Office, 1977.

U.S. Bureau of the Census. Money income and poverty status of families and persons in the United States: 1978. *Current Population Reports*, Series P-60, No. 120. Washington, D.C.: U.S. Govt. Printing Office, 1979.

Wallace, H. M. Status of infant and perinatal morbidity and mortality. *Public Health Reports*, 1978, *93*, 386–393.

NINE

THE SELECT PANEL REPORT AND THE CHALLENGE OF THE NEW RIGHT

JONATHAN B. KOTCH

INTRODUCTION

It is no understatement that the November, 1980 national elections substantially changed our perception of the political climate in Washington and in the United States as a whole. The dual prospects of the incoming conservative administration of Ronald Reagan and the Republican majority in the Senate cast a pall over the presentation to Congress of the report prepared by the Select Panel (1981) for the Promotion of Child Health on December 2, 1980. The length of time it took for the report to be published by the Government Printing Office led to unconfirmed rumors that the new administration was trying to suppress it. Representative Andrew Maguire of New Jersey, an early proponent of the Select Panel in the House, had been defeated, and Senator Edward M. Kennedy, who had served as chairman of the Senate Health Subcommittee, was reduced to the status of senior minority member of the Senate Human Resources Committee by the Republican victory. The

Health Subcommittee has not even been established in the 97th Congress, permitting Human Resources Committee Chairman Orrin Hatch to have personal control over both the parent committee and all health-related matters.

Whereas the November election appeared to signal a dramatic "turn to the Right," Lipsett and Raab (1981, p. 30), quoting Louis Harris, have argued that the Republican electoral victories in fact resulted from nothing more than a slight conservative shift in political and economic opinions. According to Harris, there has been no change in the electorate on social issues, including those affecting maternal and child health (MCH).

America has experienced many periods of political reaction from right-wing moralists. As early as 1800, a pamphlet appeared warning Christians of dire moral consequences were Thomas Jefferson to be elected. In the 1850s, the Know-Nothing party played a substantial role in American politics, largely as a reaction to increased immigration of Catholics and others. William Jennings Bryan's 1896 and 1900 presidential campaigns were a populist protest against the Eastern establishment and the commercial interests represented by President McKinley. The 1920s saw the Ku Klux Klan "rise again," together with fundamentalist Protestantism. More recently, Senator Joseph McCarthy symbolized the right-wing political paranoia of the early 1950s (Lipsett & Raab, 1981, p. 27).

It may be that we are now entering another such period. It is certainly useful (and comforting) to put contemporary political events into an historical context. I hope that, by examining the movement which calls itself the New Right, it may be possible to assess the relevance of the Select Panel Report in a changing political environment.

THE NEW RIGHT

The New Right is a coalition of single-issue pressure groups and politically active religious fundamentalists, loosely linked together by a network of political structures financed and operated by a small group of well-organized, highly professional political zealots. A right wing has always existed in this country, but the first enduring radical right-wing groups, such as the John Birch Society, did not make their appearance until the 1950s. The use of the term "New Right" is intended to distinguish contemporary right-wingers from Eastern conservative intellectuals, such as William F. Buckley, Jr. (Crawford, 1980). According to Epstein and Forster (1967), however, what distinguishes New Right organizations from their predecessors is:

A greater use of the mass media for propaganda purposes . . . . An increased emphasis on the potential of activities at the grass roots level. A strong, almost united front attack on the civil rights movement—as well as stepped up attacks on the churches and schools as factors in the alleged Communist conspiracy. And probably most important, an increased emphasis on openly *political* thinking, *political* organization, and *political* action.

In short, the attack from the extremist position is now broad and well integrated, in many areas well financed, and everywhere more determined than ever to achieve success. (p. 5; italics in original)

New Right politicians and propagandists have captured many issues as their own. It is useful to divide these into political and cultural issues. Although admittedly arbitrary, I would lump such specific concerns as the Panama Canal treaty, recognition of Taiwan, nuclear energy, national defense, and gun control as political issues, together with more general issues such as taxation and government regulations. Cultural issues are those such as abortion, the Equal Rights Amendment (ERA), sex education, homosexual rights, family rights, "scientific creationism," school prayer, Christian schools, "secular humanism," and pornography. Ultimately, all these issues are political in the sense that any resolution of the conflicts surrounding them involves political processes. Yet, it helps to appreciate that the issues around which the New Right has rallied do not necessarily hang together. For example, one can be interested in restricting the access of children to pornographic literature without necessarily being committed to full diplomatic recognition of Taiwan.

Corresponding to many of these issues is a single-issue organization, frequently with a well-known personality at its head. Good examples are Phyllis Schlafly of Stop-ERA and Anita Bryant of Save Our Children, Inc. Recent years have also seen the emergence of New Right organizations concerned with family rights issues (including abortion, homosexual rights, sex education, ERA, pornography, humanism in the schools, and textbook censorship) but with less well-known leaders. These include the Pro-Family Forum and the National Pro-Family Coalition. Perhaps the granddaddy of all single-issue pressure groups on the right is the National Rifle Association (NRA), which has succeeded against all odds in preventing any reasonable consideration of handgun control in this country.

With the exception of the handgun issue, which the Select Panel appropriately identifies as an important issue in child health, most of the challenges to cherished MCH principles originate from those groups and individuals rallying around the issues classified as "cultural." Yet, it is precisely these groups that are least likely to be subsumed by any New Right super organization. For example, Alan Crawford reports that

Phyllis Schlafly will not sell her mailing lists, and that right-to-lifers do not necessarily share the more political concerns of the New Right's political cadres. A 1974 attempt to unite local groups involved in textbook protests met with limited success (Crawford, 1980). It is important, therefore, not to view the New Right as a unified political movement.

On the other hand, there is no doubt that very skillful and highly motivated professional organizers are trying to create such a movement. The *Conservative Digest* (The New Right, 1979, p. 14) identified its own "Big Four" organizers—Paul Weyrich, John Terry Dolan, Howard Phillips, and Morton Blackwell. Weyrich, press secretary for former Colorado Senator Gordon Allcott, together with Joseph Coors of Rocky Mountain brewing fame, founded the Committee for the Survival of a Free Congress (CSFC), one of the best financed of the New Right's political action committees (PACs). Ironically, liberal reforms of campaign finance laws in the wake of Watergate abuses led to increased influence of such PACs which could pool small contributions (now limited to $1,000 per candidate per contributor) from vast numbers of people to promote or oppose specific candidates or causes. John Dolan heads the National Conservative Political Action Committee (NCPAC), which, besides being a highly successful money raiser, also provides technical political assistance to those right-wing candidates who are ideologically pure enough to merit such beneficence. Howard Phillips, founder and head of the Conservative Caucus, was campaign manager for Richard Schweiker (now Secretary of the Department of Health and Human Services) when he first ran for the Senate in 1968. Finally, Morton Blackwell, editor of the *New Right Report*, also chairs the Committee for Responsible Youth Politics, an organization which trains young political activists for House and Senate campaigns and places trainees on the staffs of leading conservative Senators and Representatives. The average age of the Big Four is 37 years.

Missing from both *Conservative Digest*'s Big Four and its "Leadership Network" of 14 is the man who Hank Lacayo (1979) of the United Auto Workers' calls the "top enchilada," Richard A. Viguerie. In a network of overlapping interests and interlocking directorates, the ability to raise large sums of money from large numbers of people is the key to power, and Viguerie is the master of the mailing lists. Starting with an organization called "Young Americans for Freedom," Viguerie raised $6 million for George Wallace's 1968 presidential campaign. Since then, Viguerie has been involved in fund raising for organizations such as the CSFC, Conservative Caucus' Committee for Responsible Youth Politics, NCPAC, Americans for Effective Law Enforcement, and the NRA, as well as for Senators Jesse Helms and Roger Jepsen and for presidential candidates John Connally and Phillip Crane. From its offices in Falls

Church, Virginia, the Richard A. Viguerie Company (RAVCO), with a staff of 300, sends out 100 million pieces of mail a year from 300 mailing lists containing 25 million names. RAVCO grosses about $15 million yearly in direct mail solicitations (Crawford, 1980, pp. 48–49).

These New Right leaders meet regularly at weekly "Kingston" sessions. Sometime in the summer of 1979, Jerry Falwell, the fundamentalist minister from Lynchburg, Virginia, and other evangelicals met with Washington area New Right leaders and formed the Moral Majority and two other fundamentalist political groups, the Religious Roundtable and Christian Voice. The circulation of radical right-wing organizational talent between the religious groups on the one hand and the New Right political groups on the other demonstrates how the network operates. For example, Viguerie has raised money for all three fundamentalist organizations. Robert Billings, first executive director of Moral Majority, had been president of the National Christian Action Coalition. He left Moral Majority in mid-1980 to act as religious liaison with the Reagan campaign. Ed McAteer, formerly field director for the Conservative Caucus, became the director of Religious Roundtable, and Gary Jarmin, a former legislative director for the American Conservative Union, became the head of the Political Action Committee of the Christian Voice (FitzGerald, 1981).

The extent to which the evangelicals have developed real political power is controversial. Despite *Conservative Digest*'s banner headline that "Pollster Harris Credits Moral Majority Vote for Reagan's Stunning Landslide Win," more sober analysts have reserved judgment (Lofton, 1980, p. 13). An election day poll of voters leaving voting booths suggested that fewer born-again white Protestants voted for Reagan than did other white Protestants. At the same time, Carter lost less support among born-again Protestants than he lost among other white Protestants (Lipsett & Raab, 1981).

Despite estimates in 1980 that between 20 and 25% of American adults—or about 20 million—qualify as evangelicals, other indicators of religiosity in America continue to decline. Only 40% of the adult population attended church regularly in 1980, the lowest figure ever recorded (Beckwith, 1981). Furthermore, a Gallup poll commissioned by the National Council of Churches in 1977 found "a marked decline in the importance people placed on religion" (Beckwith, 1981, p. 13). Even closer to MCH concerns was the National Opinion Research Center survey of a national sample of Catholic adults. Only 18% of those interviewed in 1974 accepted the church's position on two of three family issues—divorce, premarital sex, and birth control—compared with 42% in 1963 (Beckwith, 1981).

Although it would be a mistake to think of those who have supported rightist issues and candidates as monolithic in their views, some have noted an apparent similarity among members of some New Right organizations. Frances FitzGerald (1981) describes the congregation of Falwell's Thomas Road Baptist Church:

> Winter and summer, the congregation looks like nothing more or less than the solid midsection of this town. It consists mainly of couples with two or three children, but there are a number of young adults and a number of elderly people . . . . There are proportionately about the same number of blacks in the congregation as in the choir—which is to say, very few . . . . What is startling about the congregation is its uniform aspect . . . .
> In the early fifties, Lynchburg had a relatively unskilled work force and very small middle class; today, it has a highly skilled work force and a much larger middle class. Falwell's parishioners stand, as it were, on the cusp of this new middle class. They are clerical workers, technicians, and small businessmen, and skilled and semiskilled workers in new factories. (pp. 69–70)

Like the parishioners in Lynchburg, many New Right sympathizers are recent migrants to the world of middle-class perquisites. As such, they are still somewhat marginal with respect to the dominant social stratum. In the words of Ben Wattenberg, these Americans are "unyoung, unpoor, and unblack" (Crawford, 1980, p. 148). Their grip on the middle-class life style, then, seems tenuous. White evangelicals, for example, aggregate below the American mean in income and education. They fall in the group which would feel an economic pinch the most (Lipsett & Raab, 1981).

SOME CHARACTERISTICS OF THE NEW RIGHT MOVEMENT

The foregoing description suggests several features which characterize the New Right movement. One such feature is status insecurity, a phenomenon not unknown in American political history among upward-striving groups. Lipsett and Raab (1981) argue that issues of status far outweigh moral issues in importance to members of these groups. The status of those "on the cusp" of the middle class is most threatened by the rising expectations of minorities, by the seeming lack of permanence characterizing values associated with a status only recently achieved, and by the lack of respect afforded these individuals in their new social and economic roles.

Such insecurities lead to the resentment which inspires what Crawford (1980) calls the "politics of grievance" (p. 265). A common strategy of the New Right is to target conspicuously liberal legislators for attack and to focus the diffuse hostility associated with an emotional issue such as abortion, ERA, or the Panama Canal "giveaway" against a vulnerable political target. More often than not, the New Right is against something or someone. Senator Jesse Helms of North Carolina, for example, has voted against so many bills since his election in 1972 that liberal pundits have labeled him "Senator No."

This strategy of attacking vulnerable politicians has often backfired, as when single-minded efforts to bump off a moderate have led to the election of a liberal. Two examples from the 1978 off-year elections are those of Clifford Case of New Jersey and Edward Brooke of Massachusetts. Both of these moderate Republicans were somehow the more despised for despoiling the ideological purity of the Republican party. In New Jersey, the New Right candidate, conservative Jeffrey Bell, defeated Clifford Case in the Republican Senatorial primary. Bell, however, was subsequently trounced in the general election by the Democratic candidate, Bill Bradley. In Massachusetts, Brooke defeated right-wing primary challenger Avi Nelson, but went on to lose the election to Democrat Paul Tsongas (Crawford, 1980).

Ideological purity is a characteristic most highly revered by the right, so much so that "moral victories," such as those described above, are valued as highly as the real thing. Such idealism is not a conspicuously political way to do things, for pragmatic politics inevitably involves compromise. As a strident but powerless minority, the New Right maintained loyalty to its most extreme positions on political and cultural issues. What the assumption of political power will do to the New Right remains to be seen. Barry Goldwater, for example, the standard-bearer of American conservatism for nearly two decades, was drummed out of the ranks of the New Right when he supported Gerald Ford's candidacy for the Republican presidential nomination in 1976. As Viguerie put it: "A new generation of conservative leaders is needed" (Crawford, 1980, p. 114). Conservative columnist David Brudnoy wrote: "Barry Goldwater is through as Mr. Conservative." His crime? Putting "expediency before principles" (Crawford, 1980, p. 16).

The New Right has so narrowly defined its issues and so insists on strict adherence to its program that even the conservative heroes of an earlier age are not spared criticism. Chief among such victims is William F. Buckley, Jr., whose friendship with the late Allard Lowenstein of New York was enough to earn him a permanent position on the New Right hit list. Moreover, Buckley represents a whole spectrum of things that the New Right is "ag'in," namely, effete intellectualism, elitism, and the Eastern establishment.

If it can be said that the New Right is for anything, it is for a utopian image of free enterprise that "cannot be said to exist anywhere in the world" (Crawford, 1980, pp. 208–209). There is, moreover, a certain romanticism in this myth, wrapped up as it is in the aura of Western man as pioneer and hero. This is a man's world, one in which women sacrifice their claims for equal status in favor of certain protections. Relieved of the responsibility (or, as the case may be, satisfaction) of participating in the labor force, the New Right woman is provided for, either through the financial security of an intact marriage or through alimony and child support in the case of divorce. In return, the New Right woman stays at home and raises children, leaving the hearth periodically to censor textbooks or to protest busing and gay rights.

The commitment to a perception of reality which cannot be viewed as the modal family structure in this country—either today or in the past—provides tremendous motivation for those called upon to defend it. The opponents of ERA, family planning, abortion, homosexual rights, secular education, and public support for day care centers are able to rally under the banner of "family rights" because of fears that "international humanist/socialist planners" (Pro-Family Forum, 1978) are plotting to take children away from their parents under the guise of "children's rights." As biased as such an interpretation may appear, we turn now to a case study which demonstrates that such a movement did succeed in blocking the evolution of a promising joint public–private effort to set up child health planning committees in North Carolina counties.

THE NORTH CAROLINA CHILD HEALTH PLAN

The fate of *A Child Health Plan for Raising a New Generation* (Joint Child Health Planning, 1979), a 75-page document jointly published by the North Carolina Chapter of the American Academy of Pediatrics (AAP) and the North Carolina Department of Human Resources (DHR), provides an excellent case study of the convergence between New Right and fundamentalist forces to defeat a common enemy. In this case, the enemy was a presumed conspiracy to undermine the traditional family, but the more immediate target was the governor of North Carolina, who was running for reelection. This example demonstrates the New Right's willingness to obscure the facts in order to redefine issues in its own terms. Once having done so, New Right leaders can exploit the anxieties of its working- and middle-class constituency to attack a political figure, a law, or a document (for a full description of this case, see Kotch and Johnson, 1981). Lessons drawn from this example may inform our efforts to keep the Select Panel Report viable.

As part of health planning efforts inaugurated by Public Law 93-641 (the National Health Planning and Resources Development Act), both the North Carolina Chapter of AAP and the DHR had independently established child health planning committees in the fall of 1977. The pediatricians participating in DHR's effort, one of whom was also on the AAP's committee, suggested a merger, which was officially consummated on May 5, 1978. The Joint Child Health Planning Committee then hired a consultant who facilitated a series of committee and subcommittee meetings which led to a final draft of *A Child Health Plan*. This plan was presented to North Carolina's governor in March, 1979.

As it happened, *A Child Health Plan* became public at the same time that a piece of legislation called "The New Generation Act," advocated by the governor, was being debated in the House. Two "pro-family" legislators got it into their heads that the New Generation Act, which merely set up an interagency coordinating committee for children's services at the state level and recommended that counties do the same, was a covert effort to compel implementation of the child health plan. For its part, the proposed health plan was designed as a template for interdisciplinary child health planners at the county level. Because of the concerns of the physicians and others on the Joint Child Health Planning Committee, the health plan mentioned many contemporary MCH issues, including infant mortality, infants at risk, comprehensive health care, adolescent pregnancy, and genetic counseling, to name a few. Furthermore, *A Child Health Plan* repeatedly called for the use of a "health care home" (Joint Child Health Planning, 1979, p. 17) to coordinate children's health services. Such a facility would accept primary professional responsibility for promoting children's health through preventive care and by arranging for, or providing, primary care and whatever services were deemed necessary. This benign concept became the target of a deliberate distortion by New Right demagogues. One state legislator stated that the New Generation bill and *A Child Health Plan* were part of a conspiracy "for the government to take over the family's responsibility for child-rearing" (Skube, 1979). A prominent New Right spokesperson in the battle against "secular humanism" wrote that the health care home was intended to be a compulsory group residence. By a perverse intuitive leap, the author concluded that "raising a New Generation" was new-speak for raising a master race (Morris, 1979).

It did not take long for New Right politicians and fundamentalists to jump on the bandwagon. Two fundamentalist preachers, who had previously scored a major political victory by getting Christian schools in North Carolina exempted from even minimal state academic standards, started preaching and writing against the *Child Health Plan* and the New Generation Act. The Congressional Club, a direct-mailing organization established—with the help of Richard Viguerie—to elect Jesse Helms in 1972, provided some of the resources for the opposition. The

New Generation Act became a campaign liability for the governor, who was challenged in the Democratic primary by a former governor, and in the election by a former right-wing Democrat, turned New Right Republican.

Whereas the New Generation Act remains on the books, *A Child Health Plan* is now all but forgotten. The one county planning effort which grew out of it was forced to be abandoned by local pressure, and a $195,000 federal grant to test innovative Medicaid reimbursement strategies for comprehensive care was returned because of its association with the *Child Health Plan*. Political strategists advised that a vigorous defense of the *Plan* would backfire, and in fact the controversy receded from the headlines as election day approached. Unfortunately, not only did the controversy recede, but the *Child Health Plan* disappeared altogether. So far, there has been no attempt to revive it.

SOME THINGS LEARNED[1]

The report of the Select Panel (1981) shares some liabilities with North Carolina's *Child Health Plan*. It would be impossible to produce a meaningful document about child health today without addressing the very issues which bring legions of moral crusaders out of kitchens that look "like the ones that appear in detergent advertisements on television" (FitzGerald, 1981, p. 70). These issues include family planning, sex education, abortion, day care, and even gun control. Yet, despite the strength that single-issue pressure groups appear to command, in every case the majority of Americans, when polled on particular issues addressed by the Select Panel Report, side with the Panel's recommendations. A majority of such Americans (who are not necessarily those who vote) favor federal registration of handguns, support sex education in public schools, and oppose the proposed Constitutional amendment to outlaw therapeutic abortions (Harris, 1980).

The use of direct-mail solicitations, the use of a cadre of professional political technicians, the use of electronic media, and the use of scare tactics abutting (and in some cases crossing) the line between hyperbole and falsity have succeeded in some cases in turning a minority sentiment into a majority vote. Single-issue groups can turn out a high percentage of their supporters on election day, whereas voter participation among the general population is abysmally low. Therefore, low voter participation is behind many so-called New Right "upsets" (Crawford, 1980). The best example is the 1980 presidential election, in which fewer than 54% of eligible participants bothered to vote (compared to nearly 86% in the presidential run-off in France this year; Wicker, 1981).

Since Reagan got 51% of the vote, he only received the expressed support of 26.5% of the American electorate, which hardly amounts to a mandate for anything.

Although the Panel observes in its Preface that its purview was limited to health services by the Congress, such blinders may ironically make it easier to defend the Panel's recommendations. When North Carolina's child health planners wandered from strictly medical care concerns, they used professional jargon such as "anticipatory guidance," "parenting skills counseling," and "clarifying personal values." Such expressions are much more likely to raise a red flag than a discussion about referral patterns between primary care providers and specialists. The strength of the Select Panel Report lies in its recommendations regarding universal health services for all pregnant women and children. Aspects of the report which offer improved quality of health services for all citizens need to be emphasized rather than obscured by arguments over any one issue. Such skirmishes divert attention from the larger and more important goals of high quality, accessible health services for all children and for women of reproductive age.

Many of the characteristics of the New Right discussed above may ultimately redound to the benefit of MCH advocates: inability or unwillingness of some single-issue groups to work with others; the need for ideological purity, which precludes the effective use of political compromise; the use of less than scrupulous campaign and public relations tactics; the pattern of being against, rather than for, anything except huge military expenditures and a romantic dream of life on the frontier; and, ultimately, the possibility that New Right successes may be perceived as harmful to the personal interests of many Americans.

MCH advocates can take advantage of these weaknesses. The report of the Select Panel (1981) offers a comprehensive program which merits support from the many constituencies under the MCH umbrella. Like the New Right groups, MCH advocates have not always demonstrated an ability to form lasting coalitions. Frequently, turf battles and professional boundaries have kept child advocates in different fields apart. Recently, however, MCH advocates demonstrated an ability to compromise over an issue critical to one constituency but threatening to another. Thus, the MCH Section of the American Public Health Association, meeting in Detroit in 1980, withdrew its support from the Child Health Assessment Program (CHAP) after it had been saddled with antiabortion amendments in Congress. It is encouraging that child health advocates were able to see that long-term advantages lay in sacrificing a short-term and uncertain gain (CHAP) in favor of a united opposition to the antiabortion movement in Congress.

What is missing from the MCH coalition at this time is any meaningful involvement of the MCH constituency at the local level. The early success which some MCH advocates (notably the American Academy of Pediatrics and the American Public Health Association) have had in finding support for maintaining a categorical MCH program at the national level did not result from mobilizing a vast citizen constituency; rather, it resulted from the involvement of professionals and experts. Yet, success in the long run may depend upon demonstrating the commitment of such a constituency at the local level. Some MCH areas, conspicuously family planning and some "disease of the month club" organizations, have such local constituencies. Those programs identified as primarily for the poor do not.

Therefore, it stands to reason that the resentful American on the right, who claims to have had it with programs which appear to redistribute his income to those less worthy, is a potential supporter of an MCH program which would directly benefit his family. The Select Panel Report calls for setting standards for third-party insurers—including employee benefit plans—which could reduce the out-of-pocket cost of medical care for the families of working people. Knowing as we do that the majority of Americans support some form of national health insurance (Goodman, 1981), it follows that there is likely to be support for child health programs which are neither hung up on the certification of eligibility nor are associated with public welfare programs.

North Carolina's *A Child Health Plan for Raising a New Generation* had no political constituency except for the professionals who wrote it. As a result, politicians did not rush to its defense when it came under attack. The potential constituency behind the Select Panel Report must be mobilized, but it will not be won over if the report is interpreted as just another program for poor people. Its strength lies in the prospect of universal benefits. Advocates must not lose sight of this theme should self-styled moralists take exception to one or another specific recommendation. And while family life education, day care, and birth control—to name some of the more vulnerable recommendations—deserve our continued and unstinting support, circumstances are different from those only a year ago. The MCH message remains as important as ever. Only the audience has changed.

FOOTNOTE

[1] With apologies to Jessie Bierman (1969).

REFERENCES

Beckwith, B. The decline in American religious faith since 1913. *The Humanist*, 1981, *41*, 10–14, 54.

Bierman, J. Some things learned. *American Journal of Public Health*, 1969, *59*, 930–935.

Crawford, A. *Thunder on the right*. New York: Pantheon, 1980.

Epstein, B., & Forster, A. *The radical right*. New York: Vintage, 1967.

FitzGerald, F. A disciplined, charging army. *New Yorker*, 1981, *57*, 53–141.

Goodman, L. J. Proposal for a national health insurance and health policy: Social survey results. *Medical Care*, 1981, *19*, 329–341.

Harris, L. Reagan leading as election leads into its final hours. *ABC News-Harris Survey*, November 2, 1980.

Kotch, J. B., & Johnson, K. The fate of joint public-private planning for child health in North Carolina. *Journal of Public Health Policy*, 1981, *2*, 136–152.

Joint Child Health Planning Task Force. *A child health plan for raising a new generation*. Raleigh, N.C.: North Carolina Department of Human Resources, 1979.

Lacayo, H. *The New Right: A special report*. United Auto Workers Interoffice Communication, June 17, 1979.

Lipsett, S. M., & Raab, E. The election and the evangelicals. *Commentary*, 1981, *71*, 25–31.

Lofton, J. D., Jr. Pollster Harris credits Moral Majority vote for Reagan's stunning landslide win. *Conservative Digest*, 1980, *10*, 13–14.

Morris, B. Hitler is dead but not Hitlerism. *National Educator*, 1979, *5*, 13.

Pro-Family Forum. *Parents, have you heard about kiddie-lib?* Fort Worth, Mimeo, 1978.

Select Panel for the Promotion of Child Health. *Better health for our children: A national strategy* (4 Vols.). Washington, D.C.: U.S. Govt. Printing Office, 1981.

Skube, M. Hunt bill is facing opposition. *Winston-Salem Journal,* April 26, 1979, p. 16.

The New Right: A special report. *Conservative Digest,* 1979, *9,* 9–21.

Wicker, T. Giving voters a break. *New York Times,* May 19, 1981, p. 15A.

TEN

COMMENTARY AND AFTERWORD

LISBETH BAMBERGER SCHORR

The foregoing chapters offer a rich diversity of perspectives that will enhance the consideration of the Report of the Select Panel (1981). Some of the papers lead me to believe that, on certain issues, it may be useful to place into clearer focus the viewpoint and intentions of the Panel. Availing myself of the welcome invitation of the editor to add a final comment to this volume, I will not attempt a general review of the papers, but will limit myself to clarifying positions of the Panel which may not have been fully understood.[1]

These comments fall into five general categories: (1) how the Panel's recommendations may fare in a changed political climate; (2) how the recommendations fit into the wider context of health services financing and organization that goes beyond maternal and child health; (3) the constraints within which the Panel was operating; (4) amplification of Panel viewpoints that may not have been articulated clearly enough; and (5) consideration of further steps toward consensus and constituency building.

THE EFFECTS OF POLITICAL CHANGES

Concern is evidenced throughout this volume about the possible impact of political changes, both while the Panel was engaged in its deliberations and since the completion of the Report. Several authors express concern that because of changing political circumstances both the analysis and recommendations of the Report are now dated and irrelevant.

Most of the authors point to a reality of which the Panel was continually mindful—that maternal and child health policy cannot and must not "take place in a vacuum, insulated from the harsh realities of economic and political life" (Myers, p. 42). Nonetheless, some authors see the Panel's efforts to influence policy as "insulated from changes in the economic-political stream" (Myers, p. 42). Miller observes that "although the scholarship of the Report is of a high order, it is essentially a political document" (p. 35). This is true, as it should be given the circumstances of the Panel's origins and purposes. The Panel was created by the politically sensitive U. S. Congress, and its members were appointed by a politically aware cabinet officer, Joseph A. Califano, Jr. The political context of the Panel's creation was not some brief passing moment; neither was it tied to a single rigid outlook. The Panel was acutely aware of political pressures and realities throughout its deliberations, and worked hard to produce a report that would not be so lacking in vision as to be doomed to instant obsolescence.

However, there is surely room for differing views about which aspects of the current political situation are likely to endure, which are likely to change as a result of general social, economic, and political changes, and which may be amenable to changes stemming from more effective action to improve maternal and child health. In particular, one might question the assumption of several authors that current political trends will persist well into the future. Marmor and Greenberg suggest that the agenda for the 1980s will not include "an activist, expansionist role for government" (p. 66). Myers contends that the Panel's "conclusions and recommendations are not in step with current economic and political situations" (Myers, p. 40), because "humanitarianism is no longer very popular" (Myers, p. 43), and because "there simply will be less money available for maintenance of MCH [maternal and child health] and other health and medical care efforts in the future" (p. 41). Newberger holds that "it is now clear, perhaps more than ever, that our country is even less concerned with assuring community responsibility for the young," and that "well-intended and intelligent efforts to better children's health through government action may no longer be welcomed" (p. 69).

The question of whether the Panel would have proceeded differently had we been able to see further ahead is raised by Newberger in the first sentence of his chapter. He suggests that if the Panel members had waited another 6 months before completing the Report, "their conception of children's health and the view of who is responsible for it might have changed dramatically" (Newberger, p. 68).

But election results have not altered children's health needs, the evidence on effective interventions, nor the need for systematic action to improve child health policy at every level—including the federal level. Rather, there have been changes in the acceptability of some of the Panel's recommendations, and drastic changes are indicated in the tactics likely to be effective in obtaining needed action in the immediate future.

A number of the chapters emphasize, as an immediate consequence of current political trends, the need to find ways of making existing programs work more effectively. In fact, from the outset this was a major theme of the Panel's work, and its Report is permeated with recommendations toward that end. Efforts in that direction can be undertaken despite—and in some instances perhaps because of—the current reluctance to expand government programs.

It is difficult to assess the precise level of the nation's concern with assuring community responsibility for the young at any given moment. But one can assume that this level is not fixed and that it can be affected both by general social and economic forces and by systematic advocacy efforts. Further, the nation seems to be in disagreement less about the appropriate extent of community responsibility for vulnerable persons than about desirable forms for carrying out that responsibility. Current Reagan administration proposals assume continued popular support for the dismantling of programs that promote child health, even once the effect of such cuts has been widely observed and understood. It remains to be seen if this assumption is correct, and, if so, for how long. Furthermore, the fate of efforts to better children's health through government action is not likely to be uniform everywhere, but to vary with the effectiveness of the advocacy, the purpose of the effort, and often with the prevailing climate of a particular community and state.

I believe that members of the Panel would be inclined to agree with Miller's view that "caution should attend the interpretation that recent elections represent an expression of the public will against government sponsorship of essential human support services" (p. 36). While the Panel might have modified its assessment of what could be done immediately and what would take longer, while we might have emphasized different aspects of the supporting data, and while we might have presented some of our arguments differently, I doubt that our fundamental analysis would have been any different if we had been able to foresee the election results and the changed nature of federal–state relations.

Having been given the responsibility to describe and analyze changes needed to improve maternal and child health policy, our Panel could not have stopped short of examining the full range of policy options, including those that seem unlikely to be acted on in the immediate future.

THE WIDER CONTEXT OF HEALTH SERVICES FINANCING AND ORGANIZATION

The Panel was consistently mindful of the fact that maternal and child health policy is inextricably related to every other aspect of the health system, including the policies and practices of public and private institutions and third-party payers, the availability of various provider arrangements, and the education and training of health professionals. From this perspective, Myers's analysis seems distorted and oversimplified, depicting the states as heroes and the federal government as villain, with no other forces—except the "health-based social movement"—to influence the outcome.

Nothing occupied the Panel so much as the delineation of functions among federal, state, and local governments to assure that each level would function most effectively with respect to the other levels and to the private sector as well. As our report summarized:

> State authorities insist they could do a far better job of delivering health services . . . if the Federal Government would limit its role to defining broad health objectives and transmitting funds in a manner giving States maximum discretion over how they should be spent. In the State view, present problems are the result of categorical program regulations, lack of consistency in defining program roles and client eligibility, and excessive Federal paperwork. (Select Panel Report, Vol. I, p. 63)

Others, by contrast, advocate that "Federal control of maternal and child health programs could be increased . . . so that (similar) policy objectives can be pursued with . . . equal vigor everywhere in the Nation," and they also express concern that "an enlargement of State authority and curtailment of opportunities for local communities and consumer groups to deal directly with Federal authorities might well risk limiting access to health care for many poor and minority children and mothers" (Miller, 1981).

Our detailed recommendations regarding the appropriate roles of local, state, and federal governments take both sets of concerns into account, and provide a more differentiated response than Myers's critique suggests on the respective roles of federal and state governments and on the related question of categorical programs. The Report includes a very careful sorting of state and federal roles, as well as recommendations for program simplification and for greater authority to the states in deciding how to achieve nationally determined maternal and child health objectives. We also proposed a contract rather than a regulatory model of performance audit by the federal government.

There seems to be considerable confusion about the term "categorical." The Panel uses the term to apply to delivery patterns and states that certain services "are as well or better provided in settings that are not organized to provide comprehensive care, singling out family planning services and preventive dental care as high priority services which are especially well suited to being funded and provided as categorical services." (Select Panel, Vol. I, p. 269). Miller's discussion of categorical services as contrasted with comprehensive services provided under one roof is similar to the Panel's use of the term, but he adds a second contrasting concept—services aimed at all age groups versus services aimed at children and pregnant women (Miller, pp. 26–29). Miller suggests that the record indicates that categorical services may be superior to comprehensive services in a number of respects. Certain services (he would include family planning, mental health, well-child care, and pre- and postnatal care) are often best rendered separately; services for the healthy might be advantageously separated from services for the sick; and services for children should perhaps be funded and delivered separately from services for all age groups. He believes that categorical services have the additional advantage of allowing "for priorities to be set, for specified objectives to be achieved, and for the interests of underserved people to be addressed" (Miller, p. 28).

It is not clear how Myers uses the term "categorical" when she says that, under past federal–state relationships, states "are tied into the same categorical way of viewing the world of health and MCH that characterizes the federal perspective" (p. 45), that the Select Panel emphasizes primary care and prevention only "in the context of categorical funding" (p. 52), and that "the categorical approach to the health of mother and children" has failed (p. 53). As evidence for the last rather sweeping statement, Myers claims that "none of the major programs considered by the Panel—Title V, EPSDT, WIC, P.L. 94-142, or Community Mental Health—has met its goals" (p. 53). While these were not the only programs considered by the Panel, they are the five on which the Panel made specific legislative recommendations, based on a detailed analysis of each program that attempted to distinguish between the many ways they had achieved or failed to meet their goals.

Myers, in my view, also oversimplifies when she attributes to "inflexible, long-distance federal policy" all the pressures in the health system that militate against provision of appropriate high quality care to all children and mothers. The alternatives she describes as part of the "health-based social movement" have arisen less in response to federal government pressures than to the depersonalization and high technology that now pervades in our medical care system. The medical care system is the product of many complex factors, including the way we pay for medical services and the way health professionals are trained. The "health-based social movement" she describes has not been primarily a reaction to federal interference and regulation. On the contrary, the movement has developed and been stimulated with federal support. What has been labeled by others as the "community-oriented primary care movement"—similar in most respects to Myers's "health-based social movement"—has built on the foundations of the federally-supported neighborhood and community health centers and the federally-funded and operated National Health Service Corps.

CONSTRAINTS ON THE PANEL

Some authors suggest that the Panel may have been misguided or unwise how we defined the scope of our report and in our willingness to sacrifice some precision in our manpower recommendations in return for consensus. Both criticisms merit closer examination.

Scope of the Report

Several authors were troubled by the fact that the Panel made no recommendations about such issues as poverty (Newberger, pp. 79–80), child custody, foster care, teenage employment (Marmor & Greenberg, p. 62), and other issues having an important bearing on child health. The Panel deliberated on these matters at length, and in order to avoid misunderstanding, instructed me to explain in the letter of transmittal our views of the proper scope of our Report. I summarized our position as follows:

> In accordance with our congressional mandate we have addressed and analyzed issues and policies pertaining to the physical environment, health behavior, health services organization and financing, and health research. We did not try to go beyond these, although we are fully aware that other aspects of the social environment exercise a powerful influence on health. It is true that if we could eliminate poverty and racism in this country, if high quality preschool programs and community supports for families were more available, if teachers and schools were more effective, if we had full employment and every young person could look forward

to productive work, our health indicators would improve significantly. Nevertheless, we have not focused on these issues, both because they are outside the Panel's mandate, and because we wish to help direct public attention to the extensive opportunities to improve child health by improving health policies and programs. (Select Panel, 1981, Vol. I, p. iv)

With reference to suggestions in several of the papers that too many of our recommendations were directed to the federal government and not enough to the states, localities, and the private sector, it is important to bear in mind that we were asked by the Congress to direct our Report to the legislative and executive branches of the federal government.

Content and Consensus

The Panel decided early in its deliberations to strive for consensus, if such could be achieved without compromise of strongly held views and principles. We believed at the end that we had been successful in this aim. Only one member dissented from any of the major findings and recommendations contained in the first volume of the Report, filing dissenting views on three of the Panel's more than 200 recommendations.[2] Achieving this near unanimity entailed considerable accommodation among all participants and a general willingness not to pursue every issue to every ultimate implication.

Perhaps foremost among the issues on which we exercised every conscious restraint, as suggested by both Guerra (Chap. 6) and Williams (Chap. 7), was the Panel's treatment of manpower questions. Williams is right in pointing to the "clear philosophical consistency between what has historically been a focus for nursing in the area of maternal and child health and the nature and scope of services which the Select Panel thinks must be provided to mothers and children" (p. 112). Why, then, would the Panel propose recommendations on the involvement of nurses which could be accurately characterized by Williams as "relatively passive" and "somewhat modest" (Williams, pp. 112–113)? I can think of two subtle factors that may have influenced our stand on the role of nurses. One, as suggested by Williams, is that the Panel was given pause by the prospect of a physician surplus. In the words of the Graduate Medical Education National Advisory Committee (GMENAC), "we do not know how simultaneously to preserve or extend the nonmedical services of nonphysician providers without simultaneously extending their contribution to the medical surplus" (Williams, p. 110). A second factor may have stemmed from the Panel's determination to insure that our Report would focus on the needs of mothers and children, rather than on the needs of health care providers. Not only could we not, in the time available, fully analyze maternal and child health needs in terms of the precise optimum manpower distributions, but we were eager to avoid recommendations that could be seen as special pleading on behalf of any professional group—physicians or nurses, pediatricians or family practitioners, dentists or dental assistants, psychiatrists, psychologists, or social workers. In consequence, we may, as William claims, have missed an important opportunity to point up the crucial role of nurses in assuring appropriate services at reasonable cost for all mothers and children.

PROBLEMS OF COMMUNICATION

Perhaps the most disturbing result of reviewing the papers in this volume is my conclusion that some of them reflect major misunderstandings of what the Panel sought to convey. On a number of issues Panel members and staff reached agreements which we believed were communicated clearly, only to discover from several of the commentaries that we had been misunderstood. Following are some of the most important misunderstandings.

Our Emphasis on Psychosocial and Other Nonmedical Services

Newberger states that the Panel's Report proposes "a cautious expansion of medical services for children" (p. 68). Whether the Panel was cautious or daring is a matter of judgment, but there is no doubt that central to the entire Report was a recognition of the need to expand the availability of health and health-related services. The Report is permeated by the recognition, made explicit first in our chapter on needed services (Vol. I, pp. 45–57) and throughout the subsequent discussion of the financing and organization of services, that medical services alone cannot meet the health needs of children. Indeed, our discussion of needed services is introduced by the observation that:

> health problems pertinent to mothers and children range from the biomedical to the psychosocial, not only in their causation, but also in their treatment and prevention. It is the Panel's view, therefore, that the health services needed by this population will necessarily entail not only traditional medical care, but also a range of services such as counseling, anticipatory guidance, and various information and education activities that are oriented to psychosocial issues. Furthermore, if an individual cannot physically get to a source of needed care, or cannot communicate with a health professional once there, the health service is available in theory only. Thus, the services that should be available include selected transportation, outreach, translator and related services. (Select Panel, Vol. I, pp. 177–178)

Newberger's paper dramatizes the critical nature of nonmedical services—a point which is emphasized more frequently perhaps than any other throughout the Panel's Report. Newberger's claim that on pages 50–51 (Vol. I) "the Select Panel degrades these vital supports for child health by referring to them as 'boundary' services" (Newberger, p. 79) is astonishing, since the clear import of the section of the Report cited above—as well as every other reference to this issue throughout the Report—is the precise opposite. The Report states clearly that: "The definition of health-related services that should be routinely provided in organized primary care settings needs to be expanded to include various services that are not a traditional part of curative medicine and have often been seen as 'boundary services' to be provided by others" (p. 50). The rest of the section is devoted to a discussion of how these services, which have been traditionally regarded as marginal to child health care, should occupy a more central role, and a great deal of the remainder of the report is in fact devoted to spelling out the operational implications of this view:

- The chapter on nutrition in Volume I, and our focus on the WIC program in Volume II, are based on the premise that "nutrition is a major, not marginal, component of efforts to promote health and prevent disease in this population as in all age groups" (Vol. I, p. 141);
- Our lists of needed services (Vol. I, pp. 181–191) provide an emphasis and degree of detail for an array of nonmedical services that is, to my knowledge, quite unprecedented in any similar compendium;
- The service domains singled out for priority attention in the needed services chapter include mental health and related psychosocial services, and services that promote access to care. These priorities are again reflected in our focus in Volume II on increasing the availability and accessibility of nonmedical services through improvements in P.L. 94-142, the Mental Health Systems Act, Title V, and Medicaid;
- Our chapter on changes needed in the organization of services includes recommendations to assure: (1) "a broad range of health services, psychological and social as well as medical" (Vol. I, p. 226); (2) coordination of services provided by a variety of health professionals and other agencies and providers, including those from the welfare, correctional, and educational systems (Vol. I, p. 227); and (3) a recognition of the central role of the family in all aspects of maintaining child health (Vol. I, p. 230);
- Our recommendations for changing third-party payment policies and practices (Vol. I, pp. 320–324) are aimed at removing the bias toward technology-oriented care, which discourages the "provision of time-consuming services such as counseling which are central to disease

prevention and health promotion" (p. 321). We were so concerned about the importance of making these heretofore undervalued services more widely available that we invested considerable time and effort in the design of a concrete new proposal—the Board on Health Services Standards—the primary purpose of which is to facilitate third-party reimbursement for this category of services;

- The importance of changes in the training of health professionals to improve their "understanding of the influences of genetic, familial, environmental and social factors on the health status of children and mothers" is spelled out on pages 394–396 of Volume I.

The Panel's Needs-Based Approach to Defining Maternal and Child Health Services and Needed Health System Changes

The significance of this approach seems also insufficiently understood. Guerra points out, quite correctly, that demand-based estimates would provide a more accurate basis for calculating manpower needs in the immediate future (p.   ). It was precisely because we considered it important to distinguish between actual needs and effective demand—the latter reflecting various current arrangements which the Panel hoped would not be permanent, including differences among families in ability to pay for and otherwise obtain needed services—that we decided that only a needs-based analysis would form a proper basis for long-term recommendations.

Newberger, inexplicably, states that "the Panel's approaches to change seem more focused on what providers can provide, rather than on what children need" (p. 71), even though our entire analysis of the organization of personnel to deliver such services, and the administrative arrangements undergirding health services delivery and financing programs, was based on a prior analysis of what services children and pregnant women need.

The first five papers commissioned by the Select Panel (1981, Vol. IV) were focused on the health needs of infants, children, adolescents, pregnant women, and chronically ill children. The Panel concluded at an early stage that any proposals we might make for changes in the organization and financing of health services should grow out of an assessment of what services children and pregnant women actually need, and the task of defining "needed" services became a fundamental first step in the Panel's work (Select Panel, Vol. I, p. 7). Most members of the Panel considered the needs-based analysis a significant departure from the more conventional program analysis approach, and felt that it gave our document a particularly solid foundation.

The Fundamental Characteristics of Changes Advocated by the Panel

Myers expressed disappointment in the Panel's recommendations for what she characterizes as "more of the same" (p. 40). In contrast, several other authors are concerned that the Panel's recommendations are unrealistic because they require major social reforms, massive increases in public expenditures, and other changes with sweeping and perhaps unknown consequences. We carefully analyzed which of the existing array of programs and policies were working and needed to be extended, which programs required only minor modifications, and which programs needed major changes. Most of the commentaries seemed to overlook the changes we advocated which could be accommodated within existing or only slightly augmented expenditures and with only slight modifications of existing practices. For example, home visiting is an old idea that merely needs to be sustained and perhaps revitalized; studying the efficacy of "soft services" merely requires a tiny diversion of research funds from any number of high technology, acute care topics to these services; increasing the awareness of physicians about nutrition issues requires only a miniscule revision in medical education and perhaps board examinations. Although we did advocate certain significant new departures in health policy, we also suggested many steps that could be taken within current fiscal and political constraints.

CONSTITUENCY AND CONSENSUS BUILDING

How those concerned with improving child health must adapt goals and tactics to changing political realities, and how these "realities" can be modified are matters that occupied the Panel throughout its deliberations—even as they have occupied the commentators in this volume. What are the critical elements in bringing about social change?

Marmor and Greenberg suggest that child advocates historically have been weak because they "have not bound together the social altruism and economic self-interest in the mix that has characterized other more successful political lobbying groups" (p. 65). Kotch believes that the missing ingredient has been "meaningful involvement of the MCH constituency at the local level" (pp. 142–143). Kotch also argues that the strength of the Panel's recommendations lies in their potential attractiveness to conservatives as well as liberals and in the prospect of universal benefits (p. 142). By contrast, Guerra would narrow the target groups on whose behalf improved services are sought, believing that migrants, seasonal farm workers, refugees, and aliens have needs so different from the rest of the population that they can only be met by a separate health delivery system (pp. 100–101). Miller would advocate a universal approach across income groups, but cautions against the risks of alliances which fail to single out mothers and children for priority attention (pp. 32–33).

There are considerable differences, both among contributors to this volume and among members of the Panel, on how needed changes are best brought about. On certain issues, some of us favored seeking gradual change, small modifications at the margin, as relatively feasible goals that might be jeopardized in a quest for major reforms. Others of us subscribed to such an approach on certain issues, but saw a more general commitment to incrementalism as a disastrous attempt to leap over a chasm in two—or more—steps. But despite these differences about the desirable tempo and reach of change, there was remarkable agreement, not only on the content of the necessary changes, but on the characteristics of a useful agenda for change.

First, we agreed on the importance of specificity and concreteness in any recommendations for change. Wherever possible, we translated general principles into practical steps for action. Thus, I do not believe that the principles enunciated by Newberger (p. 93) were, as he states, "insufficiently understood by the Select Panel" (p. 92). I doubt that any Panel member would disagree with any of them. We simply considered these principles less well served by further reiteration than by translation into practical recommendations that could serve as a basis for action.

Second, we saw the role of the Panel as laying out the policy issues and pointing directions, rather than one of attempting to establish a single agenda to be followed by each of the various individuals and groups in the country concerned with improving the health of mothers and children. We hope that the Panel's emphasis on consistent and coherent action in several major areas will help to counteract what Miller refers to as "policy hopscotch among a variety of defensible approaches [which] has weakened the public commitment to children's health" (p. 34). Yet we attempted to avoid setting the priorities so sharply as to present a take-it-or-leave-it choice to the potential constituency for improved child health. We wished to leave room for different groups to make a variety of choices from among our recommendations as to which they considered most important to act on, and to make different selections as political conditions change over the next decade.

Third, and perhaps most important, we agreed that even in a period of pessimism and skepticism about our social institutions, and an uncertain economic outlook, the push for equity must continue. Particularly in such a period, we must undertake renewed efforts to assure the health of the most vulnerable in our society. Pervading our deliberations and our attempts to look ahead was a shared concern that the scramble over scarce resources could be played out in ways that will further increase the polarization of American society and extinguish what is left of our sense of community. Many Select Panel recommendations are aimed specifically at reducing polarization and alienation and at restoring a sense of community among the individuals and families of this nation; we trust these recommendations are less "seriously out of date" than Myers and Marmor and Greenberg suggest. Although the nation may be temporarily readjusting its expenditures and priorities, there is no evidence that interest in the health of this nation's mothers and children is permanently moribund. National agendas change often, and because we wrote the Report for the long-term future, much of what we suggest can be built upon when the nation focuses once more on the steps that must be taken to enable all American families to share in the American dream.

Toward that end, we hope that concerned individuals and groups around the nation will find useful both the Report of the Select Panel and the commentaries in this volume. Over the next several years, it will be particularly important to keep track of the available indicators of how pregnant women, children, and their families fare as programs and policies change. Some will change for the worse, and some for the better. We will need to know precisely what the effects of reduced expenditures and changed arrangements for authority and governance turn out to be. Margolis's paper elegantly lays out some of the epidemiological evidence that must be monitored in the decade ahead, so that the agenda for needed change can be continually updated, and the urgency for social action can and will be solidly documented. All Americans must have access to reliable information about the circumstances in which the nation's children are growing up, how well we as a society are carrying out our responsibilities for their healthy development, and what needs to be done so that our actions will match our aspirations.

FOOTNOTES

[1] This chapter has not been reviewed by other members of the Select Panel, but I trust that it generally accords with their thinking.
[2] Three members filed a total of six dissents to the recommendations for changes in selected federal programs contained in Vol. II of our Report.

REFERENCES

Miller, C.A. Personal communication, July 18, 1981.

Select Panel for the Promotion of Child Health. *Better health for our children: A national strategy* (4 Vols.). Washington, D.C.: U.S. Govt. Printing Office, 1981.

ELEVEN

PRESIDENTIAL AND CONGRESSIONAL COMMISSIONS: THE SELECT PANEL IN CONTEXT[1]

RON HASKINS

INTRODUCTION

John Steinbeck once wrote that nothing original had ever been achieved by a committee. As if to defy this assertion, Western governments have a long history of assembling prestigious groups of scholars, professionals, business leaders, and government employees to study important questions of public policy and to make recommendations for action by government agencies, private groups, and individual citizens.

This volume has been devoted to critiques of the report by one such commission—the Select Panel for the Promotion of Child Health (1981). The authors of each paper have carefully examined a particular aspect of the Select Panel Report and its policy recommendations. In this concluding chapter, however, my intent is to provide perspective for evaluating the work and recommendations of the Select Panel by examining previous presidential and congressional commissions. My primary purpose is to study commissions as a method of conducting policy analysis and recommending governmental action. The chapter's first section will be devoted to analyzing the composition and functions of presidential commissions, with occasional attention to congressional commissions, and then to examining the means by which commission impact on public policy is achieved and can be increased. The second—and much briefer—section of the chapter will examine the Select Panel Report (1981) with particular attention to the possible short- and long-term impact of the Panel's recommendations.

COMMISSIONS: COMPOSITION AND FUNCTIONS

Commission Composition

As suggested by the information in Table 1, commissions are often composed of up to five distinct groups, though in practice three are more common and more important. The first and primary group, of course, is the official members of the commission itself. The second most important group—and some might argue that this group is actually the most important—is the commission staff. A third important group is consultants hired by the commission. In addition to these three groups, two other groups may participate directly in commission proceedings; namely, technical or advisory boards, and government agencies.

Commissioners. The characteristics of federal commission members have been thoroughly described by Popper (1970). In general, commissioners tend to be lawyers, over 50, white, male, and of impressive background. Above all, commission members must be politically acceptable, which nearly always means that they hold moderate views on the issue addressed by the commission, as well as on most other policy matters. In recent years, blacks, Hispanics, and women have been included on commissions, though usually only one or two of each. It is especially desirable to have a commissioner who fits into more than one of these categories. Patricia Harris—a black female—was a member of two presidential commissions. As suggested by the example of Patricia Harris, many commissioners tend to serve on more than one commission. According to Popper (1970, pp. 17–18), between 1950 and 1970, seven people served on three presidential commissions, and 25 people served on two such commissions. Popper estimates that between 10 and 25% of most commissions are composed of members who have served on previous commissions. Finally, a number of commissions include U. S. Senators or Representatives, in which case there is usually an equal number of Republicans and Democrats.

The actual work of commissioners consists of attending commis-

TABLE 1: SUMMARY TABLE OF CHARACTERISTICS AND RECOMMENDATIONS OF SELECTED NATIONAL COMMISSIONS

Commission title	Dates of operation	Chairman	Composition	Summary of recommendations
Committee on Economic Security (1935)	1934–1935	Frances Perkins	5 members plus technical board, citizen's advisory council, and 7 other advisory groups	6 major recommendations concerning employment assurance, unemployment compensation, old age security, income security for children, maternal and child health, and program administration
Commission on Organization of the Executive Branch of the Government (1949)	1947–1949	Herbert Hoover	12 members plus staff of about 60	18 reports and a summary report recommending 281 changes in organization of the Executive Branch including the creation of the Department of Defense and the Department of Welfare
President's Panel on Mental Retardation (1962)	1961–1962	Leonard Mayo	27 members plus staff of 12, organized into six task forces on prevention, education, law, biological research, behavioral research, and coordination	8 general recommendations regarding research, preventive health measures, clinical services, legal services, manpower, education for the retarded, public awareness, facilities, and methods of care
President's Commission on the Assassination of President John F. Kennedy (1964)	1963–1964	Earl Warren	7 members; a general counsel and 14 assistant counsels; 12 staff members	11 conclusions concerning specifics of the assassination itself; 1 conclusion consisting of 6 parts concerning weaknesses in the security provided for presidents; 12 recommendations about strengthening security for presidents

President's Commission on Law Enforcement and Administration of Justice (1967)	1965–1967	Nicholas Katzenbach	19 members, about 60 staff, 175 consultants	About 200 specific recommendations in measuring incidence of crime, juvenile crime, police, courts, corrections, organized crime, narcotics and drug use, drunkenness, control of firearms, science and technology, research, and national anticrime strategy
National Advisory Commission on Civil Disorders (1968)	1967–1968	Otto Kerner	11 members, 2 advisory panels, staff of more than 100	Over 150 recommendations in 4 areas: 6 *employment* programs including 1,000,000 new jobs in public and private sector each year for 3 years; 4 *education* programs including the elimination of de facto segregation, quality education in ghetto schools, better vocational education; 11 recommendations to reform *welfare* including family planning, higher payments, and guaranteed income; and 12 recommendations to improve *housing*
President's Commission on Income Maintenance Programs (1969)	1968–1969	Ben W. Heineman	21 members, staff of about 70	10 primary recommendations including universal income program with guarantee level of $2,400 and 50% reduction rate, increase guarantee level as rapidly as possible to the poverty level, end AFDC, reduce state contribution to the program, broaden unemployment benefits and raise benefit levels, cash out food stamps, better manpower and training programs, expand family planning services

National Commission on the Causes and Prevention of Violence (1969)	1968–1969	Milton Eisenhower	3 commissioners; staff organized into 7 task forces including group violence, assassination, firearms, the media, law enforcement; task forces did their own research including a national survey	Published 13 volumes plus a summary; 81 recommendations including "establish justice," old and young should try to "bridge the generation gap," higher welfare expenditures, reduce military budgets, better housing for the poor, a job for everyone, stop production and sale of "junk guns," government produce annual report on social indicators
Commission on Obscenity and Pornography (1970)	1968–1970 (law passed in 1967)	William Lockhart	19 commissioners plus professional staff of 22; 4 working panels on: traffic & distribution, effects; positive approaches; legal; spent $1 million on research, performed mostly by the staff itself; also held public hearings	10 recommendations, 6 involved legislation, 4 did not; recommended massive sex education in schools, control mailing and public displays of explicit sex materials, restrict sale of sex materials to adolescents; MOST IMPORTANT: repeal all federal, state, and local laws prohibiting sale of sex materials to consenting adults
Commission on Population Growth and the American Future (1972)	1970–1972 (both Congressional & Presidential)	John D. Rockefeller, III	24 members plus staff of about 20 (C. Westoff, chair). Held 5 public hearings; commissioned new research in population growth and use of resources; also demographic projections; also a public opinion poll	Issued an interim report; published final report in 3 sections; recommendations on reproduction, immigration, population distribution, and government collection of population statistics; general thrust was *not* to limit immigration, but to achieve zero growth by eliminating unwanted pregnancies

sion meetings, attending public hearings sponsored by the commission, reading and criticizing staff reports, listening to and querying staff members about their reports, and negotiating with other commission members to decide on commission recommendations and the approach to, or actual writing of, sensitive parts of the commission report.

As a rule, commission members do not actually conduct research or gather materials, nor do they actually write the commission report; these tasks are given to members of the commission staff. Occasionally, of course, individual commissioners will be very committed to the topic under investigation and may attempt to play a very active role in directing the staff, influencing other commissioners, and shaping the recommendations and final report. In some cases, commissioners may even involve members of their personal staff in gathering and analyzing information or in writing sections of the commission report.

Staff members. All national commissions include a staff of professionals, many of whom have a substantial background in some aspect of the issue addressed by the commission. One has the impression that many—perhaps most—senior-level staff positions are filled by lawyers and social scientists, with the former group being predominant. It goes without saying, of course, that the makeup of committee staff is significantly influenced by the particular issue at hand. Thus, lawyers dominated the staff of the President's Commission on Law Enforcement and Administration of Justice while social scientists were heavily represented on the staff of the Commission on Population Growth and the American Future.

A number of important practical considerations appear to influence the composition of commission staffs. Primary among these is the short life of a commission—usually a year or 18 months. Thus, people accepting staff positions must live in Washington for a relatively short period with few, if any, prospects that their staff position will lead to permanent employment. This consideration tends to greatly reduce the number of able people who will seriously consider staff appointments. Accepting such a position means temporarily leaving one's current employment, dropping all ongoing work, and often moving one's family to Washington, D.C.

Anonymity of authorship further limits the recruitment of prospective staff members from the academic community. As suggested by the "publish or perish" dictum, talented, young, and even well-established academicians are evaluated largely by the quantity and quality of their publications. Since the authorship of commission reports is not usually attributed to individual staff members, academicians who agree to serve on a commission staff will almost certainly lose a year to 18 months in their effort to embellish their vitas.

I would emphasize the importance of these practical difficulties in recruiting qualified commission staff members. For reasons that will subsequently become clear, one might argue persuasively that staff members are substantially responsible for the originality and quality of commission work. Thus, claims such as that by Cater and Strickland (1975) that the Surgeon General's Advisory Committee on Television and Social Behavior "failed to enlist fully the best skills of social science" (p. 6) must be taken seriously. The problems of recruiting highly qualified staff members must stand as a serious shortcoming of commissions.

This is especially the case since commission staff members perform nearly all the routine and much of the substantive work of commissions. In most cases, commissioners meet every 1 to 3 months during the life of the commission, with somewhat more frequent meetings as the final report is being drafted. Between meetings, of course, commissioners return to the responsibilities of their jobs and families, usually outside Washington, D.C. Meanwhile, commission staff members continue working full-time conducting the primary work of the commission.

In particular, staff members perform three functions. First, they collect information needed to describe, understand, and attack the problem being addressed by the commission. This function usually involves reviewing demographic information, results of physical or social science research, and various survey statistics published by the government or other organizations. The outcome of this activity is a synthesis of available information pertinent to describing the issue under investigation, as well as the identification of possible alternative policies that the government or private sector could use to address the issue.

The second primary function performed by commission staff members is the preparation of background materials for commissioners. Although commissioners will occasionally use their own time and resources to obtain and synthesize information about the issue, there seems to be general agreement that commissioners are dependent on information prepared for them by staff members (see Cater & Strickland, 1975; Popper, 1970; Witte, 1962). It is, of course, also true that commissioners usually make decisions about which particular aspects of their problem area the staff should investigate, but even this degree of direction leaves substantial room for initiative—and the influence of personal perspectives of senior staff members—in information collection and synthesis.

The third primary function of commission staffs is to write preliminary versions of the commission report or reports. It seems safe to conclude that in most cases commission reports are a collaborative effort between commission members and staff. The usual procedure is for staff members to write preliminary versions based on discussions during commission meetings and on a general outline of major points agreed to beforehand by commission members. This draft is reviewed and critiqued by commissioners who then provide directions for specific revisions of the final report. Although it is difficult to gauge how involved commission members are in final report preparation—and it certainly varies from commission to commission and commissioner to commissioner—the specific wording of major conclusions and recommendations has been known to produce intense conflicts among commission members (see Epstein, 1966; Larsen, 1975).

We can conclude that the role of commission staff members is crucial, even pivotal. There is no question that staff members do the great majority of a commission's work and in particular that they gather and synthesize nearly all the information on which the commission's final report is based. Commission staff members also write initial drafts of commission reports, but commission members play a direct role in the wording of important parts of the final report, and especially of conclusions and recommendations.

Consultants. Many, perhaps most, commissions rely to some degree on information supplied by consultants in one of two primary ways. Some commissions, such as the Surgeon General's Scientific Advisory Committee on Television and Social Behavior (1972) and the Commission on Obscenity and Pornography (1970), spend a substantial proportion of their funds sponsoring original research by outside investigators. Such research is usually conducted by qualified, and often eminent, academicians whose only connection with the commission is the research contract. Once the contract is agreed upon, the researcher is free to draw whatever conclusions seem appropriate from the research results and also to publish the results in professional journals. In any case, consultants who conduct research can, and often do, provide the commission with new information relevant to the problem under consideration. It also seems appropriate to note here that the research sponsored by both the Surgeon General's Advisory Committee and the Commission on Obscenity and Pornography provided the major source of information for commission recommendations.

The second primary way in which commissions make use of consultants is by asking them to prepare background papers on selected aspects of the problem under study. These papers are usually literature reviews that summarize scientific knowledge concerning a particular topic and often include policy recommendations as well. The Select Panel (1981), for example, commissioned 22 such papers on various aspects of maternal and child health and published these papers as Volume IV of its final Report.

Both types of information—new knowledge produced by original

research and summaries of available research and scientific knowledge—are used by commission staff members in preparing background
papers and in reporting to commission members. In this way, information produced or synthesized by consultants can prove quite valuable
to commissions and can have a substantial impact on commission conclusions. Further, and a point to which I will return, the knowledge
generated or synthesized by consultants, especially in the case of original
research, may have a lasting influence on various scientific communities—and even on future commissions and government agencies.

These three groups—commissioners, professional staff, and consultants, usually with assistance from government agencies and advisory
groups—perform the primary work of commissions. But to what end is
this work directed?

Functions of Commissions

Although some social critics have viewed commissions in a rather
jocular vein (e.g., Drew, 1968)—and not altogether without reason—it
is nonetheless true that commissions have filled a variety of policy-related functions. Most of these functions are closely related, and in practice the distinctions between them are far from clear, but it is useful to
distinguish four purposes for which commissions have been appointed.
These four functions—to deflect, endorse, educate, and discover—are
dealt with in the following sections.

Deflect. Beginning with perhaps the least worthy function of
commissions, we find that presidents (or the Congress) may appoint
prestigious commissions to serve as "lightning rods" (Drew, 1968, p.
46). In another version of this role, the president may decide that commission recommendations are controversial and then dissociate himself
and his administration from such recommendations on the grounds that
they are too radical or impractical. Such action on the president's part
may allow him to come across as moderate on the issue at hand and to
portray himself and his administration as the voice of reason and sanity.

It might be argued that presidential commissions serve to draw
heat away from the White House. Particularly if a commission is highly
publicized, such as the Kerner Commission or the Warren Commission,
the news media may focus their attention on commission deliberations,
interim reports, or public hearings and thereby allow the president to
avoid, or at least minimize, media attention and public pressure on the
issue being addressed by the commission. If pressed, the president can
say that he has appointed a "blue ribbon" commission to look into the
matter, and he doesn't want to influence their dispassionate deliberations by taking a public stand on the issue.

In the version of deflection in which the president dissociates himself from commission recommendations, his reception of, and response to, the commission's final report is often an important sign of his political purpose. A clear example of this presidential approach to commission reports is provided by the National Commission on Technology, Automation, and Economic Progress which reported to President Johnson in 1966. Sociologist Daniel Bell (1966)—himself a member of the commission—has described the fate of this report in some detail. As the 14-member commission was preparing drafts of its final report, White House staff assistants were kept well informed of the commission's work and its probable recommendations. Near the end of January, 1966, the commission's final report was ready, and commission members were notified that it would be presented directly to President Johnson at the White House. As it turned out, the report was never presented to him. Rather, it was released by the White House to the press without advance notice and with no members of the commission present to answer questions—a procedure designed to minimize impact of the commission report. The reason? Bell speculated (1966, p. 5) that such treatment was accorded the commission because its recommendations—which included a guaranteed annual income and tremendous expansion of the federal government's role in providing jobs to the unemployed—were "too controversial," and Johnson was interested in putting as much distance as possible between himself and the commission's report. The commission had attracted considerable press attention during its deliberations on automation and unemployment, which had been a burning issue when the commission was appointed in 1964. But by the time the commission's report was completed in 1966, unemployment was declining and the president could afford to ignore the important long-term issues raised by the report.

Endorse. Commissions may also serve to endorse a program wanted by the president. Elizabeth Drew (1968) has referred to this function as "getting them [commission members] aboard" (p. 46) on something the president wants to do.

Although it seems logical enough that a president would appoint commissioners to endorse programs he wants, on closer inspection it turns out that the function of endorsement is a very complicated matter indeed. To be sure, presidents nearly always stack commissions with two types of members. A number of authors (e.g., Drew, 1968; Ohlin, 1975; Popper, 1970) have noted that, particularly in the case of commissions addressing sensitive issues such as riots or assassinations, the president will appoint at least one or two personal friends who will not only represent his perspective and interests, but who can also serve as a potential source of information for the White House, should that become necessary. Second, as pointed out above, nearly all commission members are "safe"; i.e., they are conservative or moderate members of the establishment, are often lawyers with extensive experience in government, and have often served on previous commissions (Popper, 1970). Certainly no president has been known to appoint commission members who are radically opposed to his programs or political philosophy. Nor have presidents typically appointed members of groups—such as the poor—who are directly affected by the problems studied by commissions.

But to acknowledge that presidents appoint their friends and other moderates to a given commission is certainly not strong evidence that commissions serve to rubber-stamp presidential programs. At least three factors can be cited to refute the notion that commissions simply endorse presidential programs.

First, as presidents often discover in making Supreme Court nominations (Eisenhower's appointment of Earl Warren being one dramatic example), political appointees do not always behave the way they are expected to, or even in a manner consistent with their previous public positions on given issues. A particularly instructive example of this phenomenon is provided by the President's Commission on Law Enforcement and Administration of Justice (1967). In its unanimous report, the commission—which included William Rogers, later President Nixon's secretary of state, and Lewis Powell, later a Nixon appointee to the Supreme Court—produced the rather immoderate conclusion that:

> [the commission] has no doubt whatever that the most significant action that can be taken against crime is action designed to eliminate slums and ghettos, to improve education, to provide jobs, to make sure that every American is given the opportunities and freedoms that will enable him to assume his responsibilities. (quoted in Vorenberg, 1972, p. 69)

Similarly, the very carefully selected Kerner Commission attributed riots and other signs of racial tension in America to white racism:

> What white Americans have never fully understood—but what the Negro can never forget—is that white society is deeply implicated in the ghetto. White institutions created it, white institutions maintain it, and white society condones it. (National Advisory Commission on Civil Disorders, 1968, p. 1)

And perhaps most remarkable of all, the Commission on Obscenity and Pornography (1970), based largely on research conducted by its staff, concluded that exposure to pornography did not influence behavior. Thus, one of its primary recommendations, supported by 12 of the 17 commissioners, was that

> . . . federal, state, and local legislation prohibiting the sale, exhibition, or

distribution of sexual materials to consenting adults *should be repealed.* (my italics; p. 51)

A second factor contributing to the difficulty of commissions serving to rubber-stamp presidential programs is that all commissions hire a large professional staff that reviews available information concerning the problem in question and its possible solutions. Further, most commissions involve outside consultants, who are almost completely independent of the commission itself, to prepare review papers and make recommendations. In addition, many commissions actually conduct or fund original research into some aspect of the problem they are charged to investigate.

The involvement of professionals both as staff members and consultants serves to throw open to individual opinion and reasoning many of the questions addressed by the commission. Such opinions are often based on idiosyncratic views of the available evidence. Although one may argue that social scientists are no more objective about evidence than ordinary citizens, one needs very little experience with social scientists and other professionals to understand that it is often difficult to pressure them to toe the party line. In fact, one could hardly imagine a more hopeless task than approaching a senior and respected member of the academic community with the message, "We would like you to do some research for us, and here is how we would like it to come out."

Nor is it always possible to control the findings of social science research. A brief excursion into the history of commissions reveals a number of cases in which research generated surprising results that shaped commission recommendations. Perhaps the most dramatic example is provided by the Pornography Commission referred to above. As described by the sociologist Otto Larsen (1975), who was a member of the commission, a variety of carefully planned research was conducted to examine the effects of exposure to pornographic material. Indeed, the commission produced 39 studies, 14 of which were experimental, to determine whether exposure to pornography had effects on consumers. Much to the surprise of both commissioners and researchers, the research failed to show effects of a "damaging personal or social nature" (see Larsen, 1975, pp. 33–34). As a result, the commission report was explicit on the policy implication of these findings:

> If a case is to be made against "pornography" in 1970, it will have to be made on grounds other than demonstrated effects of a damaging personal or social nature. Experimental research designed to clarify the question has found no reliable evidence to date that exposure to explicit sexual materials plays a significant role in the causation of delinquent or criminal sexual behavior among youth or adults. (Commission on Obscenity and Pornography, 1970, p. 139; also quoted in Larsen, 1975, p. 34)

And what resulted from such a straightforward conclusion based on a substantial body of research? The report was denounced by President Nixon and many members of the Congress. For our purpose here, the point is that to the extent that commissions involve professionals, scientists, and scientific research in their efforts, it becomes increasingly difficult for the president to control commission recommendations or to expect the commission to endorse his positions.

A third factor that tends to prevent commissions from endorsing preconceived views is that, as argued above, much of the work of commissions is usually produced by the staff and not by the commissioners themselves. Thus, although the president and his advisers may carefully select members of the commission, they usually exercise less influence on the selection of staff members, and even less on selection of consultants should the commission decide to solicit original research or review papers. As Drew (1968) and others have pointed out, commission members and staff members do not always get along well and indeed are often in conflict. Thus, even a commission that wanted to endorse a presidential program could experience difficulty in making its staff fall in line.

Having argued that commissions do not serve to merely endorse programs already supported by the president, I would like now to argue that there is a sense in which commissions do endorse presidential programs—or more accurately, a sense in which presidents endorse commission recommendations.

As I shall argue in detail below, perhaps the best omen for a successful commission is to be appointed by a president who wants to have a program of his own in a given area, but doesn't know exactly what he wants to do. Thus, in order to simultaneously achieve several purposes, he may appoint a commission to study the area and make specific policy recommendations. In so doing, the president can get advice about the nature and dimensions of the problem, can obtain recommendations for policies and programs that could deal with the problem, can draw media attention to his interest in the area, and can point to the fact that any commission recommendations which he decides to pursue are supported by an illustrious and experienced group of specialists and wise citizens. More than this, in some cases the president can also count on ready-made leadership for subsequent legislative proposals in the House and Senate. Thus, a number of commissions have included senators and congressmen who later provided support for legislation to implement commission recommendations.

Educate. A third function of commissions is to educate. In particular, there are a number of audiences that commissions might be expected to educate. One of these is policymakers at the federal, and sometimes state, level. It has been said that policymakers in the legislative branch of government have something less than thorough familiarity with many issues on which they vote. But even if commission reports are not carefully read by policymakers themselves, members of their personal or committee staffs can be expected to read these reports, and thereby increase their knowledge of the issues addressed by the report. Under some circumstances, commission reports can educate and perhaps influence policymakers in this rather indirect way.

The media is a second audience that commissions attempt to educate. As efforts by presidents and other policymakers to influence the media would suggest, this audience is one of special importance if a commission is to have its assessment of the problem and its recommendations receive widespread attention. The importance of educating the media and thereby producing coverage sympathetic to a commission's view of the problem and its solution is not a recent development. In his remarkable book concerning the Committee on Economic Security (1935), which was appointed by President Roosevelt in 1932, Dr. Edwin Witte (1962), Staff Director of the Committee, repeatedly discusses how the commission attempted to bring the press over to its view of economic security and the means by which it should be achieved.

A third audience addressed by commission reports is the American public. This mythical but powerful beast is usually conceived in the abstract, and we are asked to believe that somehow "the people" will have the final word on important issues. They will make their will known on the various issues of the day and thereby bring the many legislative and executive policymaking and policy implementing bodies into line with their wishes. This being the case, any individual or group trying to influence public policy must be conscious of the average citizen and his views on the issue in question.

A somewhat more realistic view of the American public is that it usually does not influence political decisions. Most policy decisions produced by our system are made by legislators and administrators who are subjected to strong influence by interest groups, often represented by professional lobbyists, who are directly affected by the issue at hand (Ziegler & Peak, 1972).

Nonetheless, especially on general issues that affect most citizens such as taxation, social security, and the level of government expenditures, the public acts either as a constraint on possible decisions or as a more or less direct influence in favor of a particular decision. The former type of public opinion serves to set some general limits on policy choices; if these limits are violated, policymakers risk incurring the wrath of a general public outcry. Recent issues of this type include the Vietnam

War, government taxation, and busing. Similarly, the fear of public outcry often serves to limit the particular programs that receive careful attention from policymakers. National health insurance, guaranteed annual income, and universally available day care have been examples of such programs for many years. Even now, when these strategies have been part of "normal" political debate for some years—and indeed have been recommended by a number of commissions—they are still considered radical proposals by many citizens, and public figures usually exhibit extreme caution in discussing these programs.

But public opinion does not always work in this indirect fashion. On occasion, the public will express itself directly in the form of letters, telephone calls, and telegrams to members of Congress or the White House. As I write this chapter, for example, the Democratically controlled House of Representatives has just passed President Reagan's tax cut proposal. Although the vote was expected to be close, and indeed for months had been expected to go against the President, the final tally was 238 to 195 in support of the President's proposal. As recently as the day before the vote the major television networks, the *New York Times*, and the *Washington Post* were all labeling the vote "too close to call."

What happened? In the opinion of some observers, a major force in the House vote was the mail, telephone calls, and telegrams from constituents urging particular representatives to support the tax cut. The *New York Times* (President Becomes Master, 1981), for example, claimed that:

> Both Democrats and Republicans spoke with awe of the President's having generated public support for his tax package with his Monday night television appeal . . . . (p. D21)

It would, of course, be unwise to overemphasize the direct role that public opinion plays in the American political process. Even in the tax cut example, many other powerful forces worked to shape the decisions of the 238 congressmen who supported the president's legislation. Nevertheless, this discussion of public opinion and the influence of ordinary citizens on the political process demonstrates both that policymaker's perceptions of public opinion exercise constraints on the programs they are willing to seriously consider and that the public can directly intervene to influence, sometimes decisively, particular political decisions. Thus, the task of commissions to educate the public is a very important function.

Discover. Most social problems with which the federal government must deal have a common characteristic; namely, complexity. Although advocates, and even some professionals, may claim that favored social programs are sure-fire ways to introduce the millennium, in point of fact there are no such programs (except, of course, national health insurance, early education, and a guaranteed annual income). Indeed, the recent attention to social policy analysis (MacRae & Haskins, 1981) is attributable in part to the facts that public programs addressed to social problems have not been notably successful and that we need to carefully analyze problems and potential solutions before spending money. Thus, regardless of whether one believes commissions are the appropriate vehicle to handle this work, there is an important mission to be fulfilled here.

In its broadest defition, the major part of this mission is what has come to be called "policy analysis" (Haskins & Gallagher, 1981; MacRae & Wilde, 1979; Stokey & Zeckhauser, 1978). Setting aside for the moment a number of the purposes of this discipline, let us say that before programs are established, we need dispassionate analysis to: (1) define the problem, (2) decide by what criteria we would judge potential solutions to be successful; (3) select one or few strategies for attacking the problem; and (4) estimate costs and possible effects of the program.

There are, then, two senses in which commissions can fulfill the function of discovery. First, commissions can generate new knowledge to accurately define the problem at hand. Three of the more notable examples of commissions producing this type of knowledge are the empirical studies on effects of pornography produced by the Commission on Obscenity and Pornography (1970), the national probability survey of crime conducted by the President's Commission on Law Enforcement and Administration of Justice (1967), and the ground-breaking experimental studies on TV and violence produced by the Surgeon General's Scientific Advisory Committee on Television and Social Behavior (1972). In each of these cases, and a number of others as well, commissions have been directly responsible for producing new knowledge relevant to particular policy domains. These contributions are especially noteworthy because, like all good data, they make a lasting contribution to the long-term process of policy formulation—and this regardless of the political fate of recommendations made by the commission that supported the study.

Second, commissions can discover by proposing new solutions to old problems. Such new solutions may consist of fresh, untested, or innovative programs or of a broad range of programs that are unique only in their comprehensiveness.

There are very few truly novel solutions to social problems, most solutions having been previously proposed by social thinkers, the subject of experimentation, or implemented in another country. Nonetheless, analysis of the strengths and weaknesses of possible programs and selection of a preferred program or programs can advance the process of policy formulation by bringing a specific proposal, together with its supporting arguments and evidence, to public attention. Such analysis can serve to focus public debate, and in some cases, can thereby bring previously radical proposals into the arena of "normal" political discussion.

THE IMPACT OF COMMISSIONS

But if commissions are to fulfill the various functions just discussed, and especially that of policy analysis, how can we determine whether they actually have any impact on public policy? Indeed, from the perspective of one concerned with the effectiveness of government programs, the major question about commissions is whether they have a beneficial impact on the problems they address. Commissions are, after all, only one among many bodies and individuals that study social problems and recommend solutions. If the "solutions" recommended by commissions were rarely implemented or if they did not have their intended effect, it would be necessary to question the utility of commissions as a tool in public policy formulation. In this section, then, my intent is to identify and discuss the types of impact a commission report might have, and the conditions that influence such impact.

We can organize this discussion by stipulating a simple three-stage model of commission impact. In the first stage of *preliminary impact*, the report comes to the attention of the media, the public, and, hopefully, policymakers. In the second stage of *intermediate impact*, commission recommendations are translated to either changes in current policy or new policy in the public or private sector. In the third stage of *ultimate impact*, the behavior of individuals, families, governmental units, corporations, or other organizations changes in the manner foreseen by the commission recommendations. A word or two is now in order to amplify these three hypothetical stages of commission impact.

Preliminary Impact

As outlined above, a primary objective of final commission reports is to educate media personnel and to help the media carry the commission's message to the American public and policymakers. At least three factors can be identified that maximize the impact of commission reports on the media.

The first is to release the report in the splashiest possible way. In this regard a White House press conference in which the report is announced by the president is highly desirable. Such an occasion will insure coverage by the White House press corps and will increase the probability of coverage by the major television networks and by the major weekly print media.

A second factor influencing media coverage is the clarity, conciseness, and originality of the commission's conclusions and recommendations. There is, of course, no question that the nature of the topic addressed by the commission has a powerful effect on the type and extent of coverage the media devotes to commission proceedings and its final report. Some topics are inherently newsworthy, while others are inherently less so. Thus, the Warren Commission (President's Commission on the Assassination of President Kennedy, 1964) was assured extensive media coverage because the assassination of President Kennedy was one of the biggest news stories of the past 20 or 30 years. And because crime is a perceived threat by a majority of the American public and an issue of great political significance that has played a major role in the past three or four presidential elections, the President's Commission on Law Enforcement and Administration of Justice (1967) was assured substantial press coverage. By contrast, commissions such as the President's Commission on Income Maintenance (1969), the President's Panel on Mental Retardation (1962), and the Advisory Council on Public Welfare (1966) seem less newsworthy and are not by any means assured of extensive media coverage.

Nonetheless, a commission can promote more extensive and better news coverage by having a clear and understandable message for the public, especially if the message can be stated in such a way that its long-term significance is apparent. Even complex reports on complex policy problems, then, must be reduced to one or a very few straightforward and unambiguous messages that can be featured in the media. The Kerner Commission's conclusion that America was becoming two separate societies—one white and one black—and that white racism was the major cause of our society's race problems is an excellent example of how a long and complex report can be translated to an understandable—and eminently newsworthy—message.

A third factor that influences the extent and quality of media coverage for commission reports is the number of times a commission attempts to conduct activities or release information that may be of interest to the media. Many commissions, for example, hold hearings that are covered by the media. Such hearings can contribute to a sense of urgency about the commission's topic and a sense of anticipation for the commission's conclusions and recommendations.

Another technique to generate media coverage—employed with great success by the National Commission on the Causes and Prevention of Violence (1969)—is to issue preliminary reports or reports by commission task forces before the final commission report. To the extent that such reports are newsworthy in the sense discussed above, they can serve to build anticipation for the commission's final report. The Violence Commission, for example, issued both a progress report and a series of task force reports over an 11-month period preceding its final report. Some of these reports, especially the *Walker Report* (1968) on police violence at the 1968 Democratic National Convention in Chicago, received a great deal of publicity and were subsequently published commercially (see Short, 1975). Thus, in addition to stimulating interest in the commission and its final report, release and publication of task force reports also kept the issues addressed by the Violence Commission before the public long after the news media had lost interest in the commission.

The point of media coverage is to bring the problem addressed by commissions, as well as commission recommendations, to public attention. As argued above, however, we should not overrate the long-term impact of public attention. The American public is characterized by an extremely short-term memory, and the idea that public outcry will lead quickly to legislative action is almost never correct. Nonetheless, public reaction, especially when manifested in letters, telegrams, and phone calls by individuals and groups to policymakers, can contribute to further action on the problems addressed by the commission.

Intermediate Impact

Which brings us to what I have labeled the "intermediate impact" of commission reports; namely, influence on legislation, regulation, or administrative action in the public or private sector. The sources of influence on these types of political action are legion, and a thorough examination of how commissions can promote their intermediate impact is not appropriate here. Nonetheless, it is possible to suggest a number of mechanisms by which commissions can increase their intermediate impact.

First, in the case of commissions appointed to influence public policy, the major recommendations should be translated into legislative language. Two commissions which achieved substantial intermediate success—the Committee on Economic Security (1935) and the Crime Commission (President's Commission on Law Enforcement, 1967)—both participated in drafting federal legislation. In the former case, members of the commission staff actually drafted legislation that was available when the final report was released. Subsequently, much of the draft legislation was enacted—word for word—as the Social Security Act of 1935. In the latter case, commission staff members worked with administration officials in writing draft legislation, and much of this legislation was enacted in the Safe Streets Act of 1968. Most notably, the creation of the Law Enforcement Assistance Administration (LEAA) in the Department of Justice was directly attributable to legislation originally drafted by commission staff. As these examples suggest, it should be a requirement of all commissions that they translate their recommendations into specific legislative proposals.

The second step commissions can take to increase their intermediate impact is to insure that well-established groups of some sort will lobby for commission recommendations. A major shortcoming of commissions as a force for new policy is that when their final report is finished, the commission disbands and its members and staff quickly lose interest in the issues addressed by the commission (Popper, 1970). Thus, if there is to be long-term pressure on Congress, state legislatures, or the private sector to adopt commission recommendations, it must come from organized groups that have a vested interest in commission recommendations. It must be admitted, of course, that commission resources are usually limited, and many commissions may need to use all their resources to produce a high-quality report.

Perhaps the most original and effective approach to creating a constituency to support commission recommendations was used by the Crime Commission (President's Commission on Law Enforcement, 1967). Realizing that any reform of police departments, the courts, or correction facilities would require substantial cooperation from state and local officials, the Crime Commission awarded grants of $25,000 for the creation of state planning committees. About half the states applied for and were awarded these grants. These committees, then, served to "involve states and localities in the concerns of the Commission and prepare them to continue the work of the Commission" (Ohlin, 1975, p. 112).

Third, commissions should include one or two U.S. Senators and Representatives, plus policymakers at the state and local level, who can provide leadership for the enactment of commission recommendations. These policymakers should be selected on the basis of two criteria: a history of interest in the problem and political influence. The former criterion will insure that the policymaker is motivated to carry on the commission's work and convince colleagues that commission recommendations are important; the latter criterion will increase the probability that the policymaker can take effective action—such as scheduling committee hearings, getting powerful floor sponsors for the legislation, and providing leadership to get bills out of committee and through the congressional maze.

Fourth, especially in the case of commissions that make many recommendations, the commission report must clearly indicate priorities among the recommendations. Thus, commissions could indicate the few—not more than three or four—recommendations that should be immediately enacted. The choice of recommendations for immediate priority would be based on judgments about the relative importance of the recommendation in attacking the problem and on the feasibility of enactment and implementation. The remainder of the recommendations, then, would be proposed for long-term action.

The fifth measure commissions should take to increase the likelihood of intermediate impact is to provide estimates of the cost of each recommendation. Ideally, the commission should provide estimates of both costs and benefits for each recommendation, thereby discovering whether each recommendation would actually produce benefits that exceeded its costs—and in the process producing a powerful argument in support of implementing the recommendation. However, because data requisite to benefit–cost analysis are not always available, and because the process of producing benefit–cost figures for every recommendation may prove impractical, commissions should attempt to produce cost estimates for all their recommendations, and benefit–cost estimates for their most important recommendations.

Ultimate Impact

Even should legislative or administrative action based on commission recommendations be achieved, analysts still should not judge the commission a success. As any number of examples would show, legislation does not always have its intended effect, and indeed some legislation seems to produce no measurable effects at all. Thus, in order to evaluate the effectiveness of commissions as a tool of public policy formulation, we must attempt to measure whether their recommendations have the intended effects at the local level.

As it turns out, this criterion of commission success is quite stringent. Nonetheless, the main order of business for commissions—as it is for any individual or group who would use government to promote the general welfare—is to select those policies that will be efficacious in solving the problem at hand.

Although there have been few studies that examine the implementation and effect of commission recommendations, such studies as do exist have produced information that highlights the need for long-term follow-up of commission impact. One such study was conducted by the Committee on Expenditures in the Executive Department (1949). This committee of 13 U.S. Senators was appointed to report to the Congress on progress in implementing the recommendations of the Hoover Commission (Commission on Organization of the Executive Branch, 1949).

As outlined in Table 1, President Truman had selected the Hoover Commission to propose organizational changes in the executive branch of the federal government. This commission of 12 distinguished men—including former President Hoover, future Secretary of State Dean Acheson, Senators Aiken and McClelland, and future Secretary of Defense Forrestal—supervised the work of a large staff organized into 24 teams. The commission produced 19 reports including a summary report. These reports—which dealt with such topics as records management, departmental management, budgeting and accounting activities, federal regulatory commissions, and organization of the various executive departments—proposed what is essentially the current structure of the federal government and many of the basic practices by which the government conducts its routine business.

It should be noted that the Hoover Commission had many of the characteristics that I have argued are essential to a commission that produces high intermediate impact. In particular, the commission was appointed by a president who wanted to take immediate action on the problem addressed by the commission, it was widely believed that the historical situation demanded some type of government reorganization, and the commission included a number of powerful political leaders from the Congress who in fact participated in translating commission recommendations to legislative and administrative action.

Not surprisingly, these conditions led quickly to implementation of most commission recommendations. Indeed, a mere 6 months after publication of the commission report, the bipartisan Committee on Expenditures (1949, pp. 2–3) was able to report that approximately 80% of the commission's 281 recommendations had been considered by the appropriate agency and most of these had been implemented.

A second example of follow-up evaluation of commission ultimate impact is provided by a careful examination of the Crime Commission (President's Commission on Law Enforcement, 1967) conducted 5 years after the commission report was published. Written by James Vorenberg (1972), who had been executive director of the Crime Commission staff, this evaluation underlines the importance of distinguishing between the intermediate and ultimate impact of commissions. It will be recalled that the Crime Commission was notably successful in having its recommendations implemented by legislative action. Upon receipt of the commission report, President Johnson had promptly submitted legislation—some of which had been written by commission staff—to the Congress. In 1968 the Safe Streets Act became law, and several hundred million dollars began to flow to the states in support of a national war on crime. Without question, the Crime Commission had achieved a level of intermediate impact enjoyed by very few commissions. As Vorenberg (1972) notes:

"Even those of us who had two years earlier been a bit cynical about the reasons for the Commission's creation and doubtful about what it would accomplish were optimistic" (p. 63).

Nonetheless, in reviewing the Crime Commission's impact at the local level after 5 years, Vorenberg (1972) found an extremely bleak picture. By 1970, the rate of crimes against property had increased 147% in 10 years; crimes of violence had increased 126%. Furthermore, in the first 9 months of 1971, violent crimes and crimes against property were up 10% and 6%, respectively, over the previous year (pp. 63–64). Why?

The Crime Commission had made recommendations for reform in three important parts of the justice system; namely, the police, corrections, and the courts. Moreover, recommendations in each of these areas had been backed by federal legislation and federal money. And yet, Vorenberg found that, although there had been some minor improvements in police departments, there had been virtually no change in the corrections system or the courts. More specifically, there had been little movement toward the commission's goal of reducing the dependence on prisons and increasing the use of community-based alternatives to incarceration; nor had the courts taken action to reduce overloaded dockets and long delays.

Thus, although the Crime Commission had produced remarkable intermediate impact, it had nonetheless produced little ultimate impact. In this respect, the commission must be judged a failure. On close inspection, however, the failure is attributable, not simply to faulty program recommendations, but to inadequate implementation of the recommendations. In Vorenberg's view, the commission had misjudged the feasibility of their recommendations—local bureaucracies were extremely resistant to change, private citizens were hostile to reforms such as use of community-based alternatives for rehabilitation of criminals, and Congress had insisted on block grants to the states which reduced the federal government's power both to control how localities spent money and to press for changes in the criminal justice agencies as a condition of receiving federal funds.

Vorenberg's thoughtful analysis leads me to two conclusions. First, there is no necessary connection between the intermediate and ultimate impact of commissions. Second, by carefully examining what actually happens as recommendations are enacted and implemented, it is often possible to discover why recommendations did not produce their intended effect (see Gallagher, 1981, pp. 62–72).

One final example[2] will again demonstrate the importance of long-term follow-up in evaluating the ultimate impact of commission reports. In 1969, after years of unfocused debate about the role of television violence in the nation's rising crime rates, Senator John Pastore of the

Senate Subcommittee on Communcations asked the Secretary of Health, Education, and Welfare to appoint a committee of distinguished citizens to examine the possibility that television programs had harmful effects on children. Pastore, an influential Senate leader, subsequently expended persistent effort between 1969 and 1972 to determine whether and how TV violence should be controlled.

A committee was appointed by the Surgeon General within days after Senator Pastore's request, and met for the first time in June, 1969. This committee—the Surgeon General's Scientific Advisory Commitee on Television and Social Behavior (1972)—sponsored 23 original research studies. The committee's final report (Surgeon General's, 1972) consisted of five volumes reporting the original research plus a summary volume in which the 12 committee members drew their conclusions about TV and violence. Although crouched in very careful language, the committee did conclude that there was "a preliminary and tentative indication of a causal relation between viewing violence on television and aggressive behavior . . ." (Surgeon General's, 1972, p. 18).

Interestingly, the preliminary impact of the committee report must be counted as one of the greatest of any commission in the past 20 or 30 years—though much of the impact was unfavorable to the committee. Not the least important cause of media attention was the fact that, in forming the committee in 1969, the Surgeon General had asked various organizations—including the national television networks—to, in effect, blackball from a list of 40 names any prospective committee member to whom they objected. NBC and ABC did, in fact, object to a number of names, and these were removed from consideration for committee membership. Furthermore, five people closely associated with, and nominated by, the television industry were placed on the 15-member advisory committee. Subsequently, these membership characteristics led to the widely circulated charge that the committee was stacked in favor of the media.

To further complicate matters, just before release of the final report in January, 1972, the *New York Times* issued a front-page "scoop" on the contents of the report (Gould, 1972). Unfortunately, the headline to the article read: "TV Violence Held Unharmful to Youth." This, of course, was not what the committee report had concluded. As one might imagine, the television networks widely disseminated the *Times* story, which in turn prompted the Surgeon General to call a Washington press conference during which he declared that the report "shows for the first time a causal connection between violence shown on television and subsequent [aggressive] behavior in children" (quoted in Cater & Strickland, 1975, p. 80). During the ensuing uproar, the committee report was discussed in the news and editorial pages of the country's leading news-papers, as well as by the national radio and television networks.

Nor was preliminary impact the end of the committee's influence. Indeed, Senator Pastore conducted thorough hearings on the committee report after it was released and then conducted hearings again about 2 years later (in 1974). The consensus reached after the first set of hear-ings—due in no small part to Senator Pastore's skill in forcing consen-sus—was that TV can produce violent behavior in some children and that some action by government or the networks was therefore probably appropriate. The committee itself, perhaps to its discredit, refused to draw policy implications from its work. Nonetheless, Senator Pastore managed to extract promises for action from the presidents of the major networks, and Dean Burch of the Federal Communications Commission (FCC) assured Senator Pastore that he would use FCC powers to reduce to near zero all needless violence on children's television, and to enhance and diversify the networks' programming for children. Finally, Pastore lobbied heavily, especially with various secretaries of HEW, for the cre-ation of a violence index to furnish information on trends in TV violence.

Thus, the advisory committee's report was at the nexus of several attempts to improve the quality of television generally, and particularly to reduce the level of violence on children's TV. Many factors seemed to favor change in the direction suggested, though not explicitly stated, in the Surgeon General's Report (1972); namely, reducing the level of violence on children's TV. First, a powerful U.S. Senator, who could and did focus considerable media attention on the problem and put government and industry officials under pressure during Senate hear-ings, used the report as "proof" that TV violence caused aggressiveness in at least some children. Second, the report and its conclusions had, by comparison with other commission reports, substantial preliminary impact and were widely discussed.

And yet, critics such as Cater and Strickland (1975) find that the FCC never "adopted a policy statement on children's television pro-gramming" (p. 123), that HEW has made little progress toward devel-oping a violence index, and that there has, in fact, been little decline in the actual level of violence on TV programming. Thus, we are again alerted to the importance of distinctions between levels of commission impact. For this highly publicized and controversial commission pro-duced very little in the way of either intermediate or ultimate impact.

Summary of Commission Impact

Table 2 summarizes the forces that influence each of the three levels of commission impact. Three points will serve to highlight the

TABLE 2: FORCES INFLUENCING THREE LEVELS OF COMMISSION IMPACT ON POLICY

Source of influence[a]	Preliminary impact	Intermediate impact	Ultimate impact
External	Temper of times Presidential support "Newsworthiness" of commission topic	Political mood of the country State of the economy President's commitment to commission recommendations Support from important public figures Support from congressional leaders Support from organized groups	Political mood of the country State of the economy Continuing commitment by oversight committees and agencies
Internal	Succinctness of conclusions and recommendations Recommendations given in priority order and include cost estimates or benefit–cost analysis Amount and attractiveness of pre-final report, news releases, preliminary reports, and hearing Manner of releasing final report	Recommendations given in priority order and include cost estimates or benefit–cost analysis Recommendations stated as legislative proposals Commission members that can provide legislative leadership Degree to which commissions can create or activate supportive constituent groups	Quality of problem analysis and "correctness" of recommendations

[a] External to the commission means those factors over which the commission has no influence; internal to the commission refers to those factors over which it can exert influence or even control.

187

essential message of both Table 2 and the above discussion of commission impact. First, recognizing the existence of three levels of commission impact prompts us to realize that it is improving the status of individual children and families that has been the ultimate goal of most national commissions. In the long run, commissions can be judged successful only when their recommendations have produced positive effects at the local level.

Second, there are many forces that shape the impact of a commission's report that are totally beyond the commission's control: (1) commissions can rarely influence a president's response to their report; (2) the feasibility of their recommendations may be determined in large part by the state of the economy and the political mood of the country at the time their report is released; and (3) their legislative or intermediate impact is controlled to a large extent by the congressional leaders and lobbying groups that support or oppose commission recommendations. But it should not be concluded from the existence of such powerful external forces that the fate of commission recommendations is entirely beyond the commission's control. In fact, there are a number of measures that commissions can take to maximize the probability of impact at each of the three levels. Notable among these are producing a succinct and well-written report, identifying high priority recommendations, producing benefit–cost figures for the high priority recommendations, and attempting to create political support among congressional and other constituencies before termination of the commission's life.

Finally, I would draw attention to the fact that success at the preliminary and intermediate levels bears no *necessary* relationship with ultimate impact. The basic task of any commission is to move the nation toward solution of the social problem they are created to address. Thus, their value as an instrument of public policy hinges on the skill and accuracy with which they analyze the problem and use available evidence to propose policy that can effectively reduce or solve the problem. In this respect, commissions cannot be more successful than the quality of their policy analysis.

THE SELECT PANEL REPORT: PROSPECTS FOR IMPACT

Having reviewed the composition and function of commissions, and having proposed a simple model for measuring commission impact, let us now briefly focus attention on the Select Panel. As I write this paper, it has been less than 9 months since the Select Panel Report was published. Thus, one cannot be at all confident in making judgments about its intermediate and ultimate impact. Nonetheless, I will offer some speculations.

Initial Impact

The Select Panel Report (1981) was released at a press conference attended by Senator Kennedy (chairman of the Senate Subcommittee on Health and Scientific Research), Congressman Waxman (chairman of the House Subcommittee on Health and the Environment), Lisbeth B. Schorr (chairperson of the Select Panel), nearly all members of the Select Panel, and Dr. Julius Richmond (Surgeon General). Media coverage of the press conference was moderate. Although none of the national television networks aired a story about the Panel Report on the evening news, there was fairly widespread coverage by major newspapers. The *Washington Post*, for example, carried a story on page 13 of its main section (Rich, 1980), and the *New York Times* carried stories on both November 30 (Tolchin, 1980) and December 3 (Brody, 1980). In addition, both the United Press International and the Associated Press carried stories about the Select Panel Report that appeared in many daily newspapers around the country.

It seems clear, then, that the Report's initial impact—at least as reflected in media coverage—was fairly substantial. Although the "giant four-volume report," as the *Washington Post* put it, was an intimidating document, the press release prepared by the Select Panel boiled down the Report to five primary recommendations. Their central recommendation, featured in the lead paragraph of the press release, was that all pregnant mothers should be guaranteed prenatal care, that all children should be guaranteed preventive care to age 6, and that family planning should be easily accessible for all families. Further, the Panel estimated that such an expansion of health care would cost about $5 billion above current health expenditures.

This central conclusion emphasized in the press release is clear and straightforward and suggests that if implemented, such programs could well pay for themselves in the long run. Furthermore, given the Proposition 13 climate of reduced government expenditures that has pervaded the country since 1979, the recommendation is bold and controversial. Nonetheless, it did not succeed in producing substantial long-term media interest.

Although I would not wish to charge that the media or the American public is indifferent to children's health, it does seem that children's health has never generated consistent public interest. A few stories about children's health have gained a measure of media attention in the past two decades—especially hunger in the South, lead poisoning, and Medicaid cost overruns—but these issues had special features that made them more attractive to the media. The fact that some families and children in modern America suffer from malnutrition carries a certain shock value—as Senator Hollings discovered in the early 1970s—that makes the story newsworthy. Similarly, lead paint poisoning suggests that landlords in big city slums have little regard for black children who consume paint chips, and Medicaid fiscal abuses can be covered by the media from the perspective of greed and dishonesty on the part of doctors. In short, these "health" stories received media attention for reasons not entirely determined by the public's demand for information about children's health.

My own conclusion, then, is that children's health is not a news story of inherent interest to the American public. This is especially true when the story involves complex solutions rather than a mere expose' of problems. Thus, that the Select Panel Report did not generate long-term media attention is understandable.

Intermediate Impact

As suggested by Table 2, two important factors determining intermediate impact of commission reports are the political and economic mood of the nation. These factors—which comprise conditions such as the party in power, the state of the economy, and levels of unemployment, as well as less tangible conditions such as the public's attitude toward regulation, social programs, and government spending—are ones over which commissions have virtually no control. Unfortunately, these factors are also most important in determining the intermediate success of commission reports. The commissions with greatest intermediate impact have been those that address topics that are part of a national crisis or at least a widely acknowledged problem for which people believe—or can be made to believe—the nation should find a solution. Thus, for example, the Committee on Economic Security (1935), which essentially wrote the Social Security Act of 1935, was appointed and operated during the depths of the Great Depression when both the American public and policymakers were willing to try almost anything. Similarly, the Hoover Commission (Commission on Organization, 1949) reorganized the administrative branch of the federal government after World War II when everyone agreed that the government's tremendous growth during the Depression and World War II necessitated reorganization and new administrative procedures. And the Crime Commission (President's Commission on Law Enforcement, 1967)—the recent commission that has achieved perhaps the greatest intermediate success—issued its report at a time when politicians of both parties were concerned that the courts and prisons were overloaded and inefficient and when increases in crime rates, dramatically reported by the media, had galvanized public opinion into a feeling that something must be done about crime.

Unfortunately, the Select Panel Report has not been issued during an age of political support for new initiatives in child health. In fact, the mood of the nation, and especially its policymakers, has been one of disenchantment with social programs, of opposition to federal authority and interference in families, and of outright hostility to government regulation. These factors, of course, do not give one optimism that the Panel's recommendations will find immediate legislative support.

Further, the commitment of the president to commission recommendations is an important factor that shapes the intermediate impact of commission reports. Thus, to issue a commission report coincident with a change in administrations, even in the best of times, may spell trouble for commission recommendations. But to have issued a report that is in large measure inconsistent with the incoming president's political principles and objectives, as was the fate of the Select Panel, almost insures a minimal intermediate impact for the commission's recommendations.

This line of reasoning leads me to conclude that few if any of the Select Panel recommendations will receive serious congressional attention over the next few years. Having stated this conclusion, however, I would like to offer two caveats. First, a commission report should not be judged solely by the speed with which its recommendations are implemented. One might well argue that there is an inverse relationship between the originality and comprehensiveness of a policy proposal and its political feasibility. Should we conclude from this argument that commissions and other policy advisory bodies should refrain from recommending policies with low feasibility? On the contrary, the history of social policy enactment shows that policy ideas often occupy the public agenda for many years before enjoying the metamorphosis into legislation. In the politics of legislative action, persistence can often produce victory in the long run. Thus, for example, a central recommendation of the Select Panel is what amounts to national health insurance for pregnant women and children under 6. Our nation is not about to pass such a plan, but solid arguments on its behalf—especially arguments of the benefit-cost variety—may hasten the day when we have some program of national health insurance for children.

The second caveat is that in a time of retrenchment on social initiatives, small victories can be important. It would appear, for example, that the Select Panel Report (1981) played some role in convincing the Congress to favor separate block grants for health programs and resisting the Reagan administration proposal to put a cap on Medicaid funding.

Despite these caveats, it does seem fair to argue that the Select Panel could have taken action to increase the intermediate impact of their recommendations. In particular, the Panel could have reduced their number of recommendations (see the analysis by Burnett in Appendix A), placed their recommendations in priority order, and built a strong benefit–cost case for at least three or four central recommendations. In this regard, the focus on child health insurance and family planning demonstrated in the Select Panel's press release is much clearer (see also Select Panel, Vol. I, pp. 192–202) and more easily translated to concrete action than many of the recommendations contained in the Select Panel Report itself. Although the Panel was charged by the Congress with surveying the entire field of maternal and child health, it still should have been possible to indicate a clear priority—accompanied by supporting arguments and data—for only a few recommendations. By so doing, the Panel may have served as a powerful catalyst for individuals and groups interested in legislative action.

Ultimate Impact

It is, of course, far too early to make predictions about the long-term impact of the Select Panel Report. Some feel that the papers commissioned by the Panel and published as Volume IV of its Report will make a lasting contribution to analysis of health policy (Janis, 1980); and nearly everyone seems to agree that the data summaries in Volume III will be widely used by health policy analysts and government officials interested in health.

But in turning to the ultimate impact of the Panel's work on children's health, I see no substantial reason for optimism about the Panel's recommendations. Our nation will have very few federal initiatives in human services policy over the next 4 to 8 years; thus, there appears to be little chance that the Panel's program recommendations will be enacted in the immediate future. As a result, we will not know any time soon whether implementation of Select Panel recommendations would have a beneficial impact on maternal and child health.

On the other hand, two considerations lead me to some moderate optimism about the long-term impact of the Select Panel's work.[3] First, the fact that we now have a report on children's health by a major commission may signal a recognition of the special health needs of children. As Arden Miller (Chap. 2) points out, the health needs of children are often overlooked—and indeed are sometimes directly sacrificed to the health needs of adults. Witness, for example, the fact that in 1975, the average per capita health care expenditures for children, adults, and the aged were $212, $472, and $1,360, respectively (see Davis & Schoen,

1978, Table 3-2). A scholarly assessment of children's health status and suggested reforms in current health policy, then, marks a welcome recognition of children as a population in need of more and better health services. Further, since many other populations are also in need of better health services (as well as other services), a particularly welcome aspect of the Select Panel Report is the repeated argument that basic health services for children and families are a good investment—that the long-term value of improved health and the value of increased human productivity will exceed the initial expenditures. One might wish that the Panel had made this case even more strongly and displayed it even more conspicuously in their Report, but the basic outline is nonetheless there (see Vol. I, pp. 192–202).

A second long-term value of the Select Panel Report is the Panel's emphasis on preventive services, or even more particularly, on making such services universally available. The concept of universally available basic health services, sometimes masquerading as national health insurance, has frequently been endorsed by highly respectable groups and individuals since its approval by the Committee on the Cost of Medical Care in 1932. Universally available health care, like a guaranteed annual income, is a policy ideal that has long been on the public agenda. The modification offered by the Select Panel is, in effect, to have universal care for pregnant women and children. This is a policy proposal that is immediately attractive to advocates of programs for children and could also be supported by advocates of national health insurance as a step toward a federal program with more general coverage.

Of course, this discussion seems rather disconnected from reality at a time when federal support for social programs has been sharply cut, with further cuts almost a certainty. But, due to economic and political forces that seem somewhat beyond our powers of rational analysis, we should expect and plan for a future day when federal programs will once again test our abilities to distribute beneficence. The Select Panel, like most other commissions examined here, can be expected to make a small but real contribution to such beneficence.

FOOTNOTES

[1] I thank Flo Purdie, Kitty Pope, and Amy Glass for their help with library work; Sherree Payne for typing and retyping; Jim Gallagher, Dale Farran, Craig Ramey, Duncan MacRae, Eli Rubinstein, and Arden Miller for their comments on an earlier draft of this manuscript; and Susann Hutaff for editorial assistance. I especially thank Lisbeth Schorr for her careful, incisive criticism of this chapter.

[2] Another interesting study of commission ultimate impact was conducted by Urban America and the Urban Coalition (1970) 1 year after publication of the Kerner Commission Report (National Advisory Commission, 1968). After examining changes in poverty, education, housing, violence, crime, ghetto development, and so on since the Kerner Commission Report was issued, the authors concluded that "a year later, we are a year closer to being two societies, black and white, increasingly separate and scarcely less unequal" (p. 118).

[3] I acknowledge discussions with Lee Schorr and Arden Miller that have influenced my thinking on both these points.

REFERENCES

Advisory Council on Public Welfare. *Having the power, we have the duty: Report to the Secretary of Health, Education, and Welfare.* Washington, D.C.: U.S. Govt. Printing Office, 1966.

Bell, D. Government by commission. *Public Interest*, 1966, 3, 3–9.

Brody, J. E. Child health: Money and a national plan advocated. *New York Times*, December 3, 1980, p. B8.

Cater, D., & Strickland, S. *TV violence and the child: The evolution and fate of the Surgeon General's Report.* New York: Russell Sage Foundation, 1975.

Commission on Obscenity and Pornography. *The report of the commission on obscenity and pornography.* Washington, D.C.: U.S. Govt. Printing Office, 1970.

Commission on Organization of the Executive Branch of the Government. *Concluding report.* Washington, D.C.: U.S. Govt. Printing Office, 1949.

Commission on Population Growth and the American Future. *Population and the American future.* Washington, D.C.: U.S. Govt. Printing Office, 1972.

Committee on the Cost of Medical Care. *Medical care for the American people: The final report on the cost of medical care.* Chicago: Univ. of Chicago Press, 1932.

Committee on Economic Security. *Report to the President.* Washington, D.C.: U.S. Govt. Printing Office, 1935.

Committee on Expenditures in the Executive Department. *Progress on the Hoover Commission recommendations.* Washington, D.C.: U.S. Govt. Printing Office, 1949.

Davis, K., & Schoen, C. *Health and the war on poverty: A ten-year appraisal.* Washington, D.C.: Brookings, 1978.

Drew, E. B. On giving oneself a hotfoot: Government by commission. *Atlantic,* 1968, *221*(5), 45–49.

Epstein, E. J. *Inquest: The Warren Commission and the establishment of truth.* New York: Viking, 1966.

Gallagher, J. J. Models for policy analysis: Child and family policy. In R. Haskins & J. J. Gallagher (Eds.), *Models for analysis of social policy: An introduction.* Norwood, N.J.: Ablex, 1981.

Gould, J. TV violence held unharmful to youth. *New York Times,* January 11, 1972, pp. 1; 75.

Haskins, R., & Gallagher, J. J. *Models for analysis of social policy: An introduction.* Norwood, N.J.: Ablex, 1981.

Janis, J. *The legacy of the past two decades: Implications for child health programs and policies in the 80's.* Paper presented at the Bush Center in Child Development and Social Policy, Yale Univ., New Haven, Ct., May 1980.

Larsen, O. N. The Commission on Obscenity and Pornography: Form, function, and failure. In M. Komarovsky (Ed.), *Sociology and public policy: The case of presidential commissions.* New York: Elsevier, 1975.

MacRae, D., & Haskins, R. Models for policy analysis. In R. Haskins & J. J. Gallagher (Eds.), *Models for analysis of social policy: An introduction.* Norwood, N.J.: Ablex, 1981.

MacRae, D., & Wilde, J. A. *Policy analysis for public decisions.* North Scituate, Mass.: Duxbury Press, 1979.

National Advisory Commission on Civil Disorders. *Report of the National Advisory Commission on Civil Disorders.* Washington, D.C.: U.S. Govt. Printing Office, 1968.

National Commission on the Causes and Prevention of Violence. *To establish justice, to insure domestic tranquility.* Washington, D.C.: U.S. Govt. Printing Office, 1969.

Ohlin, L. E. Report on the President's Commission on Law Enforcement and Administration of Justice. *Sociology and public policy: The case of presidential commissions.* New York: Elsevier, 1975.

Popper, F. *The president's commissions.* New York: Twentieth Century Fund, 1970.

President becomes master of Congress. *New York Times,* July 30, 1981, pp. 1, D21.

President's Commission on the Assassination of President Kennedy. *Report of the President's Commission on the Assassination of President John F. Kennedy.* Washington, D.C.: U. S. Govt. Printing Office, 1964.

President's Commission on Income Maintenance Programs. *Poverty amid plenty: The American paradox.* Washington, D.C.: U.S. Govt. Printing Office, 1969.

President's Commission on Law Enforcement and Administration of Justice. *The challenge of crime in a free society.* Washington, D.C.: U.S. Govt. Printing Office, 1967.

President's Panel on Mental Retardation. *A proposed program for national action to combat mental retardation.* Washington, D.C.: U.S. Govt. Printing Office, 1962.

Rich, S. Guaranteed complete health care urged for pregnant women, children under 6. *Washington Post,* December 3, 1980, p. A13.

Select Panel for the Promotion of Child Health. *Better health for our children: A national strategy* (4 Vols.). Washington, D.C.: U.S. Govt. Printing Office, 1981.

Short, J. F. The National Commission on the Causes and Prevention of Violence: Reflections on the contributions of sociology and sociologists. In M. Komarovsky (Ed.), *Sociology and public policy: The case of presidential commissions.* New York: Elsevier, 1975.

Stokey, E., & Zeckhauser, R. *A primer for policy analysis.* New York: Norton, 1978.

Surgeon General's Scientific Advisory Committee on Television and Social Behavior. *Television and social behavior: Reports and papers* (6 Vols.). Washington, D.C.: U.S. Govt. Printing Office, 1972.

Tolchin, M. More health funds for children urged. *New York Times,* November 30, 1980, p. 35.

Urban America, & Urban Coalition. *One year later: An assessment of the nation's response to the crisis described by the National Advisory Commission on Civil Disorders.* New York: Praeger, 1970.

Vorenberg, J. The war on crime: The first five years. *Atlantic,* 1972, 229(5), 63–69.

Walker, D. *Rights in conflict: Report to the National Commission on the Causes and Prevention of Violence.* New York: Bantam Books, 1968.

Witte, E. E. *The development of the Social Security Act.* Madison, Wisc.: Univ. of Wisconsin Press, 1962.

Ziegler, L. H., & Peak, G. W. *Interest groups in American society* (2nd ed.). New York: Prentice Hall, 1972.

APPENDIX A

SUMMARY AND CRITIQUE OF THE SELECT PANEL'S RECOMMENDATIONS

CHARLES K. BURNETT

The four volumes of the Select Panel Report (1981) contain the most comprehensive survey to date of the health status of mothers and children in the United States. Volumes I and II present the Panel's findings and recommendations, while Volumes III and IV are devoted to health-related data and background papers, respectively. This appendix will focus on Volume I of the Report: *Major Findings and Recommendations*. After a brief discussion of the structure and substance of the Report and a description of the method used to identify and classify the Panel's major recommendations, precis of the recommendations are listed in tabular form and discussed. Recommendations specific to the five federal programs dealt with in Volume II are not included because, for the most part, they were covered in Volume I.

The Select Panel was created by Congress in 1978. Consistent with the mandate given similar commissions and panels in the past, the Select Panel was asked to "formulate specific goals with respect to the promotion of the health status of children and expectant mothers in the

United States" and to "develop a comprehensive national plan for achieving these goals" (Vol. I, p. 448). As has been the case with many previous commissions, however, many of the Panel's recommendations lack the specificity to allow their direct translation into legislative proposals (see Chap. 11). The current political climate notwithstanding, the number and generality of the Panel's recommendations would seem to reduce the likelihood of their implementation.

Stylistically, the Report's mixture of a large number of explicit and implicit recommendations inhibits the reader's ability to understand precisely what the Panel believes should be done. With the exception of the 65 summary recommendations presented in the synopsis of Volume I, the Panel's recommendations were embedded in some 350 pages of text. The 235 recommendations identified by the analysis summarized here were usually italicized, offset by bullets, or explicitly labeled. Certain other statements, similar in form or content to the explicit recommendations, were identified as recommendations in the volume's index while others were not. The Panel would have performed a much more valuable service had it made all of its recommendations explicit and easily distinguishable from the text of the report.[1]

The substance of the recommendations was divided into 12 major areas by the Panel. In contrast, this analysis used 21 categories for classifying the most salient substantive area addressed by each recommendation. While it was usually apparent what topic or area was the focus of a particular recommendation, many recommendations were vague or unclear. For example, on page 262 (Vol. I) the Panel states:

> We therefore recommend that policymakers and health care providers assign high priority to organizational reforms designed to achieve better integration of mental and general health care, and better coordination of the mental health system with other service systems including education, corrections, and social services.

This recommendation, while primarily concerned with mental health and placed by the Panel in a mental health section of the Report, also involves issues of general health care, education, corrections, and social services. Furthermore, the recommendation leaves unclear what policymakers, which providers, what kinds of organizational reforms, and what types of integration are meant. Similarly, on page 230 (Vol. I), the Panel recommends that "an awareness of the central role of the family in all aspects of maintaining child health must permeate the activities and organization of primary care units." Again, the recommendation mentions families, the maintenance of child health, the activities of primary care units, and the organization of primary care units. What this "awareness" of families means, how it is to be implemented, and by whom are not mentioned.

Despite the lack of specificity in topic and assignment of responsibility, most of the Panel's recommendations appear reasonable and potentially beneficial. On closer inspection, however, the utility of many of the recommendations is reduced by the fact that guidelines or suggestions for implementation are absent. Several recommendations, on the other hand, present concise and specific information. For example, the Panel recommends that:

> DHHS [Department of Health and Human Services], in developing regulations to implement P.L. 96-272, the Adoption Assistance and Child Welfare Act of 1980, require (sic) that care plans for children in foster care include a statement of the child's health needs, the health services being provided, and the agencies or individuals responsible for providing needed services. (Select Panel, Vol. I, p. 311)

This recommendation deals exclusively with P.L. 96-272, specifies that DHHS is responsible for its implementation, and clearly indicates that a statement of child health status be included in foster care plans. While this kind of crisp, straightforward recommendation would be most likely to lead to action, it is also most vulnerable to obsolescence. Rapidly shifting program structures and political inclinations often set policy without regard to well-reasoned suggestions for improvement. The Panel, faced with the choice between specificity and generality, apparently opted for the latter.

Early in the Report, the Panel stated that they "must be cost-conscious as well as compassionate" (Vol. I, p. 2). Perhaps, however, the Panel's position on cost considerations is best summed up by their assertion that "children matter for themselves, that childhood has its own intrinsic value, and that society has an obligation to enhance the lives of children today, quite apart from whether we can prove later benefits in adulthood" (Vol. I, p. 2). Although this is a noble sentiment, it may prove unwise to assume that improvements in the health of mothers and children will arise out of altruistic motives regardless of the cost involved. The vast majority of the Panel's recommendations would cost money—in some instances a great deal of money. To take only one example, the Panel recommends free comprehensive health care for all mothers and children in the United States without careful consideration of the cost involved or the mechanism to be used for raising the necessary funds. Other recommendations suggest expansion or increased funding of existing programs. Acknowledging the complexity of assessing cost–benefit or even cost–effectiveness of the various services addressed by the Panel, some economic criterion is necessary for informed decision-making. At the very least, the Panel should have provided cost estimates to accompany its recommendations.

Related to the sparsity of cost considerations is the Panel's decision not to prioritize its recommendations. The Panel provides little guidance as to which of its 235 recommendations should receive immediate implementation or which could be deferred. Without data on cost or the relative importance of its proposals, the Report suggests a myriad of ways to improve maternal and child health by restructuring the entire health care system in the United States. Indeed, the Panel's proposals extend beyond the health care system into environmental protection, safety, education, and business. The Panel should not be faulted for fulfilling its mandate to develop a comprehensive plan, but without an implementation strategy which considers the economic, political, and social constraints on its recommendations, the Report is a catalogue of what could be done, not what can and should be done, when, by whom, and at what cost.

The recommendations included in this analysis were taken from Volume I of the Select Panel Report (1981). All explicitly labeled recommendations and implied recommendations, if they were listed in the "Index to Recommendations" of Volume I, were analyzed. Explicit recommendations were statements by the Panel which included the words "recommend," "recommends," or "recommendation," and which were offset from the text by italics or bullets. Implicit recommendations were often italicized and took the form of action-oriented statements, frequently including the words "believe," "urge," or "should," with the Panel named or implied as the source of the statement. Where recommendations contained several closely related subparts, the subrecommendations were designated by letter, listed below the major recommendation, and not counted as separate recommendations. Due to the difficulty of determining which implicit recommendations were actually intended by the Panel to be taken as recommendations, it is likely that some errors of commission or omission have been introduced by this analysis.

Four classification variables were used to categorize the recommendations: (1) topic; (2) whether they were explicit or implicit; (3) who would be responsible for implementing the recommendation, i.e., the level of government or the private sector; and (4) whether the recommendation involved a new program or revision or expansion of an ongoing program. Categorization of *topics* was based on the predominant substantive area addressed by each recommendation. Many recommendations made reference to more than one area, but I have nonetheless classified them according to the primary topical category they seemed to address. The categories were derived by first listing the topics covered by each of the recommendations, then clustering recommendations with similar major content. Recommendations which did not readily fit into established clusters were placed in a "Miscellaneous" category. As mentioned above, recommendations were coded as *explicit* when the words: "recommend," "recommends," or "recommendation" were used; other recommendations were *implicit*.

Level of *responsibility for implementation* was defined as the sector of the economy specified by the Panel as responsible for carrying out a given recommendation. Public sector units were coded as federal, state, or local; and community groups, businesses, practitioners, and citizens were coded as private sector. Where responsibility for implementation could not be determined from the text, the recommendation was coded as "Unclear." For the *type of initiative*, recommendations which suggested modifications to existing programs or practices were coded as "Old," proposals for novel programs or practices were coded as "New," and those which did not clearly reference either extant or new initiatives were coded as "Unclear." Neither the classifications for level of responsibility or type of initiative were mutually exclusive categories since several recommendations specified more than one level of one or both of these variables. The summary of recommendations, grouped by topic, is presented in Table 1 (immediately following this chapter).

Excluding the Panel's 65 summary recommendations, 235 recommendations were identified. Approximately half (49%) of the recommendations were explicit, while the remaining 51% were implicit. Classification according to predominant topic resulted in 21 topical categories containing from 2 to 28 recommendations each. Level of responsibility for implementation was assigned by the Panel to the federal government in 43% of the recommendations, to the states in 20%, to local governments in 7%, and to the private sector in 6%. Unclear assignment of responsibility characterized 45% of the recommendations. New initiatives were proposed in 28% of the recommendations, modifications of existing programs or practices were suggested in 11%, and 64% of the recommendations were unclear as to type of initiative. The totals for level of responsibility and type of initiative add to more than 100% since some recommendations specified more than one level of one or both variables.

A closer examination of the variables by which the recommendations were classified provides additional insight into the substance of the Panel's recommendations. Table 2 presents the number of recommendations per category and the percentage of recommendations falling into each level of the three classification variables.

Beginning with number of recommendations, the seven topics most frequently addressed by the Panel were (in rank order): Collaboration, Cooperation and Consolidation; Nutrition; Research and Data Needs; Planning and Evaluation; Primary and Comprehensive Care;

TABLE 2: CLASSIFICATION OF RECOMMENDATIONS BY EXPLICITNESS, LEVEL OF RESPONSIBILITY FOR IMPLEMENTATION, AND TYPE OF INITIATIVE

Category[a]	Explicit recommendations	Level of responsibility[b]					Type of initiative[b]		
		Federal	State	Local	Private	Unclear	Old	New	Unclear
Environmental hazards, accident prevention, and safety (8)	38	88	38	50	38	13	75	88	13
Mental health (2)	100	0	0	0	0	100	0	0	100
Health education and information (7)	57	43	14	29	43	57	86	29	14
Nutrition (26)	50	38	15	4	12	46	8	12	81
Primary and comprehensive care (19)	37	32	21	5	0	53	11	11	79
Collaboration, cooperation, and consolidation (28)	39	32	14	7	4	50	0	29	71
Hospitals (18)	17	11	0	0	0	89	6	6	89
Public schools and day care (8)	38	25	75	0	0	25	13	25	63
Health care financing (14)	14	64	14	7	7	29	7	50	43
Training (8)	63	0	0	0	0	100	13	13	75
Family planning (3)	100	33	33	0	0	67	33	0	67
Dental care (4)	50	25	25	25	0	75	0	0	100
Adolescents and juvenile offenders (10)	60	30	30	20	0	70	0	10	90
Chronically ill and handicapped children (9)	67	11	44	0	0	56	0	0	100
Foster care (5)	80	80	20	0	0	0	0	40	60

TABLE 2: CLASSIFICATION OF RECOMMENDATIONS BY EXPLICITNESS, LEVEL OF RESPONSIBILITY FOR IMPLEMENTATION, AND TYPE OF INITIATIVE

Category[a]	Explicit recommendations	Level of responsibility[b]					Type of initiative[b]		
		Federal	State	Local	Private	Unclear	Old	New	Unclear
Nonphysician providers (3)	33	33	0	0	0	67	0	33	67
Research and data needs (22)	86	64	5	0	0	32	5	55	41
Minorities, migrants, and immigrants (7)	29	71	29	0	0	14	14	14	71
Planning and evaluation (19)	53	63	37	5	0	11	0	53	47
Medicaid (5)	80	100	20	0	0	0	0	60	40
Miscellaneous (10)	40	50	20	20	20	40	20	20	60

[a] Numbers in parentheses are the number of recommendations in each category.
[b] All column entries are percentages. Category percentages sum to more than 100 because they are not mutually exclusive. This is especially true for recommendations with subcomponents that were assigned to different levels of responsibility and were different types of initiatives.

Hospitals; and Health Care Financing. Those least frequently mentioned were: Mental Health; Nonphysician Providers; Family Planning; Foster Care; and Medicaid. Although many recommendations included several topics, the primary thrust of the report, as measured by frequency of recommendations, appears to have been the structure, planning, organization, financing, and evaluation of primary care and nutrition services for pregnant women and children. By contrast, the Panel mentioned, but placed less emphasis on (at least in number of recommendations), ancillary services, nonphysician providers, and special populations in need of services typically provided outside the primary care system. The small number of Medicaid recommendations may reflect the more detailed discussion of that federal program in Volume II.

Although few in number, the Mental Health and Family Planning recommendations were all explicit; that is, labeled as recommendations and offset from the text. Other categories containing relatively high proportions of explicit recommendations were: Research and Data Needs; Medicaid; Foster Care; Chronically Ill and Handicapped Children; and Training. Categories with high proportions of implicit recommendations included: Health Care Financing; Hospitals; Minorities, Migrants, and Immigrants; Nonphysician Providers; Primary and Comprehensive Care; Public Schools and Day Care; and Collaboration, Cooperation, and Consolidation. While the greatest number of recommendations dealt with structural aspects of the health care system, the Panel, with the exception of the category of Research and Data Needs, was less explicit in these areas than in the categories containing fewer recommendations.

Where it was possible to discern a clear assignment of responsibility for implementing its recommendations, the Panel favored the federal government. In 12 of the categories a predominant federal role was indicated. The states, on the other hand, received major responsibility for only two categories: Public Schools and Day Care, and Chronically Ill and Handicapped Children. A federal–state partnership was suggested for Family Planning, and division of responsibility among federal, state, and local governments was indicated in the areas of Dental Care and Adolescents and Juvenile Offenders. Interestingly, Health Education and Information was seen as a major federal and private sector responsibility. In general, the Panel did not assign much responsibility to the private sector or to local governments for implementing its recommendations. The major exception to this generalization was the area of Environmental Hazards, Accident Prevention, and Safety where a collective effort was suggested.

Classification of the Panel's recommendations as "old" or "new" was quite difficult because many recommendations could have implied new initiatives, modifications to existing programs or policies, or the more widespread application of practices currently in limited use. New initiatives, however, were frequently proposed in the categories of Collaboration, Cooperation, and Consolidation; Health Care Financing; Foster Care; Research and Data Needs; Planning and Evaluation; and Medicaid. Modifications of existing practices were stressed in the areas of Health Education and Information and Family Planning.

Consistent with its mandate, then, the Panel apparently focused most of its attention on the structural and organizational role of the federal government in planning, evaluating, and financing primary and comprehensive maternal and child health care. The rather limited roles proposed for state and local governments, possibly reflecting the Panel's mandate and the political climate within which the Panel was formed, seem somewhat inconsistent with President Reagan's New Federalism.

FOOTNOTE

[1] I am informed by Panel Staff that the decision not to make the recommendations stand out from the text was made in the interest of increasing the readability of Volume I.

REFERENCE

Select Panel for the Promotion of Child Health. *Better health for our children: A national strategy* (4 Vols.). Washington, D.C.: U.S. Govt. Printing Office, 1981.

TABLE 1:	SUMMARY OF SELECT PANEL RECOMMENDATIONS BY CA-
		TEGORY[a]

Environmental hazards, accidents prevention, and safety

1.	Motor vehicle safety (F,S,L,P/O,N/E/82)
	Independent and collaborative effort to improve motor vehicle safety for children and
	pregnant women
		• involving parents/schools/corporate leaders/labor leaders/health care person-
			nel/private organizations/policymakers
	A.	Encourage use of automobile restraint systems for children from infancy on
	B.	Further efforts by manufacturers to develop inexpensive and effective child re-
		straint systems
	C.	National Highway Traffic Safety Administration should strengthen child motor
		vehicle safety
		• resist delays for requiring passive restraints
		• mandate proven safety technology unless manufacturers voluntarily act
			within next 5 years
		• intensify efforts in next 5 years to specify child passenger safety standards
	D.	State authorities should:
		• review and adopt if indicated, state mandatory child restraint laws
		• require car leasing agencies to provide free child car seats
		• enforce 55 mph speed limit
		• enact/enforce helmet laws and helmet/licensing for mopeds
2.	Home and neighborhood accident prevention (F,S,L,P/O,N/E/86)
	Develop and promote broad policies of home and community accident prevention
	for children
		• involving public authorities/corporate leaders/labor leaders/professional or-
			ganizations/private organizations/schools/parents
	A.	Local governments should upgrade housing and building codes
		• state governments should provide incentives for home safety
	B.	Fully implement and broaden federal efforts to reduce child asbestos exposure
	C.	Consumer Product Safety Commission should require child-proof caps
	D.	Local/state organizations should develop child–parent consciousness-raising
		campaigns on minimizing child accidents
	E.	DHHS should promote dissemination of universal danger symbol for children
		2 and older
	F.	Congress should ban handguns except for police, military and pistol clubs
		• until banned, disseminate child and adolescent gun safety protection stand-
			ards
3.	Recreational facilities/space/programs should promote appropriate exercise and min-
	imize accidents (L,U/U/I/87)
	A.	Require urban planners and architects to consider recreational impact of new
		urban construction
		• include child/youth recreation as part of environmental impact statements
	B.	Boards of Education should consider physical education and recreation essential
		and work with parents and local governments to provide recreation in and out
		of school
	C.	Proper supervision/protective equipment/sports safety education for organized
		sports
	D.	Greater attention to and financing for improved contact-sport safety equipment

E.   Expand swimming and water safety classes/strengthen state and local laws on pool and water safety

4.   Develop broad federal child accident prevention strategy (F,S,L,P/O,N/I/88)
  •   involve MCH authorities in DHHS in cooperation with other DHHS department/other federal agencies/regional/state/local/parents

  A.   Establish national and state/regional policy-oriented epidemiological data base on accidents/poisoning/injuries

  B.   Computerized information network and increased information capacity of centralized accident and poison-control centers

  C.   Congressional funding for accident prevention under Emergency Medical Care networks

  D.   Congressional mandate to Secretary of DHHS to assess and expand Bureau of Community Health Services, accident control demonstration projects

  E.   Accident prevention should be an integral part of all federally funded primary health care programs

5.   Minimal federal legislative, regulatory, and administrative steps to address chemical and radiation hazards (F/N/I/94)

  A.   Congress should legislate and appropriate funds for public–corporate partnership to clean up chemical dump sites
    •   priority to sites with imminent risk to pregnant women and children
    •   EPA establish monitoring system and risk indicators under P.L. 94-469 (Toxic Substances Control Act, 1976)

  B.   Premarket tests and exposure/ingestion tolerances for pesticides for infants/children/pregnant women

  C.   EPA should give special attention to pesticides levels for migrant and other rural families

  D.   Comprehensive national policy for removing lead and educating parents should be developed by DHHS, HUD, EPA, DOE, and other federal–state agencies

  E.   FDA should establish national guidelines for x-ray exposures
    •   providers should protect patients from unnecessary x-rays and educate patients

  F.   OSHA & NIOSH should collaborate with federal/state/professional organizations on comprehensive reproduction hazards policy

6.   FDA establishment of food safety research priorities (F/O,N/I/97)

  A.   FDA development of coherent national drug testing and research policy

  B.   Further work on nutritional imbalances and toxic exposures in food
    •   exploration of implications for more coherent national policy

  C.   New research on communicating safety/nutrition information
    •   also labeling policies

  D.   More intensive investigation of relationship between food and child behavior/school performance/adaptation

7.   FDA should collaborate with other federal, state and local agencies to inform them of drug and food hazards (F/O,N/E/98)

  A.   Expand drug-labeling to nonprescription drugs
    •   special attention to sensitivities of children/pregnant women
    •   collaborate with alcohol, tobacco, firearms/other federal agencies/industry/professions

8.   Availability of clean and healthful community water supplies (F/O,N/I/101)

  A.   Federal assistance to states and communities for fluoridation
    •   if community not fluoridated, schools should be

B. Collaboration of state and federal agencies initiated by PHS to correct inadequate water systems

C. Federal funding for national study of diseases from contaminated water

Mental health

1. Mental health services for chronically ill and handicapped children should be readily available through Community Mental Health Services Act and other public and private sources in settings where children may be found (health settings, schools, etc.) (U/U/E/305)

2. Families of chronically ill and handicapped children should have access to wide range of psychosocial support services (U/U/E/306)

Health education and information

1. Greater emphasis in health care settings on education/guidance/counseling for health promotion and prevention (U/O/E/128)
   A. Counseling and education component in family planning services
   B. Counseling and anticipatory guidance on behavioral risk in all prenatal care
   C. Increased availability of childbirth education with special efforts for low-income and high-risk women
   D. Increased emphasis on parent education/guidance/counseling in prenatal and infancy periods
   E. Priority given to preadolescent and adolescent health education/counseling/guidance

2. Federal policymakers adopt broad national strategy to stimulate health education and counseling within health care (F,U/O/O/129)
   A. MCH authorities in DHHS should expand educational functions and dissemination by the department/media/voluntary organizations/providers
   B. Standards and monitoring of federally supported health programs should reflect importance of counseling and education for parents/children/adolescents
   C. Further support through federal programs and policies to education and counseling
   D. Include training in counseling/guidance/education in all professional training and disseminate information by DHHS/private foundations/professional associations/certifying bodies
   E. Increased emphasis on counseling/guidance/education in professional continuing education

3. Public education at all levels should make strong commitment to health education/promotion (L,U/U/I/130)
   A. Health education should be essential component of curricula at all grade levels
   B. School boards, superintendents and principals should ensure health education cooperation of personnel/parents/community health resources
   C. Physical education programs should foster self-esteem and competence with exercise/lifetime fitness/health maintenance and team sports
   D. Adequate teacher training in curricula/methods/materials prior to certification
   E. School personnel should be encouraged by school boards/superintendents/principals to seek relevant preparation and continuing education
   F. Parents should play active role in school sex education and education within the family

4. Strengthened federal leadership in health education (F/O,N/E/132)

A.   Adequate appropriations for School Health Education Program (P.L. 95-561, part 1)
B.   Increased support for Office of Comprehensive School Health
C.   Strong interagency coordination
D.   Incentives for state and regional education agencies to employ health education professionals for coordination and administration
E.   Strengthen health education in Head Start and other preschool programs through guidelines/dissemination/monitoring
5.   Parents/communities/advocacy groups counter media pressures to adopt deleterious behaviors (P,U/O/E/134)
A.   Continue and broaden dialogue with networks and provide accurate information to TV industry
B.   Assist in development of critical viewing skills
C.   Encourage parents to monitor TV viewing and provide alternatives to children
D.   Promote endorsement of health behaviors by celebrities to children and adolescents
6.   Federal/state/foundation policymakers should strengthen role of TV in promoting health (F,S,P/O,N/I/134)
A.   Increased research and periodic national reports on effects of TV and programming on children
B.   Adequate children's programming for license renewal
C.   Reestablish FTC authority to investigate and regulate children's TV advertising and programming
D.   Continuation of education programs and federal support for new programs
E.   More health public-service announcements during children's prime time
F.   Media campaigns, e.g., special health risks to pregnant women
7.   Voluntary associations and community agencies renew efforts for community-based parent education (L,P/O/I/137)
A.   Increase availability of support groups and networks
B.   Increase industry/organizations/school cooperation for health content and job training and recreation in adolescent community programs
C.   Increase use of Cooperative Extension Program of Dept. of Agriculture to reach rural families

---

Nutrition

---

1.   Federal leadership in nutrition education including norms for appropriate nutrition (F/U/I/155)
2.   Comprehensive school-based health education including major emphasis on nutrition and development of curricula and materials (U/U/E/155)
3.   USDA/DHHS/Dept. of Education/state/foundations collaborate on development and evaluation of school nutrition curricula (F,S,P/U/E/155)
4.   The Expanded Food and Nutrition Education Program and the Nutrition Education and Training Program should design programs consistent with established principles of nutrition, information, and education (F/U/I/157)
5.   Employers and providers should encourage breast feeding (P/U/I/157)
6.   Major manufacturers/distributors/marketers of food ensure availability of nutritious food and nutrition education (P/U/I/158)
A.   Vending machines, especially in schools, should provide nutritious foods
B.   Supermarkets should educate for sound nutrition principles

    C. Restaurants should provide adequate, nutritional foods

7. Public and private sector health care policies should ensure provision of nutrition services (U/U/E/159)

8. Providers should include patients' nutritional needs in health care services and coordinate with community nutrition services/professionals (U/U/I/159)

9. Provider training should include basic principles of nutrition (U/U/I/159)

10. Social services/teachers/day care staff, etc., should receive nutrition training and continuing education (U/U/I/159)

11. Public and private third-party payers reorient financing policies to reflect importance of MCH nutrition services (U/U/I/161)

12. Regulations and support for Title V should sustain and strengthen eligibility and provision of nutrition services (F/U/E/162)

13. Collecting of more specific information on recipients, staffing, impact, and cost-effectiveness of Title V nutrition services (U/U/E/162)

14. Monitoring by HCFA of state implementation of EPSDT nutritional assessment guidelines (F/N/E/163)

15. Title XIX should reimburse appropriate nutrition services (U/N/E/163)

16. States should develop cooperative arrangements with WIC and other programs for referral (S/U/E/163)

17. State and local authorities should extend Head Start nutritional model through linkages with other community services and day care centers (S,L/U/E/163)

18. Enlarge (over the long run) WIC to serve all eligible women, infants, and children (F/O/E/166)

19. MCH programs should be expanded and incentives provided for collaboration with WIC for nutrition services (U/U/I/166)

20. Strengthen state and local health care systems through additional funding of MCH programs under Title V and Medicaid/EPSDT for Nutrition Services (F/U/E/166)

21. The Food Stamp program should be expanded both in number served and benefit levels (F/O/E/168)

22. Continued support for school breakfast/lunch programs and state encouragement of local support for breakfast programs (F,S/U/E/169)

23. (Over time) commodity supplemental food program should become more closely related to provision of primary and preventive health care services (F/N/I/170)

24. Research to better define and understand children's diet, nutrition, and health status (U/U/I/170)

25. Research to identify behaviors increasing child disease risk and development of effective strategies to change bad nutrition practices (U/U/I/171)

26. Research to better understand and document effects of early feeding on nutrition and development and adult health (U/U/I/171)

Primary and comprehensive care

1. Universal and unconditional access to minimum basic services (U/N/I/192)
- prenatal, delivery and postnatal care
- comprehensive health care for children 0–5
- family planning services

2. Primary care units should provide broad range of psychological and social as well as medical care (U/U/I/226)

3. Primary care units should be accessible in location/transportation/absence of psychological barriers/hours of operation (U/U/I/226)

4. Primary care units should have the capacity for community outreach (U/U/I/226)
5. Primary care units should be locus for coordinating all needed health services (U/U/I/227)
6. Primary care units should encourage strong relationship between patient, family, and practitioner(s) who can provide continuity of care (U/U/I/227)
7. Primary care units should establish collaboration among various health professionals to provide effective service delivery at reasonable costs (U/U/I/227)
8. Primary care units should review process and outcomes of care for quality improvement (accountability) (U/U/I/229)
9. Primary care units should establish systematic connection with consumers to assure responsive services and community support (U/U/I/229)
10. Awareness of central role of family in all aspects of child health must permeate all aspects of primary care (U/U/I/230)
11. Federal and state governments should continue to regard community and migrant health centers /MIC centers/C & Y centers/NHSC personnel as best means for increasing availability and access to primary care (F,S/O/E/240)
12. Congress should increase grant support to these [in 11] primary care centers (F/O/E/240)
13. States should support and expand MIC and C & Y projects (S/U/E/240)
14. DHHS should further develop and facilitate support of comprehensive care centers (F/U/E/240)
15. Priority given by federal/state/local authorities to support of comprehensive health department care rather than individual components of primary care (F,S,L/U/E/246)
16. State health departments and Title V agencies should assist in identifying areas for health department-sponsored comprehensive care centers and foster development or extension of existing services to comprehensive care (S/U/I/246)
17. Primary care for chronically ill and handicapped children should be available as well as necessary specialized care (U/U/E/305)
18. National Health Service Corps should maintain and increase complement of providers for MCH services (F/U/E/402)
19. Policy should be changed to permit placement of NHSC personnel in comprehensive primary care facilities in underserved areas without reimbursement by local agencies (F/N/I/402)

Collaboration, cooperation, and consolidation

1. "Over the long run" individual primary care physicians be encouraged to practice with other physicians and health professionals (including dentists) (U/U/E/232)
2. Better links must be developed between office-based practices and community sources of care and services (U/U/E/232)
3. Public and private funds should be used for demonstrations of encouragement and use of health-related services by office-based practitioners (U/U/I/232)
4. Improved linkages between outpatient departments and community services (U/U/I/235)
5. Facilitation of contractual relationships to link school-based services with medical schools/hospitals/private practices (U/U/I/250)
6. Federal interagency agreements among OHDS, PHS, and HCFA to encourage implementation and find funds for health assessments and follow-up for children not covered by other sources (F/N/E/254)
7. Policymakers and providers assign high priority to organizational reforms to better integrate mental health with general health care and coordinate with other providers (U/U/E/262)

8. Federal/state/professionals/voluntary organizations/hospitals/medical schools/public should support selected regionalized health services for children, newborns, and pregnant women (F,S,L,P/U/I/281)

9. Further development of regionalized perinatal care networks for all high-risk pregnant women and newborns (U/U/I/281)

10. Encourage trend toward regionalized genetic services (U/U/I/281)

11. Extend regionalized networks to improve care for accidents, certain chronic illnesses, and handicaps (U/U/I/281)

12. Support regionalized referral back-up services (U/U/I/281)

13. Develop better methods of communication between medical centers and primary care providers (U/U/I/281)

14. Support improved regionalized ambulance services (U/U/I/281)

15. Each community should designate lead agency to coordinate services to pregnant adolescents and teenage parents, reviewed by state MCH planners (L/N/E/291)

16. All agencies using individual service plan format for chronically ill and handicapped children should coordinate accounting and programmatic requirements with community lead agencies and community teams to coordinate services (U/U/I/307)

17. Greater interagency cooperation in series of cooperative projects for assisting migrant children with DHHS as lead agency and including departments of Agriculture/Education/HUD/Labor/EPA (F/U/I/313)

18. Every state governor's office should review options for consolidating all MCH services and place authority over funding in office of state health unit (S/U/E/349)

19. Title V Crippled Children's Funds should be linked to state MCH authority for data collection, planning, and quality assurance (if not already housed in MCH agency) (S/U/E/350)

20. DHHS should familiarize states with minimal consolidation/coordination with other states' policies and practices for improved consolidation/coordination (F/U/E/350)

21. Joint or concurrent applications and reporting forms for all federal programs (F/N/I/354)

22. Interagency agreements to identify responsibilities, define process, and set time frames for goals (F/N/I/355)

23. Secretary of DHHS establish Maternal and Child Health Administration as agency of Public Health Service [See text for details] (F/N/E/373)

24. Secretary of DHHS give consideration to restructuring HCFA-PHS relationship to ensure HCFA emphasizes health promotion and high quality service as well as efficiency (F/N/E/385)

25. Periodic House and Senate Joint Committee hearings on MCH programs to assess adequacy of program coordination and complementarity (F/N/E/388)

26. Team modes of practice should be encouraged by training and organizational and financial arrangements (U/U/I/395)

27. State or regional systems should be developed to provide clinical and managerial support to MCH care (S/N/I/402)

28. Efforts needed to encourage closer collaboration between public health and private care and preventive and therapeutic services (U/U/I/403)

Hospitals

1. Hospitals should establish primary care centers with help of public and private funds (U/U/I/234)

2. Encouragement of further development of hospital-based group practices (U/U/I/235)

3. Some hospitals should assume responsibility for creation and operation of decentralized, neighborhood primary care centers (U/U/I/235)

4. OPD's and ER's should assure systematic transmittal of medical information to primary care providers and encourage use of primary care providers for those without (U/U/I/235)
5. Grants under section 328 of PHSA should be expanded to support more hospital comprehensive care centers (F/O/I/236)
6. Improved management and efficiency of hospital-based ambulatory care (U/U/I/236)
7. Modified methods of defining and allocating costs within hospitals (U/U/I/236)
8. Hospital commitment to children should be reflected in operating and staffing policies/environmental design/care philosophy (U/U/I/276)
9. Hospitals should encourage, support, and provide accommodations for parents (U/U/I/277)
10. Hospitals should allow parents and siblings to visit hospitalized children at any time (U/U/I/277)
11. Hospitals should make systematic provision for preparing children and parents for major procedures (U/U/I/277)
12. Cost of basic psychosocial care should be included in hospital per diem rate and covered by third-party payers (U/U/I/277)
13. Hospital children's policies should be considered in accreditation and federal loans for hospital construction (F/N/E/277)
14. Hospitals offering obstetric care, if have not already done so should adopt policies to: (U/U/E/278)
    A. Arrange for or sponsor childbirth classes
    B. Permit father or other person in labor room for support
    C. Allow rooming-in of newborn
    D. Maximize contact between newborns and parents, especially intensive care infants
15. All hospitals with emergency rooms which treat children should have specialized equipment, trained staff, and child-sensitive arrangements (U/U/I/279)
16. All ER's should encourage selection and use of regular source of primary care and transmit medical information to primary care providers (U/U/I/279)
17. Enlarged public and private support for children's hospitals as regional centers for specialized care (U/U/I/281)
18. Public, third-party, and charitable funding should encourage hospitals to design systems maximizing homelike settings and hospice care (U/U/E/305)

Public schools and day care

1. All states and federal government should establish preconditions and flexibility to expand school-based primary care (F,S/U/I/250)
2. Adoption of state laws and policies to permit full use of primary care personnel in broad school-based programs (S/N/I/250)
3. Training and support for preschool/day care personnel to ensure immunizations and comprehensive health assessments (U/U/I/252)
4. Training and support for preschool/day care personnel to ensure setting and adherence to safety/nutritional/infection control/accident prevention standards (U/U/I/252)
5. DHHS regulations for preschools and day care centers should be promptly implemented with support for states and Title XX agencies (F,S/O/E/253)
6. State Title XX funds should pay costs of day care center staff time to implement DHHS regulations (S/N/E/253)
7. State health agencies should assist state Title XX agencies and providers to arrange necessary services for children in day care and coordinate with child's other care sources (S/U/E/253)

8. State laws mandating school screening should be modified to assure more than isolated screening including linkage with sources of care (S/U/I/275)

Health care financing

1. New methods of paying for primary care in hospitals developed with public and private demonstration funds (U/N/I/236)
2. Federal authorities should take steps to make enrollment of low-income children and parents more attractive to HMO's (F/U/I/242)
3. Federal grants should be used as partial subsidy for HMO's enrolling low-income clients (F/N/I/242)
4. Medicaid regulations should be waived to allow HMO's to offer same benefit package to low-income clients as others (U/N/I/242)
5. Further efforts to develop realistic models of prospective reimbursement to HMO's for low-income care (U/U/I/242)
6. Further support of demonstrations of Medicaid reimbursement of school-based child health services (U/O/I/250)
7. Health insurance purchasers/public and private payers and providers modify and create alternatives to current reimbursement schemes and encourage their use (F,S,L,P/N/E/322)
   A. Revision of payment schedules and methods to reflect value of counseling and time-intensive primary care and decrease incentives for technical procedures
   B. Various payment methods for service packages such as lump sum, annual, or monthly retainer fees and capitation payments and salaries for providers in organized settings
   C. Reimbursement methods with equal incentives for training professionals in ambulatory and inpatient settings
8. States voluntarily have insurance commissioners review private insurance policies and grant certification for marketing only to those adequately meeting needs of children and pregnant women using criteria from Board of Health Service Standards (S/N/E/326)
9. National health financing program with universal entitlement to all (F/N/I/330)
   A. If not universal, then up to age 18; if not to 18, then to age 5
10. All needed services should, over the long run, be fully covered without cost-sharing (F/N/I/332)
11. Expanded grant programs to subsidize development of resources in geographic areas where services unavailable and finance demonstrations of new service delivery mechanisms (F/U/I/335)
12. Expanded grant programs to pay for needed services more appropriately financed through grants than third-party payers and where more information is needed on best payment method (F/U/I/335)
13. Expanded grant programs to pay for comprehensive services for persons (e.g., handicapped children) with distinct service needs (F/U/I/335)
14. Expanded grant programs to pay for needed services for those lacking other sources of payment such as migrants, illegal immigrants and poor not Medicaid-eligible (F/U/I/335)

Training

1. Training in OPD's for continuing, personalized care and collaboration with all other professionals (U/U/I/236)

2. Financing of teaching in OPD's by subsidies or increased third-party payments (U/U/I/236)
3. Training on all fronts regarding chronically ill and handicapped children (primary care/related professions/community members/parents/nonhandicapped children) should be expanded with UAF as professional model (U/O/E/306)
4. Training programs for health and social services personnel should underscore psychosocial needs of families of chronically ill and handicapped children (U/U/E/307)
5. Training in psychosocial factors and increased emphasis on promotion and prevention for providers, especially primary care providers (U/U/I/394)
6. Pressure to cut back support for training MCH professionals should be resisted (U/U/E-397)
7. Training in public health should be combined with training in public policy and administration (U/N/E/403)
8. Research training opportunities be increased in ambulatory and prevention/promotion settings (U/U/E/425)

Family planning

1. Expansion of categorical funding for family planning services, including counseling, to serve all wishing services in variety of settings (U/O/E/270)
2. Family planning should be integral component of every primary care unit and also in free-standing clinics (U/U/E/270)
3. State and federal authorities should work closely together to assure federal support for family planning (Title X, Medicaid, Title V, Title XX) used in complementary, mutually-reinforcing ways (F,S/U/E/270)

Dental care

1. Preventive dental services for children be made available in sites providing economies of scale and simple access (U/U/E/271)
2. Provision of preventive dental services should involve extensive use of dental auxiliaries (U/U/I/271)
3. Preventive dental services should be funded through new federal grants and state and local revenues and, possibly, Medicaid and Title I of ESEA (F,S,L/U/I/272)
4. Dental health programs and policies should incorporate care for special dental needs of chronically ill and handicapped children (U/U/E/305)

Adolescents and juvenile offenders

1. Policymakers and health system leaders increase attention to adolescent health needs and public and private sectors intensify development of organizing models (U/U/E/286)
   A. Provision of adolescent outreach systems
   B. Provision of health education to adolescents in the health care system
   C. Availability of family planning services without parental consent
   D. Adolescent health services, especially VD, family planning, pregnancy testing, crisis counseling, should be provided free or at reduced cost
   E. Adolescent health care staff should be sympathetic and communicate well with adolescents
2. Policymakers and public and private third-party payers support variety of models to serve adolescent health care needs (U/U/E/289)
   A. Acute care hospitals serving significant number of adolescent patients should organize adolescent units

    B.   Family planning clinics serving significant number of adolescents should provide special sessions and programs with vigorous outreach for teenagers

    C.   Private physicians should include review of health habits and peer and family relations and behavioral issues in routine exams

3.   Federal and state leaders of EPSDT and Title V should review and revise policies and programs to ensure needs of adolescents met and given sufficient priority (F,S/U/E/290)

    A.   EPSDT should increase outreach to adolescents

    B.   State Title V agencies with federal encouragement should review service programs to assure adolescents are included and increase training programs

    C.   State level health planning systems should assess extent to which EPSDT and Title V give adequate attention to adolescents

4.   Public and private funding sources increase support of multiservice, single-site systems for adolescent care (U/U/E/291)

    A.   Administrative changes to ease pooling of funds from categorical sources and develop common reporting forms for expenditures and program activities

    B.   Include strong evaluation component in extended support

5.   Special consideration in ambulatory and hospital settings should be given to developmental concerns of chronically ill and handicapped adolescents (U/U/E/306)

6.   Juvenile offenders with mental health problems should not be placed in detention/correctional settings lacking services to meet special needs (physical and mental) (U/U/I/309)

7.   All juvenile facilities should include suicide prevention and full range of preventive mental and physical health care (U/U/I/309)

8.   Detention and correctional facilities provide full medical evaluation to all juveniles on entry, periodically thereafter, and ready access to primary and emergency health care (U/U/E/309)

9.   Federal/state/local governments absolutely prohibit confinement of juveniles in adult jails; until accomplished, provide maximum protection and comprehensive medical and educational services (F,S,L/N/I/310)

10. Every juvenile detention facility should designate health authority responsible for all levels of care, routinely accountable to state MCH authorities (F,S,L/U/I/310)

Chronically ill and handicapped children

1.   Hospice or home care should be available for handicapped or chronically ill children (U/U/I/277)

2.   Public health/social services/private providers should provide training and aid for home care of chronically ill and handicapped children (U/U/E/306)

3.   All public and private programs should take into account "hidden" costs (transportation/special modifications/equipment/lost work time, etc.) of caring for chronically impaired children (U/U/E/306)

4.   Parents who are full-time caregivers of handicapped children should have ready access to respite care (U/U/E/306)

5.   Special tax credits should be created for parents caring for handicapped children at home (F,S/U/E/306)

6.   Enhancement of availability and accessibility of prevention services recommended elsewhere in report for chronically ill and handicapped children (U/U/E/306)

7.   State health authorities should play major role in early identification of handicaps in children under 5, expanding early intervention programs, and coordinating with private sector and school programs (S/U/E/306)

8.   Clarify state designation of policy-making groups for developmental disabilities and

health planning aimed at creating and maintaining community team approach with special backup medical services for every handicapped child (S/U/I/307)

9. State MCH authorities should give technical assistance for health-related aspects of MR programs to accompany continued categorical programs (S/U/I/307)

Foster care

1. Research on health needs of foster children and availability and adequacy of services should be given high priority by DHHS (F/U/I/311)
2. In implementing P.L. 96-272, DHHS should require care plans for all foster children, including health needs, services provided, and responsible service providers (F/N/E/311)
3. Parents willing to care for handicapped or chronically ill foster children should receive higher basic support payments (F/N/E/311)
4. Medicaid reimbursement should be extended to cover all physical and mental health services for all foster children (F/U/E/312)
5. State EPSDT and P.L. 94-142 conduct outreach to foster parents and institutions to inform them of available programs and assist in obtaining needed services (S/U/E/312)

Nonphysician providers

1. Federal support for development of nurse practitioners and nurse midwife clinics (F/N/E/241)
2. Schools without comprehensive care should utilize nurses to provide direct service and linkages with other providers (U/U/I/251)
3. Training and use of mid-level practitioners should be supported and expanded (U/U/I/398)

Research and data needs

1. Continuation and expansion of categorical research programs on determinants of illnesses/handicaps/retardation (U/O/E/306)
2. Each state should develop strategy for collecting and using policy-related epidemiological data on status and access/fund receipts and management data/program evaluation data (S/U/E/364)
3. Public and private support should encourage research in all health sciences and facilitate integrated approach (U/U/I/408)
4. No one agency should be charged with administering all MCH-related research (F/U/E/410)
5. Asst. Secretary for Health be charged with identifying major gaps in research/helping coordinate research/encouraging multipurpose research agencies in DHHS (F/N/E/411)
6. Asst. Secretary should give consideration to establishing national registry of MCH research (F/N/E/412)
7. Asst. Secretary should give specific attention to encouraging cooperative MCH research between public and private sectors (F/N/E/412)
8. Support for fundamental research be sustained and increased/essential role of fundamental research become major component of planning and funding policies (U/N/E/414)
9. Congressional appropriations to agencies conducting longitudinal research should reflect importance, expense, and need for longitudinal research (F/U/E/414)
10. Where statistically sound, cross-sectional rather than longitudinal designs should be used (U/U/E/414)

11. Funding be included in NCHS budget for follow-back (retrospective cohort) surveys (F/U/E/415)
12. OMCH earmark portion of research funds for state-initiated MCH research with collaboration of state health departments and universities and disseminate results (F/N/I/419)
13. Special priority be given to developing new health outcome measures for MCH services (U/N/I/419)
14. Research on risks of environmental substances be included in national research agenda and regulations reflect knowledge from research (F/U/E/420)
15. New funds be allocated to increase analytic staff in agencies collecting health information (U/N/E/421)
16. New funds and personnel be allocated to support research with existing data bases by universities and selected private institutions (U/N/E/421)
17. NCHS be encouraged and supported to tabulate by smaller age categories/cooperate with census/increase compatibility of various data collections (F/N/E/421)
18. NCHS be provided with increased funding and personnel to provide technical assistance to states (F/N/E/422)
19. MCHA, NCHS, and others review adequacy of and improve perinatal data collection, establish state surveillance systems and increase state's and NCHS's ability to link infant birth and death records (F/U/E/422)
20. NCHS be provided resources to continue and expand data collection and analysis of physical/motor/intellectual/social/emotional development of normal children (F/U/E/423)
21. NIH, NCHS, and others develop functional categories to accompany diagnostic categories in surveys (F/N/E/423)
22. MCHA review current state and federal record-keeping and reporting requirements and consolidate and integrate data collection processes and forms (F/N/E/423)

Minorities, migrants, and immigrants

---

1. Migrant student record transfer system should be extended to children in Head Start, all health programs, and additional federal programs such as WIC (F/O/I/313)
2. MCH plans developed by states under Title V should contain explicit provisions to meet migrant health care needs (S/U/I/313)
3. Indian health service focus greater attention in 1980s on psychological, social, and behavioral problems along with traditional efforts in infant mortality and infectious disease (F/U/E/314)
4. Congress provide support needed to sustain and expand Indian health service programs (F/U/I/314)
5. Public health service office of Refugee Affairs assess problem of access to care of refugee children with attention to difficulty of obtaining Medicaid eligibility for poor refugees (F/U/E/315)
6. No distinction in determining health care eligibility should persist between refugees and "entrants" (U/N/I/315)
7. Congress, DHHS, and states should provide more fiscal relief to communities where municipal health services care for significant numbers of illegal immigrant families (F,S/U/I/316)

Planning and evaluation

---

1. As a first priority PHS promulgate standards for contact periodicity and quality of minimum basic services for use by all providers (F/N/E/192)

2. Creation of a board on Health Services Standards or existing institutions strengthened, better coordinated, or consolidated (F/N/E/215)
3. As a very high priority, Secretary of DHHS convene ad hoc group in consultation with congressional committees, Asst. Secretary of Health, and HCFA to outline nature, composition, and authority of Board and that Congress act rapidly to establish Board (F/N/E/218)
4. Federal responsibilities in state–federal relations (F/U/I/352)
   A. Identify personal health services that should be available to all/special health services needed by special populations/population health promotion and prevention
   B. Establish and fund programs
   C. Establish comprehensive MCH planning system to identify, describe, and help improve MCH services
   D. Establish common reporting system
   E. Provide technical assistance
   F. Determine if states meet criteria for providing needed services
5. State responsibilities in state–federal relations (S/U/I/352)
   A. Work cooperatively with other state-level planning bodies to identify needed services and develop plan
   B. Authorize programs and appropriate funds
   C. Support and encourage communities and regions to develop services
   D. Develop and support regional services which, due to cost, cannot be done locally
   E. Provide health promotion and prevention statewide and encourage local development of same
   F. Interpret federal standards of care and monitor local services
   G. Use federally determined planning and reporting methods
   H. Carry out additional research and demonstrations, development, advocacy, and program coordination
   I. Create conduit for consumer ideas for improvement in services
6. Federal accountability mechanism should stress federal role in establishing broad objectives and standards and states should demonstrate progress toward objective with wide latitudes in means (F,S/U/I/354)
7. New set of coordinating criteria to be met by all new or existing MCH programs (U/N/I/355)
8. Minimal community responsibilities for MCH care (L/U/I/358)
   A. Assign lead agency for needs assessment
   B. Charge lead agency with publicizing findings/participating in state and regional planning/exercising community leadership
   C. Contribute local tax dollars to match state and federal funds
   D. Increase coordination among providers
9. State agencies administering Title V and related programs should contribute more significantly to planning by establishing clear and simple requirements and enlarging planning agency's role in state efforts (S/U/I/360)
10. State MCH authority should share overall responsibility for MCH planning with HSA's, SHPDA's, and SHCC's (S/U/E/361)
11. HSA's, SHPDA's, and NHPC need direction and guidance for planning and allocating resources for health promotion (S/U/E/361)
    A. HHS Secretary should specify MCH as a national health priority and establish goals
    B. HSA's should be required to closely coordinate with state MCH departments
12. Federal MCH agency should work with NCHP and BHP in developing materials for

effective relations between state MCH authorities and state planning agencies (F/N/E/362)

13. Federal and state MCH authorities should continue to expand activities in quality assurance (F,S/U/E/363)

14. New funds necessary for demonstration projects of more efficient local service structures/federal and state program and funding coordination/coordinating services (U/N/I/366)

15. Federal policy should build cadre of state professionals in state health units to communicate and translate national into local goals (F/U/I/367)

16. Legislative creation of National Commission on Maternal and Child Health [see text for functions] (F/N/I/386)
   A. Commission should be composed of citizen members appointed by DHHS Secretary for 3 year terms
   B. Commission should include one present or former member of state MCH council
   C. Chairman of each committee in Congress submit nominees to Secretary of DHHS for commission
   D. Secretaries of Agriculture/Transportation/HUD/Education/Defense observers to commission
   E. Commission ex-officio slot for DHHS Secretary's representative for ensuring MCH interdepartmental coordination

17. If presidential health sciences planning body is established, MCH should be given adequate attention and representation (F/N/E/411)

18. MCH programs at local to federal level be required to develop evaluation plan and widely disseminate evaluation results (F,S,L/N/E/418)

19. MCHA, NCMCH and/or Congress review extent to which program funds are used to generate appropriate evaluation data and correct misuses (F/N/E/418)

Medicaid

1. Federal and state Medicaid authorities should assure in implementation of EPSDT that children actually receive diagnosis and treatment, are linked to regular primary care, and parents retain responsibility (F,S/U/I/275)

2. Federally legislated uniform national Medicaid income and resource standard and extension of eligibility to all pregnant women and children meeting test, regardless of family status or other conditions (F/N/E/329)

3. Medicaid coverage of a uniform national package of services [See Vol. II] (F/N/E/329)

4. Medicaid inclusion of all qualified providers with mechanism and rate structure ensuring availability of comprehensive, high-quality, care for all eligible children and pregnant women (F/N/E/329)

5. Federal incentives to states to provide expanded access to Medicaid services and continuity of care (F/U/E/329)

Miscellaneous

1. All corporations and government agencies give explicit attention to employee needs for family planning, prenatal care, and other supports (F,S,L,P/U/E/136)

2. Provision of additional funds through Title V to strengthen regional clinical centers (F/O/I/161)

3. Increase public awareness and commitment to increase AFDC allowances (U/U/I/170)

4. Federal, state, and local authorities should substantially increase support of home visiting programs (F,S,L/O/I/260)

    A. Permit substantial number of states and communities to use home visits by public health nurses and others

    B. Enable health departments/hospitals/CHC's and others to establish or reestablish home visiting as routine MCH care component

    C. Allow evaluation of prototype programs

5. Policymakers and providers should design screening programs on assumption that screening is done in context of individual assessments for limited number of conditions as means of linking children to ongoing care and check on adequacy of care (U/U/I/275)

6. Board on Health Service Standards should periodically review which screening tests appropriate for comprehensive care and which for high-risk groups only (F/N/I/275)

7. Criteria for hospital length of stay should be developed for children which includes psychosocial needs (U/N/I/277)

8. Routine care should be in the home or setting as near to normal as possible (U/U/E/305)

9. Substantially increased support levels for advocacy from private sector (P/U/E/369)

10. Regional MCH staff should be adequate in number, training, and experience (F/U/E/389)

    A. Expertise in other disciplines (speech/hearing/occupational therapy) should be available to cover 2 or more regions

    B. Regional staff should be permitted to work full-time with assigned states as advocates, advisors, and "prodders"

    C. Regional staff should attend not only to MCH, but also DHHS programs with MCH components

---

[a] Key to letter codes: Letter codes and numbers in parentheses indicate the levels of the classification variables assigned to each recommendation. The following format was used: (Responsibility for implementation/type of initiative/explicitness/page number)

Responsibility for implementation	type of initiative	explicitness
F = federal government	O = old	E = explicit
S = state government	N = new	I = implicit
L = local government	U = unclear	
P = private sector		
U = unclear		

Key to Abbreviations:

AFDC	Aid to Families with Dependent Children
BHP	Bureau of Health Planning
CHC	Comprehensive Health Center
C & Y	Children and Youth
DHHS	Department of Health and Human Services
DOE	Department of Energy
EPA	Environmental Protection Agency
EPSDT	Early Periodic Screening, Diagnosis, and Treatment
ER	Emergency room
ESEA	Elementary and Secondary Education Act
FDA	Food and Drug Administration
HCFA	Health Care Financing Administration
HMO	Health Maintenance Organization
HSA	Health Systems Agency
HUD	Housing and Urban Development
MCH	Maternal and Child Health
MCHA	Maternal and Child Health Administration
MIC	Maternity and Infant Care Project
NCHS	National Center for Health Statistics
NCMCH	National Commission on Maternal and Child Health
NCHP	National Council on Health Planning
NHPC	National Health Planning Council
NHSC	National Health Service Corps

NIH	National Institutes of Health
NIOSH	National Institute of Occupational Safety and Health
OHDS	Office of Human Development Services
OMCH	Office of Maternal and Child Health
OPD	Outpatient department
OSHA	Occupational Safety and Health Administration
PHS	Public Health Service
PHSA	Public Health Service Act
SHCC	State Health Coordinating Council
SHPDA	State Health Planning and Development Agency
UAF	University Affiliated Facility
USDA	United States Department of Agriculture
WIC	Supplemental Food Program for Women, Infants, and Children

Author Index

SUBJECT INDEX